JAMES CROWDEN is an author and poet living in Somerset, England. He is the author of *Ciderland* (2008) which won the André Simon Food and Drink Award in 2008. He visits India whenever he can.

Praise for *The Frozen River*:

'The singular virtue of Crowden's prose is to create a sense of enormous immediacy … he acts as a transparent lens that gathers all that fierce Zanskari winter light and illuminates the primary colours of both the place and its people. In so doing, he creates a tour de force of luminous writing'   MARK COCKER, *Spectator*

'A revelation … the most gripping and fascinating reads I have enjoyed for a very long time'
MARTIN HESP, *Western Morning News*

'The adventure brings out the best in Crowden's writing, which in full flow has a compelling lyrical energy'   OLIVER BALCH, *TLS*

'In prose hard as the frost and gritty as the rocks, James Crowden weathers a Himalayan winter in snow-bound Zanskar and recalls the boundless hospitality and ingenuity of his wind-furrowed hosts. Crowden and Zanskar are a match made on high'
JOHN KEAY, author of *India: A History*

'Terrific. Crowden is a meditative swashbuckler: imagine John Buchan, cross-legged in a mountain monastery, smelling of sandalwood incense, or Wordsworth on speed, with a belt jangling with karabiners'   CHARLES FOSTER, author of *Being a Beast*

ALSO BY JAMES CROWDEN

Ciderland

JAMES CROWDEN

THE FROZEN RIVER

Seeking Silence in the Himalaya

WILLIAM
COLLINS

William Collins
An imprint of HarperCollins*Publishers*
1 London Bridge Street
London SE1 9GF

WilliamCollinsBooks.com

First published in Great Britain in 2019 by William Collins
This William Collins paperback edition published in 2020

1

Set in Berling LT Std with Albertus MT Pro display
Printed and bound in Great Britain by
CPI Group (UK) Ltd, Croydon

'The valley of the Zangskar River is quite impassable,
except when the winter's frost makes a road
over the waters of the river.'

Frederick Drew, 1875

CONTENTS

Ladakh and Zangskar in 1976

Dras

Kargil

Sonamarg

Zoji La

Srinagar

Suru Valley

Panikar

Parkachik

Ran
Gor

Zhuldok

Tashi Tanz

Nun Kun

Pense La

Durung Drung glacier

Hagshu La

HIMALAYA

Chenab

Chenab

SINKIANG

CHINA

HUNZA

Gilgit

Indus

Karakoram
Pass

AKSAI
CHIN

Kargil

KASHMIR Zoji La
Srinagar Pass

Benihal
Pass

Padum

Manali

LADAKH

Leh

Zangskar

TIBET

PAKISTAN

Amritsar

NEPAL

Delhi

0	10	20	30 miles
0	10	20	30	40	50 km

Roads   Trails

Rivers   Chadar

THE PURSUIT OF SILENCE

The valley

Silence, snow and solitude have got hold of me and will not let go. I am possessed by mountains, cold and ice. Winter has a very firm grip upon my soul. It is like a disease, a form of spiritual possession, mountain fever. And yet there is no escape. I am here for the duration, locked into a little-known Tibetan Buddhist valley at high altitude, sandwiched between the main Himalayan range and the Karakoram.

One by one all the high passes have shut behind me and will not re-open again for six or seven months. The local people, the Zangskaris, spend half their lives huddled round small stoves burning yak dung and tamarisk scrub to keep warm. It is dark in their houses. How they survive and how they live over the winter surrounded by so much snow and ice is still something of a mystery. Only one other Westerner has spent a winter in Zangskar, an eccentric Hungarian linguist called Alexander Csoma de Kőrös. But that was over 150 years ago, and of the Zangskari winter he left no record.

Imagine if your family had lived in the mountains for a thousand years or more; what effect would that have upon your mind and your thinking, on your awareness and the way in which you perceived things? Imagine how much silence your family would have absorbed and accumulated along the way. Zangskaris try to preserve the teaching about the silence that emerges between words. The teaching is at times very formal but also very subtle, hinting at the space which exists when words run out. And then there is the silence of Dzogchen and the mountains, which cannot really be taught – only passed on from teacher to pupil. The language of Buddhism and compassion runs through their daily lives in Zangskar like an invisible thread.

To the south lies the vibrant and colourful Indian subcontinent. To the north, the dry, sandy deserts of Central Asia; to the west, Kashmir, the jagged front line with Pakistan; to the east, the lonely, vast nomadic plateau of Tibet. A place of meditation, debate and monastic scholarship. Zangskar is remote even by Himalayan standards.

Deep silence, deep snow and deep solitude. These are the inner coordinates that matter most to me. For various reasons I have sought out this seclusion, this retreat from the world. Ultimate peace and quiet. Remoteness is a state of mind – you either possess it, or you have to go and find it. But once you have found that particular form of solitude and tasted its fruits, you will go back time and time again to touch base with the wilderness and emptiness that live within the mountains. To embrace such mountains is perhaps part of the human condition.

The prospect of travelling down the frozen Zangskar river beckoned just as strongly as the silence of winter. Sleeping rough, sleeping in caves, sleeping out in the snow – you live on your wits. One false step, one major crack in the ice or serious slip that catapults you towards the open water and you are lost. The river is fast, deep and cold. A heavy pack drags you down very quickly. A swift end. Zangskar is dangerous in winter.

More than anything else in the world I wanted to make this journey down the frozen river. To the best of my knowledge no Westerner had ever sampled its delights and dangers. Although it was a challenge that I relished, I had much to learn. The mountains were calling in a silent language that I had yet to decipher. I longed for ice and the solitude, but the mountains had many tricks up their sleeve.

The ice road

Sometimes if the ice was clear I could see right through to the very bottom of the river bed where pebbles lay in many colours: grey, rusty brown, black, orange, even mauve. The water had a wonderful greenish tinge. At other times the ice was so thick, strong and opaque that you could almost drive a tank along it. When the ice gets thin the river becomes truly dangerous, wafer-thin ice with hidden whirlpools silently churning away down below. A trap that lies in wait for the unwary.

As you tread upon its surface, the frozen river leaves its indelible mark upon your consciousness. It becomes the mirror of your soul. You develop an inner strength and confidence that stays with you for the rest of your life. A yardstick. A rite of passage. An initiation. Zangskaris call the frozen river *chadar*: the ice sheet, ice road, ice blanket, frozen one. They respect it. It is a central part of their winter.

You quickly learn to read the ice, taking in old fractures and broken lines at a glance, seeking out inconsistencies that upset the river's own intention and intrigue. The river is alive with subtle shifts of direction and momentum. Solid currents woven into intricate patterns. Streams of trapped bubbles. Long lines of them, as if a diver were down below. Oval, mirrored, many-layered. Hypnotic. The flow in suspension. Encased in ice. Preserved in aspic, solidified, mute.

The feeling of being trapped in the gorge for days on end is not at all unpleasant. Almost comforting, like being embraced by mountains. There is a sense of expectation that has a certain edge to it, as if trespassing, a frisson shared with cold, sharp, early morning air. You are very alive. Adrenalin kicks in. Your breathing changes, you become aware of every sound. You plumb the depths of the silence. You are not just trapped in the gorge, you are running on a sinuous course that curves and then cuts through a vast mountain range. Geology sliced through, laid bare. Millions of years of sedimentary rocks, twisted, contorted, at times almost vertical, Buddhist time and geological time on a par with each other. You slide, skate and shuffle as if the river is pulling you along. The journey has a momentum all of its own, like running on a silver thread.

When you are on the *chadar*, the frozen river, everything changes. Your life has different parameters. Your world is narrowed down to this gorge. You become very focused, as all climbers must be. Balance becomes vital. You test yourself against the rock, against the ice, against the frozen river itself. You become tall and confident, attuned to the river's voice. You learn to read its character by tapping the ice with your stick and patiently listening to the echo, and the echo of the echo, to gauge its solidity, for you are tapping into the river's own energy, reading its mind as it twists and turns, almost like the mind of a wild animal, predicting the flow of the river under the ice and at certain times the flow of water over the ice. Like sonar or asdic, you wait for the returning ping. Resonance and pitch are vital. Tap, tap, tap. You listen to the echo bouncing back. Each vibration has a fragility. You read the ice visually as well. Each little imperfection registered, logged just in case the levels change. You navigate by the odd stunted juniper tree, small side *nallahs* (gullies, side valleys or steep ravines and watercourses that are often dried up), caves, tall frozen waterfalls, old avalanche cones, certain outcrops of rock, odd patterns in the strata, changes of direction in the colours and the shifts of light. Your mind logs them all.

You learn that rivers freeze in different ways at different times. Sometimes the frozen river breaks rank and rears up a dozen feet or more in the air, solid and chaotic, pack ice riding up over itself in great thick broken sheets. Sometimes the frozen river detonates like artillery as it moves and buckles, sharp cracks that echo upwards in the narrow confines of the gorge. It keeps you on your toes. Cracks accelerate. Sometimes the frozen river is silent. Sometimes it talks in riddles. You have to read the runes. Learn from the older men. Read their silence as well. The mind is always alert.

When I went down the frozen river alongside the Zangskaris I was not only aware of the danger but of intense beauty. Time had no meaning. We were as if in orbit, totally disconnected from the safety of the world as we had known it. We walked on borrowed time. We were in the grip of a journey and an adventure that was far larger than ourselves. The bonds with the rock and the mountains were as strong as the bonds between each of us.

Sometimes I felt very safe, at other times I was in great peril. Occasionally when the ice gave out I had to climb out of the sheer-sided gorge and take to the cliffs, climbing upwards to find a horizontal fault. That was when you were closest to the rock, gingerly creeping along narrow ledges fifty or sixty feet above the open water with no ropes or belays. My fingers would be numb and unresponsive. I would cling on for dear life, holding my stick and at the same time manoeuvring along the ledge with a heavy pack. When the cliff was close to your face, your nose rubbed the rock and you could smell its fragrance: intimate, earthy, hard, almost metallic.

I followed the Zangskaris, who are as agile as ibex and as wily as snow leopards. They are butter traders and carried many kilos of valuable butter on their backs to sell in the bazaars of Leh, the main town of central Ladakh. Fine yellow butter made from the female yaks on the high pastures, now stored in goatskins or crinkled sheep's stomachs, butter that is sought after for Tibetan salt tea and highly prized in winter. Butter trading is their only source of income in winter.

But the Zangskari winter is not just one winter; it is the memory of many winters rolled into one. It is the story of survival, not just of one village, but of many villages – a collective memory that is as large as the valley itself. Maybe ten thousand souls are trapped each year in the Zangskar valley, including monks and nuns, yaks, sheep and goats. Winter is nature's way of preserving itself. Only man can destroy the silence. Only man can appreciate it.

These times on the ice road were off limits. They were beyond the normal remit of village life. A strange rendezvous within the mountains. Only for a month or two each winter can the frozen river be used safely as a highway. The *chadar* is a world unto itself. Some Zangskaris make the journey every year, others twice or even three times in a single winter. They make it a central part of their lives. A dangerous economy. Trading mountains for wisdom, butter for rupees and precious supplies. Each person takes back what they can in the depths of their minds, that is all you can take from the valley, but it will last you a lifetime. Such silence is like a jewel set deep in the mountains. A natural way of being that takes root of its own accord in your consciousness.

Very occasionally men fall into the river and are swept under the ice with their packs. Others are caught by avalanches, whose power is unpredictable and swift. This was a foray into the unknown. New territory. A real challenge. I would be making the journey both ways.

In Zangskar they have their own dialect, which some say relates back to old Tibetan where the 'silent' letters in Tibetan are still pronounced. Tenzin is *Stenzin* and Padum is *Spadum*. But it is the unspoken language of winter that I want to explore, the silent language of mountains and survival.

Here the mountains are guardians of silence and the long winter a vital part of that equation. The invisible energy of winter has no name and cannot easily be defined, yet it is very real and abundant. It has a wisdom all of its own. It is traded in small caves and monasteries. Some even call it Buddhism.

White mountains

In Sanskrit *Him Alaya* translates as 'abode of snow' or 'snow dwelling'. In Tibetan or Ladakhi, the peaks are simply called *Pabu Riga* or 'white mountains'. In reality they are a vast, complicated maze of sharp, awe-inspiring mountains, swift rivers, rich pastures and long, wide glaciers – a zone where snow leopards, bears, ibex, wolves, marmots and the mythical Tibetan snow lions roam, a belt of mountains two hundred miles wide that stretches for one and a half thousand miles along India's northern borders, one of nature's most challenging and complex barriers.

The Himalaya is not one range but many. At the western end there is the Dhaula Dhar, the Pir Panjal, the main Himalayan range, and the Zangskar and Ladakh ranges, then finally the Karakoram, which in Turkic means 'black gravel' or 'black sands'. These mountains are a direct result of the Indian subcontinent shifting itself further northward each year. An enormous collision in slow motion, the mountains are young, tempestuous and unpredictable, the peaks still rising. Landslides are common. A world of its own – a spiritual reservoir, a place of pilgrimage and devotion. The source of all things in India: life and water.

Zangskar is made up of two high-altitude valleys drained by cold, fast-flowing, tempestuous rivers: Stod and Lungnak. These meet in the central plain to form the Zangskar river, which then flows north through a gorge for about a hundred miles, twisting and turning this way and that, cutting through a whole mountain range till it meets the River Indus. This junction is the northern end of the *chadar*, the ice road that connects Zangskar with central Ladakh and the old trading town of Leh, with its old bazaar and crumbling caravanserais. From Leh, ancient connections once spread out like a spider's web across the Karakoram to the old city states of Kashgar, Yarkand and Khotan, and further east to the trading oasis of Dunhuang, with its highly decorated Buddhist caves. Central Asia – a meeting place of many ideas and beliefs. The Silk Road, a slender path weaving through the mountains along which people's lives were led. Leh and its traders have many stories to tell.

Ladakh, known as 'Little Tibet', 'Western Tibet', 'Indian Tibet' or the 'Land of High Passes', is a remote Himalayan kingdom about four times the size of Wales. The four major mountain ranges that run through Ladakh are subdivided into small, secluded valleys. It is one of the highest inhabited places in the world, a remarkable enclave and a fine tribute to the inhabitants' farming skills. These mountains are also crucial to Zangskar's seclusion and individuality. The lowest pass into Zangskar from the west is at 14,500ft and the highest from the south over the main Himalayan range is over 18,000ft and only open for one or two months in the summer. These higher routes often cross glaciers riddled with crevasses. There is no easy way into Zangskar, and no easy way out.

The valley is almost entirely self-sufficient. But in late winter food and fodder can sometimes run perilously low. Solitary confinement, but of the very best kind. Seclusion. A rare commodity these days.

Dry, dusty dry, fierce Central Asian dry, the climate of Ladakh is that of a mountain desert. It lies in a rain shadow where everything is dependent on glaciers, meltwater and irrigation. Cold in winter, hot in summer.

The room

For winter and most of the next summer I lived in the middle of Zangskar in a small, draughty, mud-bricked room. This was Padum, the capital of Zangskar, which in its heyday had its own seven-storey fort-cum-palace. The palace had crumbled. The village had seen better days.

The small room jutted out of the roof of the house and was only used in summer, which is why it was so draughty. It was exposed to the elements on all four sides. There was no heating. Yet that room was vital to me. My hermit's cell. A place of retreat and contemplation. Base camp, where I spread out all my food and belongings.

To cook I had a blue compact petrol stove, which was excellent. I also had a Primus stove that ran on kerosene, but the jets often got blocked up and had to be pricked. My low-grade fuel resulted in lots of dark smoke and even steam emerging. It often spluttered till the stove really got going.

All my belongings and expedition paraphernalia lay scattered on the floor of the room, dumped higgledy-piggledy just as they had been when they were offloaded. Four sturdy packhorses had brought the supplies into the valley from Panikar, the roadhead in Suru, a journey of a hundred miles on foot over the Pense La, a relatively easy pass in summer. But this was mid-November, when snow could come down at any moment.

The walk into Zangskar took six days, with temperatures down to about -20°C. At that time there was no road into Zangskar, so the sound of an internal combustion engine had never been heard in the valley. Being a backwater had its own distinct advantages. Such deep and continuous silence was a great virtue and a rare commodity, highly prized by meditators, the true connoisseurs of silence.

Among many other things I wanted to study the effect of the road being built into the valley. Started in the 1960s, the road to Zangskar had progressed very slowly. It was as if the clock had been wound back five hundred years. Zangskar in those days was like old Ladakh – ancient Tibet – a world apart. A rare survival. A spiritual gem. A horse and sheep economy. A monastic realm of monks and nuns, where barley and yaks reigned supreme.

I also realised that by studying the valley I was possibly – in some measure – changing the outcome. In the physics of relativity this is called the 'observer effect'. I was, after all, an outsider. I also had a hunch that many more people would visit over the next few decades and thus alter the fragile balance that had evolved without modern technology. In the future Zangskar's peace and quiet would be under very real threat. Once the road was through, their world would change dramatically and in ways that could not be predicted. Younger men and women seemed to welcome the road and its connection with modern India, but others were more sceptical. It was a crucial year. There was no turning back.

Ice ferns

At first light I would lean up on one elbow and, with my arm outstretched, reach up with my right hand and with bare fingernails scrape the ice away from the inside of the window to get a better view of the mountain that lay behind the village. The window was close to the floor and only had two small panes of glass, each held within a simple wooden frame. Every night the frost slowly crept back into the room and flexed its silver muscles to take control once more. On the inner surface of the glass, icy ferns formed from the moisture of my own breath and nighttime breathing, moisture which within the very dry air slowly formed its own gallery. Long, curved, delicate ferns reached out from the borders, from the corners of the frame and eventually curled back on themselves. These patterns were a constant source of enchantment, for they grew silently above my head and in the dark each crystal curve formed its own trajectory, swirling like underwater currents. By morning each pane of glass had created its own universe in miniature, which, when observed carefully, looked for all the world like a map of the mountain range within which I was trapped, with ridges and side valleys, hidden *nallahs* and deep gorges, all unexplored and enticing.

This forest of rime and hoar frost was wondrous and every night made, as if on a whim, its own secret patterns, icy maps that I longed to study and traverse with my eye, as if flying or drifting above them in a hot-air balloon or even peering the wrong way down a telescope or the barrel of a microscope into the substrata of some little-known crystal world or the inner workings of a new species invisible to the naked eye. These icy maps reminded me of fractal geometry and Mandelbrot patterns that repeated themselves on many different levels of magnification. Even the tips curled like ferns. It seemed that these mysterious maps in some way mirrored and then charted my own mind. An intimate survey of unknown constellations where ideas and journeys grew of their own accord, flourished and then jostled for attention and space before vanishing as mysteriously as they had arrived.

As if the mind was transformed from being merely a window through which we observed the outside world and other people, into something much more interesting, where a simple pane of glass became metamorphosed overnight into a thing of wonder, a glass negative, or light-sensitive plate, such as early photographers used to use. And upon the plate, exposed, a rich, opaque sheen upon which our nocturnal ideas, our hopes and fears, our past and future peregrinations, our deepest secrets and lucid longings could engrave themselves, and where for a few precious hours at least, these notions were stored and made visible to ourselves. As if each fern were a dream that went back in time to the outer rim of the simple wooden window frame, which held the pattern secure. Back to the very source of things, where language had another dimension and even the smallest flicker of the candle mattered. Ice is simply water that has stopped in its tracks, the flow arrested. A crystal universe that has its own rules.

And so it was that every morning I would retrace my own particular journey back through other mountain ranges. It was as if by being very still for weeks and months on end, the mind could at long last catch up with itself. And in those delicate ferns and ice crystals I could see my own inner journey from one end of a long mountain chain to another. As if each peak were connected to its neighbour, and in the rhythm of the valleys and rivers each peak moved with the seasons and shed its ideas like meltwater. Mountain thinking. A rich, varied landscape that fed my soul. But winter was long in the making.

Winter, winter. A time of gathering in, of holding close, of paring down, of minimal movement, of unfolding hibernation. Time without boundaries, which in its own way cultivated a richness and a sensitivity that had been buried within me for many years, a deep sense of returning, of coming home at last. I was remote yet perfectly at peace with myself.

In that room those ice ferns and ice patterns, so thinly engraved onto the window, became my friends and relatives. I used to follow them and read into them all sorts of journeys and ideas, and yet it was impossible to detect or predict points at which the story might change course or an idea become reality. Many of these narratives stretched deep into the past, but others leapt into the future. It was a place of germination as well as rumination, an internal barometer that registered the smallest change. The dialogue was with one's self and the outer world. Yet there was no real need to retreat. The natural world was perfectly calm and the Zangskari culture a mirror into which I gazed.

Yet every day I had to destroy a part of this delicate and intricate world, and carve through this map of ice ferns, breaking the delicate ice filaments to see another natural wonder, which was of a different scale altogether and overlooked the whole valley. As I scraped away I felt the coldness of the ice crystals accumulate under my fingernails. I listened to the scraping noise, and then I would turn my head, strain my neck a little and look up, and while still lying down on the floor I would catch the first glimpse of dawn as the sudden pinkish light gently touched the mountain top that lay to the south. Very slowly I would watch as the light crept down the mountainside towards the monastery and then the village. I would wait for its warm rays to reach the room before stirring, unless of course snow was falling, which it once did for ten whole days.

There was no bed, no mattress, no blanket, no charpoy. My only luxury a sleeping bag that was laid out on a threadbare carpet. Under this was a bit of old, worn hessian sack that had been used as padding for the pack animals under their wooden saddles. This provided some small insulation, but the pressed earth floor was undulating and dusty. A little bumpy yet no real draughts. The ice crystals under my fingernails were unbelievably cold. Life was very basic. That was how I liked it. I always slept on the floor, it was warmer that way.

The window

That window was crucial to my existence. It was my eye onto the world, a lens like a porthole through which I could peer – and it lay just above where I slept. Those two panes of glass meant everything to me. They were only nine inches high by nine inches wide, and yet they would have been carefully carried on a man's back for a hundred miles or more over the mountain passes, wrapped in straw and hessian and carried on wooden frames like artist's easels to prevent them breaking. Glass in this valley was still something of a novelty and had an enchantment. It was treated with great respect and doubled if not tripled its value with its precarious journey. In their winter quarters the villagers often only had a wooden board that they opened slightly to let the smoke of the open cooking fires escape. It was often too cold to have glass in winter. Light came either from candles or small oil lamps using mustard oil. Some had old-style hurricane lanterns. One or two even had the newfangled pressurised Tilley lamps with a white mantle that glowed as they pumped it up. These ran on kerosene and were a constant source of entertainment, and for the man that owned the lantern a source of pride and status.

Even the wood for the window frame had travelled several hundred miles up the winding valleys from Kashmir, the lengths of timber carried on the backs of horses and yaks over the same passes that I had crossed (Zoji La and Pense La). Some timber also came from the south from the other side of the main Himalayan range, having been dragged across glaciers. Horses and men sometimes slipped down crevasses and had to be rescued with ropes. The temporary roadhead in Suru was a hundred miles away. That was where I had set out from in mid-November with four packhorses, a journey not without its problems.

Like most windows in this valley, the frame had open latticework at the bottom to let the air in, for this was a summer room. The passage of air was then cool and welcome, but in winter it was very different. Winds coming down from the mountains were often cruel and dusty. Whirling dervishes, dust devils, *djinns*, call them what you will, were common as the wind raced across the central plain. Cold winds that came off the glaciers chilled you to the bone.

This latticework below the window and the gaps round the window frames were temporarily blocked off with pages torn from a child's exercise book. I jammed cotton wool into the gaps with my penknife, then tried to seal the joints with precious strips of Elastoplast to keep the wind and dust out. But fine particles of snow nevertheless crept in and covered everything.

Often I would wake covered in a fine dusting of snow. But it did not melt, even on the sleeping bag, for the temperature inside the room and outside was not that different. I had two plastic greenhouse thermometers so that I could monitor the temperatures. I discovered that if it was -20°C outside it was about -10°C inside. If it was -30°C outside, it was about -15°C inside. All very scientific, till a young lad stole one of the thermometers. It was returned a day or two later but sadly it was broken.

After a while the degree of cold becomes academic. Dry cold can be very deceptive. But when you are travelling outdoors for long distances on your own it is a matter of life, death and stamina. The main thing was to avoid sweat that then freezes on your clothing, and frostbite to fingers, toes, ears and nose. Sometimes when cross-country skiing I tied a blue and white spotted handkerchief across my mouth like a bandit or bank robber to stop the freezing air entering my lungs. The main thing was to keep moving and only stop for a few minutes at a time unless the sun was out. I had to prepare myself for the frozen river.

I slept with a dark blue woollen balaclava pulled down over my head and fingerless mitts on my hands in case I got frostbite. Three pairs of socks, long johns and two sweaters, one oiled wool, a fisherman's Guernsey. Just right for the mountains and very hard wearing. Even indoors you had to be careful.

From here the village looked for all the world like a small convoy of tramp steamers with deck cargo. Flat roofs jostled with each other, covered in piles of firewood, kindling, scrub, roots, tamarisk and hay. Hatches all battened down for a storm and the odd grey-blue wisp of wood smoke wafting in the early morning air. Always quiet first thing, and if the weather was good the animals would be let out for fresh air and left to their own devices. They did not stray far and just milled around. They were very social and had their own pecking order. They valued human contact and were on almost equal terms to the people. For water, they ate snow.

Halfway down the outside wall was the third pane of glass. This was green and slightly frosted, and when the sun eventually hit the glass it cast a magnificent greenish light that gave the room the air of a monastic chapel or hermit's cell. Such joys of colour must have lifted the souls of monks long ago, encouraging them to believe in the sanctity of light and the visual spectrum of nature's palette. Such small delights made life here not just bearable but bountiful. Light was a resource in winter, and unlike the Arctic and Antarctic regions there were not the interminable hours of darkness to contend with. You made use of every scrap of sun to warm yourself, and many people worked on their rooftops spinning and weaving whenever they could.

When I first moved in I measured the room with an old wooden ski pole with leather straps and round baskets at the base, more akin to those used by Shackleton or Scott than what you might see on the chic slopes of the Alps. The room was 9ft 6in wide and 14ft 2in long. It was not a true rectangle, and the corresponding sides were about a foot longer in each direction, which gave it an interesting visual perspective. Nothing was quite square or even. This suited me fine. A rhombus, or was it rhomboid? Nothing parallel. No straight lines. Nothing vertical. Even the walls were built at 80 instead of 90 degrees. Maybe it was a parallel Buddhist universe after all. Everything was at a slight angle. Just as the Alexandrian poet C. P. Cavafy would have wished.

Hole in the wall

If the weather was good I could monitor the sun's progress down
the mountain while still in bed reading a book. I regarded that
mountain as a very particular friend. It had a curving ridge like
the prow of an old battleship. From the summit you could see K2
and the whole Karakoram, over 150 miles to the north. In
between lay a vast ocean of mountains. To the west, the Nun Kun
massif; to the east, Changtang; to the south, the peaks of Kishtwar.
An unforgettable sight. A first ascent, no less. To climb a mountain for the very first time is a strange and exhilarating experience. Everything is fresh, even the view. A quiet feeling of
euphoria. Success. Elation. Twenty minutes at the top, that is all.
Cup of tea from a Thermos. Just time to build a small cairn. Then
down before it gets dark.

Every morning sunlight made its long descent from the
summit, down the various ridges and steep slopes. Sometimes
painfully slowly, at other times in leaps and bounds. It was my
hourglass and I could plot the progress of the sun until it reached
the whitewashed walls of the Buddhist monastery. The sun then
glided down across empty terraced fields to the village, which lay
among the boulders of a vast terminal moraine.

Eventually the sun comes into the room, not through the
window as you might suppose, but through a hole in the end wall
where the door is. The door is made from three adzed planks of
wood that are dowelled together, but like all Zangskari doors it
is only three feet high and there is a sill of at least a foot over
which you have to step. It saves on wood and draughts. There are
cracks in the wood, and so I have put another hessian sack over
the door that keeps the wind and snow out. The light is dappled,
the hinges are leather. There is only a bent nail to keep it shut, so

I lean some old wooden skis against it. These stop the wind blowing in and also keep out the dogs that roam the rooftops.

Next to the door is the end wall, and in it have been driven small wooden pegs for hanging up the family's homespun cloaks. These are deep red or maroon, almost magenta, woollen and very warm. The cloaks were removed when I first arrived, but one peg came out and so there is a small hole in the wall. It is through this hole that the sun first appears, casting a diagonal shaft of silver light that slices through the dust and arrives on the opposite wall just above my shoulder, coming to rest on the green flowery chintz hanging. Normally I stop reading and watch its progress as the sun rises. It is as if I am a prisoner, but a willing one. That small shaft of light is a true delight.

Usually I find some matches and light a stick of incense, no easy matter with cold, stubborn fingers. I watch the blue smoke drift lazily around the room. It is another small part of the ritual, an offering to the local gods. And you have to keep the gods on your side. If the air is very still the smoke rises from the incense stick in a thin column that slowly widens rather like a silk stocking and then after rising a foot or two it forms very elegant ripples that get wider and wider. They curve and then invert and almost seem to catch up with each other before breaking out into turbulence, which has its own charm and elegance, as if mirroring the winds that sweep round the peaks. Indeed the smell of burning incense is an essential part of the rituals of this valley, and offerings to the local gods are vital on any journey or important occasion. The gods, like the mountains within which they live, are so much larger than oneself and have to be respected. Incense breeds humility and respect for the natural world.

So important was that first shaft of sunlight in the day that I never closed off the hole, even though it led outside to the bitter cold. It was somehow a direct connection with the world I had come to investigate. Each day had its own rhythm and insights. Slowly my mind became very quiet and alert. I became a silent observer, taking pictures in my mind. A language of images.

Only when the sun's rays reached the window directly did the ice ferns begin their retreat, and within a few minutes it was as if they had never existed. The silver gallery evaporated but I knew it would return the next evening, like a friend or a secret lover. Returning again and again. Night after night. A visible sign, a talisman akin to the single flame of the candle that I would read by until the stars came out. You were in the hard grip of deep winter but you were also in the grasp of great beauty and deep silence. Winter cast its spell not just over the village but over the valley.

Time and solitude

During the winter I had no watch or any contact with the outside world, so there was no need for timekeeping in the normal sense. Time did not really exist. It was a mere fragment of its former self, measured in snowfalls and summer pastures, in fodder and the condition of animals, in the eyes of the people and the mood of the children, in the time it took to light a fire or milk a cow or shear a sheep or plough a small field or brew a pot of beer. These were real measures of time, and beyond that there was the time it took to walk to the next valley with a flock of sheep or a small herd of yak. Instead of saying to someone, 'How old are you?' they would simply say, 'How many pastures have you seen?' Such is the importance of the migration to the lush summer pastures. They might as well have said, 'How many winters have you seen?' or 'How many yak do you own?'

Then there was Buddhist time and monastic time and the time it took to cremate a body. The time it took to walk to Lhasa and back or load a yak. The time to build a monastery, the time to grind up the rocks to make colours and the time to paint a vast Buddhist mural that would last a thousand years, the time to recite mantras and sutras, and the time to count the stars.

If you are not aware of time, then there is no sense of time passing and in a sense it is always time present. Distance is measured in days, winter in feet of snow, families in reincarnations. Life's journey is always in three if not four dimensions. Time here is cyclical as well as linear. A Buddhist spiral, or is it a vortex? The mind, it seems, can go in two different directions at once, if not three. A black hole that receives your thoughts. What is then left? Where has the mind gone, and where is the thinker if there are no thoughts? There is a logic to it, repetitive like a mantra, but the deeper you go into the mantra, or the silence of snow, the more becomes apparent. Buddhist time is curious. On the one hand there is the Tibetan calendar that regulates the monasteries, festivals and times of prayer, governed by the phases of the moon. On the other hand there is philosophical and psychological time, which can be very elastic indeed, leading to Buddhist 'emptiness', where time ceases altogether.

Winter is a time of hunger, particularly if there is a late or particularly deep fall of snow. Wolves are common and snow leopards come down into the villages if they are hungry enough. There are many wolf traps up the valley. Life revolves around animals, the seasons and the river. In summer small glittering irrigation channels rely on meltwater from glaciers high above the villages. The monks play their part in keeping track of the seasons, as do the astrologers and medicine men, the *amchis*. Agricultural time has an important part to play.

In some villages, time is hereditary. Certain families will know the jagged mountain skyline so well that they will be able to predict when it is the right time to plough the fields by the way in which the sun rises. A skyline that is handed down from father to son. The whole village depends on their timing – if the timing is wrong and heavy snow comes, the whole crop is lost. Sometimes for reference they build cairns on a ridge or take bearings on certain buildings.

There is a time for harvest and a time for marriage, a time for the festivals and a time for rebirth. Time for children to grow up. Everything is related to everything else. Each village in the valley plays its part and all are joined together in ways that cannot always be seen. Generations have traded with one another, and animals are as much a part of their lives as their children. There are invisible threads of trade and marriage, exchange of seed grain and labour, a religious continuity that has its own pace and circular form.

Time is measured in silence and meditation in years. Buddhist time often takes the very long view and is akin to geological or even cosmic time. Maybe it is no coincidence that Zangskar is home to many yogins past and present, yet you cannot see them. They live in remote caves and are sometimes walled up on long retreat for three years, three months, three weeks and three days. Occasionally you may see a man high up on a ridge or a mountainside taking food to them, but that is all. Time is also measured in respect and gratitude. In such a valley a man who chooses to live alone is never lonely. There are always mountains and mountain spirits. Here there is complete freedom, though the air is rarefied. Your life is pitched between mountain and river. An offering.

Every day I go down to inspect the river by the bridge to see how much has frozen over, and I wonder about its own journey.

I have to get to know the river in all its moods to understand its idiosyncrasies, its quirky beauty. I inspect the watering holes that are cut in the ice, the source of all the water for the village in winter. As winter progresses, the ice gets thicker and the holes get deeper. Young children have to use old tin cans to help fill the metal jerrycans. It is a long, laborious process, and then there is the walk of several hundred feet back up to the village. Their fingers and hands get very chapped. Rivers can move and so can the ice. Some nights you can hear it cracking.

Solitude, however, is not the same as isolation. Solitude is a virtue, a way of being content, a chosen path. Isolation is in effect an imposed loneliness. The two states are very different and yet they are linked. Isolation can enhance solitude, but it is not to everybody's taste. Time and solitude both feed on silence. Silence has its own energy and you have to learn to harness it. Even the cold has its own echo, ice its own symphony.

I knew deep down that this kind of solitude was a rare commodity and one that I prized above all others. I was fully aware that I needed time to be myself. I also had a strange inner feeling of being on the threshold of something extraordinary. This was exploration in another dimension. Solitude. I had come a long way to taste its fruits. You can savour silence, you can breathe it in like savouring a fine wine, yet there is no delusion. Clarity of purpose and being becomes all the more obvious. Absolute silence, like absolute zero, is a state of mind.

1

THE ROAD TO ZANGSKAR

November 1976

Zoji La

Mountains had been an important part of my life for many years. You visit them every so often and spend a few days with them. They become your friends. You think about them when they are not there. You talk about them with affection. You plan excursions around them. You travel long distances to see them. Slowly, they become part of your own character. Even mountain ranges become like extended families.

But such ambitious journeys as the frozen river do not come out of thin air. They are carefully planned. To get into the Zangskar valley by mid-November was a close-run thing. I had less than a week to get there and three passes to cross before the snow came down.

Down in Delhi airport at three in the morning the customs wallah looked at all my luggage and shook his head in disbelief. 'Where are you going, Sahib? Ladakh, Sahib? Very cold, Sahib. Too much snow.'

Instead of searching all my baggage, which would have taken him half an hour, he simply marked every bag with a chalk cross, shaking his head in disbelief. Then he looked me straight in the eye. He had sussed me out and proudly gave his verdict, saying, 'Back to nature.'

From Delhi I travelled Third Class on *The Frontier Mail*,[1] a train that once ran all the way from Bombay to Peshawar on the North-West Frontier. From the station announcements I could just make out the route. 'Platform Four – Panipat, Kanal, Ambala, Ludhiana, Jullundur, Amritsar.' *Chai* wallahs everywhere. '*Chai, chai, chai.*' Half a dozen porters in red loincloths and grubby turbans carried my luggage aloft on their heads, weaving in and out of the commuter crowds who were in turn besieged by wiry beggars. Third Class in the Punjab is an education. Seats hard, cramped and colourful.

In Amritsar I changed all my money in Grindlays Bank.[2] An old Sikh bank guard in faded army uniform sat outside with a shotgun cradled across his knees. Inside, large fans gyrated slowly overhead in elliptical orbits. Piles of paperwork in triplicate were anchored down by large stones. I was given great wodges of 5 and 10 rupee notes an inch or two thick, stapled together, which I put into an old pillow case. I'd have the equivalent of £300 to last the whole winter. Then I took a branch line to Pathankot across the Punjab by steam train at night under a full moon, followed by a bus from Jammu. I crossed the Pir Panjal via the Banihal Pass (which was now a tunnel)[3] and entered Kashmir.

There I visited the Tyndale Biscoe School,[4] where the headmaster, Rev. John Ray, let me stay in the Church Mission School hostel. The hostel was run by one Chandra Pandit, whose father had once been a sirdar on K2. Chandra was a Brahmin Christian and liked bottled beer. There was always a crate behind the sofa. On his mantelpiece, hedging his bets, were both the Virgin Mary and Lord Krishna.

In the hostel I met two charming Ladakhi boys, sons of the Queen of Ladakh.[5] Little did I realise it then, but I would help campaign on her behalf the following summer when she stood for parliament as the MP for Ladakh. What this involved was merely putting up a few posters with drawing pins on a stable door in a remote village at 14,000ft, perhaps the highest polling station in the world. Ladakhi boys were resourceful. Some of them even descended to Kashmir in January by sliding down the snowy slopes of the Zoji La[6] – *la* is a 'mountain pass' – on their satchels, a bit like bobsleighing. Several thousand feet in one go. It takes some nerve and skill.

I bought supplies at Embee Stores in Srinagar bazaar to last me six months. That concentrates the mind. Bags of rice and *atta* (flour), tea, sugar, a large tin of biscuits, six round tins of Amul processed cheese, six tins of baked beans, Nescafé, milk powder, soap, soups, jars of jams (red, yellow and green, like traffic lights), peanut butter, salt, vermicelli, macaroni, jars of lime pickle, a five-kilo slab of tamarind known as *imli*, dark, bitter and sticky, a dozen tins of sardines caught in the Indian Ocean, twelve packets of dried soya 'meat', which I hated (for emergencies only), three tins of tuna, one for Christmas Day, one for New Year and one for my birthday, three tins of pineapple slices, a Dundee cake and a Christmas pudding, nutmeg, garam masala, chilli powder, turmeric, pepper, drinking chocolate, a bag of toffees, two dozen bars of Indian Bournville chocolate and one bottle of Bulldozer high-strength lager. This had a large macho bulldozer on the label, appropriate for road building. Only they had no bulldozers in Zangskar. No road yet.

But the road was certainly coming and indeed was well on its way. It had taken over ten years to reach Panikar and now it was slowly snaking its way over the Pense La. The road workers used picks and shovels – two men, one shovel. One with the handle, the other with a rope on the business end. They worked in synchronised motion. 'All is pick and shovel.' One dug, the other pulled to one side. Ingenious. Plus the occasional compressor to power pneumatic drills to cut holes in vast boulders prior to blasting. A long, slow process. But all the workmen had gone home for the winter to Nepal and Bihar.

There was one bottle of orange gin, as well as one bottle of XXX rum bought in Kargil, no doubt liberated from the army. That rum was a godsend. But only one bottle, which had to last six months. Emergencies only. The food would also have to last six months till the passes re-opened in June.

Added to all this were two large cardboard boxes filled with fruit: thirty-six red Himachal apples and thirty-six oranges. I had wrapped them individually in sheets of newspaper, copies of last week's *Times of India* and *Hindustan Times*. News indeed, with Mrs Gandhi's Emergency still in full swing.[7] Journalists had to be careful what they wrote. Many were still banged up in prison, but the newspapers kept rolling just the same. Government propaganda in full swing too. 'Foreign minister returned from Moscow'; 'Mrs Gandhi to celebrate her fifty-ninth birthday with tribals in Guwahati'; 'Tito sends his regards'.

My fruit ration allowed one item of fruit each day for seventy-two days, which would see me through the first half of winter. An attempt to stave off scurvy. The apples and oranges all froze upon entry in Ladakh as I crossed the Zoji La, as did the cabbages. So in Padum I thawed the fruit out beside the makeshift stove, while the cabbage was best attacked with a small saw. Even hard-boiled eggs froze. I also heated old batteries up on the stove to extend their life, but if they got too warm they would explode and send bits of hot graphite flying round the room like shrapnel. It concentrates the mind when you have to think six months ahead. Like being stranded on a desert island, only there were no palm trees, no coral reefs and it was decidedly colder.

After gathering my supplies, I then boarded the last bus of the year for Ladakh. It had required a visit to the chief of police to secure a seat. The ticket wallah told me that there were no seats – he then demanded 100 rupees extra up front as bakshish ... which I did not have to spare. The whole expedition could have ground to a halt, so I got in a taxi and went to see the chief of police to make an official complaint. I just happened to mention Tyndale Biscoe and Mr Ray ... in passing ... and that did the trick. The very mention of John Ray's name sorted everything out. The chief of police made a brief phone call, berated the man on the other end of the line, saying something about no room for 'monkey business' at this time of the year. He put the phone down and smiled. His charm had worked wonders. I was very grateful.

I was given the best seat on the bus, next to the driver.

My last telegram was sent from the small and delightful post office with its 'rose beds and cosmos' on the bund. 'ZOJI LA OPEN LEAVING TOMORROW'.

Getting over the Zoji La to the frontier town of Kargil was only the beginning. I had to get into Zangskar before the passes closed. The snow was already late. I also had to find horsemen willing to cross the Pense La into Zangskar – roughly a week's walking, which was cutting it very fine indeed. I could not waste a single minute.

We passed Dal Lake, shimmering in the early morning light, then wound up through cedar forests to Sonamarg. One passenger intrigued me. He wore army uniform, a red beret and looked Tibetan. He was a Khampa[8] and belonged to the '22s',[9] a semi-official guerrilla unit that patrolled behind Chinese lines in Tibet. At one point they were supported by the CIA and operated though Mustang in Nepal, but the CIA had recently pulled the plug on them so they had regrouped in Ladakh and were operating under Ngari Rinpoche, the Dalai Lama's younger brother. I had a letter of introduction to Ngari Rinpoche, but had just missed him in Dharamsala.

There are many stories about the Zoji La. The pass is often spoken about as if it is a living person, inspiring fear and admiration in the same breath. Some still call the pass the Shurji La after Shiva, the all-powerful Hindu god who creates, protects and transforms the universe. Shiva – god of destruction; highly appropriate if your vehicle goes over the edge.

Very slowly, army convoys crawl up the steep hairpin bends. You wait for hours and then it is like a rodeo, as gaily coloured trucks and overloaded buses jostle for position. Some lorries break down and are simply dragged to the side of the road. If brakes fail, that's it. 'Trust in God' and military engineers. The pass is only open for half the year.

Below the road you could see the old trade route, just wide enough for two laden animals to pass and a single telephone line. There were stories of whole caravans being wiped out in late spring. The first caravans of the year always got the highest prices down in Kashmir. Avalanches were frequent and heavy. These days it was army convoys that got caught. Far below in the valley bottom you could see the mangled remains of several lorries and buses that had gone over the edge. In winter, snowploughs keep the pass open as long as possible. Road construction was a dangerous job and in these places close to the front line it was always undertaken by military engineers. All the way up there are wayside shrines and memorials to soldiers.

Early intimations

As the bus wound its way up the Zoji La my mind drifted a little, half tired, half hypnotised, almost in a dream state as the cedar trees flashed past and the views of snow-clad mountains opened out. I now had time to think about where my own journey had really started, where I was going and what I was looking for.

Travels often begin much earlier than you realise, usually in childhood. My grandfather, my mother's father, was an excellent navigator and was on convoys in both wars. According to his small, slim, blue P&O diary, I was born at the beginning of a very cold spell in January 1954. His entries were sparse: 'V Cold'; 'VV Cold'. So my first inkling of the outside world was of a vast white landscape inhabited only by snow and ice. If the photographs are anything to go by, the trees were white with hoar frost. A magical entrée into a cold, glistening winter world.

I was then brought up on the western edge of Dartmoor in south-west England. A fine, wild place with its granite tors and bevy of fast-flowing rivers. When I was eight years old there was a very bad winter. Dartmoor was covered in snow and ice for three months, like a polar ice cap. Temperatures went down to -20°C and rivers froze.

I lived alongside one. School was cancelled and there was a slight feeling of anarchy. You could pick up quite bit of speed tobogganing down main roads on old fertiliser bags and tin trays. Farms and villages were cut off for weeks on end, even months.

Snow creaked underfoot. Rivers became like glaciers. The maps in our minds now had crevasses. Avalanches were common.

Like Zen monks we entered a closed order, went up to the moor and observed its pale face, a vast moonscape upon which we walked slowly, like small gods. Silence and isolation were constant companions. Even the sea froze over.

These images became deeply embedded in my young mind, as if snow and ice were the natural order of things. The idea of being cut off from the outside world for half the year was therefore very appealing, a subconscious desire to return to that vast, white, endless space. If it involved mountains, even better. And so it was that the seeds of winter exploration were sown.

Wild places

But there were other layers of meaning, other images that sprang to mind. Other wild places that had original flavours, landscapes that were rugged, barren and untouched by human hand. It was the effect of the mountains on the mind that interested me most of all. Dangerous on your own or when caught out in bad weather. The beauty is within and without.

You lead a mountain life even when away from them. You are drawn to the mountains by their stark sculpture, their angular geology, the network of glaciers and snowfields. It is the nature of the rock that shapes them and gives them their individual topography. High-altitude ecology is very fragile. Certain zones can change with increased temperature, snowfall or over-grazing. Glaciers can retreat and some villages have had to be abandoned. It is something you feel within your bones. An unspoken understanding, a reverence, a deep respect.

I was also fascinated by rock in more immediate ways. By scaling cliff faces, clinging on by your fingertips, dancing on your toes, balancing on lips, cracks and ledges, struggling up chimneys, negotiating overhangs, seeking new routes up vertical walls. Rock climbing had its own strange satisfactions, but danger always lurked in your shadow. Sea-cliff climbing was a particular pleasure. I had several narrow escapes. Eventually rock climbing gave way to mountaineering.

I joined the army and signed on the dotted line for what was supposed to be a permanent career. They positively encouraged exploration. I was in the Royal Engineers, whose colonels, according to Kipling, were either 'Methodist, married or mad'. Well, I wasn't married or Methodist, so that left only one option. Scotland in winter had its interesting moments, ice gullies, ice climbing, blizzards and snow holing, crampons and ice axes. But deep down I needed a very different sort of challenge. Something timeless. In another dimension.

Travelling became a way of life. In their infinite wisdom the army posted me to Cyprus in the eastern Mediterranean, and so each summer I travelled further east. My apprenticeship – first in Turkey, then Iran and then Afghanistan. Hugging borders, crossing mountain ranges and deserts, testing altitude. Testing myself. Nosing around bazaars and backstreets, finding nomads and their black tents, entering restricted areas, evading army patrols and customs posts. The Cold War hotting up. The Middle East, or, as James Joyce probably would have called it, 'The Muddle East'.

I had tasted deep silence on Mount Ararat[10] and in the Dasht-e-Lut – the Desert of Emptiness.[11] Mountain silence and desert silence. One cold, one hot. Each had its own flavour. Such silence was addictive. On Ararat I was held up by Kurdish communist bandits at 13,000ft just below the snowline. They were on horseback and wore bandoliers and waistcoats, as well as Kurdish black and white chequered headdresses. A very different sort of silence when you realise that four carbines are trained on you.

A year later the army turned a blind eye and I crossed the Hindu Kush on foot, through Badakhshan and Nuristan. 'A Long Walk in the Hindu Kush'. Newby territory. I was held hostage for two days by a local tribesman, then snow came down on the fifth pass and not for the first time I sensed the extraordinary power of winter in the mountains. It gave me ideas.

Unfortunately I also contracted typhus in Afghanistan – 'Afghan fever'. Sweating hot and cold, semi-delirious at times. I was put in a darkened isolation ward all on my own with the blinds pulled down. When I was able to open my eyes again and my mind eventually settled, I started reading *Walden* – Henry Thoreau's classic account of living beside a lake in Concord, Massachusetts. *Walden* was good for the soul, and slowly I began to see the world through different eyes. Why not take a leaf out of Thoreau's book? Why not spend a year alone deep in the mountains? Afghanistan was a stepping stone. Fever the catalyst. Ladakh – a mountain desert.

In my letter of resignation to the army I mentioned something along the lines that 'studying early Tibetan Buddhist wall paintings might be more useful than bridging on the Rhine ...'. My contribution to the Cold War had not been very significant. The general was not amused, but to his credit my old adjutant was brilliant and managed to get me out of the army in three weeks flat, which was quite a record.[12] But it cost me £1,946, no mean sum in those days.

Uncle Kenny

As the road climbed up the Zoji La, the pass became steeper and steeper and trees slowly began to peter out. The bus only just squeezed round each tight hairpin bend. As I looked over the edge, I began thinking about Uncle Kenny, an eccentric uncle whose family had been out in India for four or five generations. He was something of a legend, and it was his colourful stories of India that had drawn me inexorably further east.

Earnest and brilliant, Uncle Kenny's knowledge and enthusiasm for Indian art was infectious. He was one of those uncles who with a deft flick of his freckled hand talked in secretive whispers about the Great Game on the North-West Frontier. He had been born at a hill station at the beginning of a particularly early and tempestuous monsoon, and was 'milk brothers' to Pathan tribesmen. He always saw India from the inside. Eccentric even by Indian army standards, he was a man of many layers, quixotic, highly intelligent and brusque. He didn't suffer fools gladly, but if he liked you and you were keen on your subject and asked the right questions, the doors of the 'Wonder House' began to open one by one.

When I was twelve I wanted to be an archaeologist and had already been on a dig. So my grandmother had a natter down the telephone line to her sister in Kent and arranged for Uncle Kenny to give me a conducted tour of the British Museum. K de Burgh Codrington was a real live professor and for many years he had also been Keeper of the Indian section at the V&A. I thought being a keeper was like a timekeeper, goalkeeper or a zookeeper, which was not far off the mark. He had indeed looked after one old Bengal tiger, 'Tippu's Tiger', a French-inspired mechanical wooden tiger captured at Seringapatam in south India. When you turned a handle, the tiger growled as it mauled an East India man, who let out a plaintive, muffled scream. Pride and joy of the V&A. *Très jolie*.

Uncle Kenny was indeed a keeper. He kept time with India. He kept India under his cloak and up his sleeve. He kept the flame of Indian artistic knowledge alive in London with wonderful exhibitions that helped change people's perceptions of Indian art. He loved museums and was also an avid keeper of secrets.

We met at the entrance to the BM, as the grown-ups called it, with all its pillars and capitals. Uncle Kenny looked me up and down as if I were a recruit for Lumsden's Guides or Hodson's Horse. He shook my paw and took me on a whistlestop tour of all the ancient carvings and Buddhist statues, pointing out any artefacts that came under his gaze, all the time telling me not 'What they knew' but 'What they did not know'. A revelation to me that 'grown-up' knowledge had black holes in it. Sometimes he would stand in front of a Buddhist statue and just absorb its beauty, then touch the statue gently as if it were a real person and move on with a slight nod of his head. These were his friends, colleagues and inspiration. This was his office, his temple, his spiritual home.

Then Uncle Kenny took me upstairs, where there were other smaller statues: gold and bronze Tibetan Buddhas and even a small, squat crystal goose from the ancient city of Taxila, thought to contain a small bone relic of the Buddha.[13] The goose flying over the mountains, a migratory path so beloved of Buddhists to the lake beyond, the flight path of the soul.

So before going to Ladakh I visited Uncle Kenny in his lair. Lunch, roast chicken. Rose Cottage, Appledore, on the edge of Romney Marsh. This time he was sorting through a great pile of Kushana coins that lay scattered on his table, with elegant Kharoshti script that danced around the Greek heads. Uncle Kenny had pepper and salt hair and a large pair of professorial horn-rimmed glasses. He spoke in sentences and half sentences. He showed me another small Buddha head. It left a deep impression. Peaceful, wise, intelligent, aristocratic, refined. The fusion of early Buddhist sculpture with Greek aesthetics; ancient Gandhara, the 'perfumed land' – a sacred place in his heart. He was always talking about Taxila, Peshawar and Kapisa, names of ancient cities that started to reverberate around my mind.

Uncle Kenny's ears pricked up when he heard that I was going to Ladakh. In spring 1942 he had tried to climb the Zoji La at night with guides, porters and burning torches. There was no road, only a slender track. He was optimistic and wanted to see the ancient Buddhist wall paintings at Alchi beside the Indus. But Shiva had other ideas and hampered his attempt to cross the pass. There had been a heavy fall of snow, and the avalanches were unpredictable and dangerous. Eventually in the early hours, when up to his waist in powder snow, he had reluctantly turned back.

Uncle Kenny's deep interest in Tibetan Buddhism had been sparked by a chance encounter as a boy in Simla when he saw a Tibetan salt trader in a rough woollen cloak squatting down outside Viceregal Lodge flanked by two British sergeants. Something was rather odd about the salt trader. He looked very refined, had long fingernails and pointed ears. When Kenny asked who he was, one of the sergeants replied, 'That, Sah, is the Dalai Lama.' His Holiness had fled Tibet to India to escape the attentions of the Chinese and was in secret talks with the British Viceroy. Must have been the 13th Dalai Lama in about 1910.

A rare historical moment as they both looked at each other …

My 'task' was therefore to continue Uncle Kenny's journey into Ladakh, to explore the culture, to decode Zangskar and to decipher the language of silence. That was quite a challenge. Creating a museum of the mind. To record as best I could a living Buddhist culture with a continuous thread going back to the time of Gandhara. That was the sort of challenge I was looking for.

When I left Appledore, Uncle Kenny wished me luck and simply said, 'Beware avalanches.' He shook my paw. I had been given my marching orders.

Dried apricots

The summit of the Zoji La was an anti-climax – a few scrappy buildings, a toll barrier and an army snowplough detachment. Sikh engineers stood around in green padded jackets and dark blue turbans, just waiting to get their snowploughs stuck in. They banged their hands together and stamped their feet. Snow swirled around ominously.

Paperwork was checked and tolls paid. Eventually the Sikh sergeant raised the red and white barrier, waving us through, then brought the bar back down again with a clang. We were in. The doors were shutting one by one. The password was no word at all. The Tibetan Khampa smiled as he looked out of the bus window. He was coming home to his family – Tibetan Buddhist territory that he understood.

Next day in the town of Kargil, right on the Pakistani front line, I bought ten kilos of dried apricots, each kilo of wizened nuggets carefully weighed out on a hand-held balance with a single smooth, rounded stone salvaged from the river in the other pan.[14] Old-style weights and measures. Brass pans. Equilibrium. Each kilo tipped into a small, dusty hessian sack. Apricots, gemstones of the mountains. Rich flavours of summer. Orange tinged with red. Blushing. Apricot oil was used in lamps. Medicine. Gives a good sheen to dark hair and is rubbed onto the skin when hands become chapped with cold. I was interested in the taste. A rich, complex sweetness that filters through your mouth. Anchors you into warmer times. Best soaked the night before and then warmed up.

Apricot wood is also used for musical instruments. In China the expression 'expert of the apricot grove' is used to refer to a good physician. Apricots are used in traditional Tibetan *amchi* medicine. Almost as sacred as juniper. Ten kilos of apricots would last me most of the winter, I reckoned. Useful down the frozen river. Luxury.

Kargil was a key town strategically.[15] In the old days you could go north to Skardu and Baltistan. But since Partition in 1947 it had been the scene of bitter fighting. In three wars the town had changed hands several times. It was even said that soldiers in the Pakistani OP (observation point) on the mountain that over-looked the town could, with a powerful pair of binoculars, see what the Indian brigadier was having for breakfast on the veranda of his army bungalow down by the river. A *masala* omelette and a chapatti or two, washed down with *masala chai*, this informa-tion no doubt relayed to the generals in Rawalpindi for analysis. One day the Indians put in an airstrike, followed by an uphill assault to reclaim the OP so that the brigadier could enjoy his breakfast in peace.

To get to Suru I took a lorry. There had been a very hard frost that morning, and to get the engine started the boy lit a fire with straw under the sump to get the sluggish oil moving and the engine turning over. Eventually the diesel spluttered into life. I travelled in the back with my baggage, a few goats and thirty men standing on sacks of flour. I hung on for dear life. This valley had once been Buddhist. Near Sanku, there was still a tall Buddha statue.

Six hours and forty miles later, after many halts, the lorry arrived at the roadhead – Panikar. I offloaded my possessions and watched the lorry going back down the valley, changing gear as it negotiated stream beds and rode over large ruts. I listened intently, maybe for half an hour, as the engine noise became fainter and fainter, slowly receding until it disappeared altogether. The silence that followed had such extraordinary depth and breadth to it. You could almost touch it. This was what I had come for. Then the dust storm hit.

The roadhead

Walking into Zangskar from Panikar in the middle of November on the very edge of winter presented its own problems. It is still a hundred-mile walk to Padum, but it felt more like a hundred years. At night I kipped out in the engineer's compound, sleeping on the concrete floor of an open lean-to shed, surrounded by all the baggage I had brought up from Kashmir – two large hampers, half a dozen hessian sacks, an assortment of bags and holdalls, two sets of skis and snowshoes, ice axes and crampons, as well as two hurricane lanterns and a Primus stove.

The local teacher helped me to find horses. To get horsemen to go to Padum on the edge of winter was not easy. They had worked on caravans all summer and were exhausted. I needed four horses. For two days we walked from village to village asking anybody we saw, without success. There were many excuses, all of which were valid.

It was too cold
  Horses had been worked all summer.
Snow might come at any time
  Snow on the pass was often very deep.
It was too far
  There was no grazing.
The men were tired
  Horses were tired.
Horses needed shoeing
  They needed extra grain.
The men were wary
  Their wives did not want them to go.
What if there was a blizzard?
  Men had died on the pass.
What if they were trapped in Zangskar?
  What then?
What if the horses were trapped
  Who would pay for fodder?
How would they even get fodder?
  It was too late in the year.
Where would they stay?
  There were wolves.
There were bears
  There were snow leopards.
There had been trouble in Zangskar
  Some kind of uprising.
Rumours that people had been killed
  That is what they are saying.
It is too cold
  None of them want to go.

In the end, I negotiated directly with two brothers in their forties, Fazal Din and Jamal Din. We agreed a price, based on double the government rate because their return journey would be unladen.[16] It seemed reasonable enough in the circumstances as it was a seven-day journey: seven days there and seven days back, which made a journey of fourteen days. If they did the journey quicker then they kept the extra money, which was a good incentive. Fifteen rupees to the pound.

> The government rate was 25 rupees a day per horse.
> 4 horses @ 25 rupees a day = 100 rupees a day for 14
>   days = 1,400 Rs
> 2 men @ 10 rupees a day with double allowance for the
>   cold = 280 Rs
>
> Grand total = 1,680 Rs

I paid them an advance. Their wives watched intently as the men counted the money and then handed it over to them. The men now had to get the horses shod and fed with barley. We would leave the next day in the afternoon.

A grave situation

In between these negotiations I went to find two graves in a willow grove at the back of the village. The teacher had tipped me off. The first was an army officer's, a fine sarcophagus:

IN EVER LOVING MEMORY OF HERBERT W. CHRISTIAN
CAPTAIN KING'S ROYAL RIFLES FIFTH SON OF
GEORGE AND MARY CHRISTIAN BIGHTON WOOD
ALRESFORD ENGLAND DIED OF FEVER AT SURU
MAY 21ST 1896 AGED 29

A corner of a foreign land that was forever Hampshire, with magnificent views of the Nun Kun massif. His regiment, the 60th Rifles, had been involved in the Relief of Chitral, a small beleaguered fortress right up on the Afghan border. He had used his leave to hunt ibex and markhor.

The other grave was that of a Ladakhi Christian, his name carved on a slate slab about eighteen inches square. Simple and minimalist.

IN LOVING MEMORY
OF SC GERGAN
LEH LADAKH BORN
29 12 1900 KILLED
BY KUTH RAIDERS
AT PENTSE LA AGED 29 ON
14. 6. 1929 WHILE ON DUTY

Both men, I noticed, were twenty-nine when they died. I had no intention of joining them just yet. As I was only twenty-two, it gave me seven years' grace.

The Gergans were well known. Back down in Srinagar in Sonwar bazaar I had met Sonam Skyabldan Gergan, Chimed Gergan's brother, and he told me the story. Chimed had been a forest and game officer for the Maharajah of Jammu and Kashmir. The previous summer he had apprehended some Kishtwari smugglers of *kuth*, a valuable plant found on the Pense La. *Kuth* had a high value as it was used as a drug, dye and medicine. Gergan confiscated their haul and took them down to Kargil to see the magistrate as they had evaded customs duties, but they managed to bribe their way out of trouble. The next year they were not afraid of Gergan, so when he tried to re-arrest them they simply knifed him, left him on the pass to die and fled back to Kishtwar.

After this tragic death, Sonam Skyabldan Gergan was given his brother's job and was able to check up on all his father's historical observations about the history of Ladakh. His father, Joseph Gergan, had helped translate the Bible into Ladakhi for the Moravian missionaries. When I told Mr Gergan that I was going to Zangskar for the winter he looked at me quizzically and simply said, 'Is that wise?'

Snuff and silver horse bell

In the mountains you were always judged by the amount of baggage you had and the number of pack animals. In the summer some caravans had a hundred horses. That was very respectable. A large caravan on the move had a wonderful rhythm and life all of its own. Now my own small caravan from Suru was made up of two horsemen and four horses. So in the eyes of the village I was only a four-horse wallah.

Loading was simple. First, rough horse blankets were slung over the backs of the horses to cushion the load and prevent chafing sores, then homemade wooden pack saddles were secured in place. Next, the girth strap, which was only two strands of rope, was tightened several times. While this was going on, the packhorses were given nosebags full of barley and chaff. Loading all the horses took at least half an hour each morning, often before dawn when your fingers were at their coldest. You got going as quickly as possible.

Each load was carefully organised, weighed and balanced. Each day the horses had the same load, and if the load slipped at any point on the journey they simply stopped and waited for the two horsemen to readjust and tighten the load. Everyone knew what they were doing. It was often far too cold to talk.

Day one. We set out in the middle of the afternoon and began to walk towards the fine snow-capped pyramid of Nun, which at 23,500ft was the highest peak for many miles. An elegant curved plume of spindrift was blowing off the summit, the speed of the jet stream probably in excess of 100 mph, icy winds that sooner or later would come down to the valley floor.

As we walked along the path beneath the mountain there was complete silence. The streams were all frozen – just the odd gurgle coming from beneath the ice. Icicles hung down from overhangs, cliffs and crevices. The road had its own path and we simply followed, not speaking a word. We knew the risks. We were just glad to get going and bask in what was left of the afternoon sunshine.

The Nun Kun massif towered above us, a wonderfully cosmopolitan mountain group that attracted climbers of many different nationalities: British and Nepalese as well as American, Italian, French and Swiss. These mountains were worshipped by the local villagers, who thought that foreign mountaineers were climbing to find God. Why else go to those lengths or heights? Maybe they were right. God was always over the next ridge. But then if there were many mountains, surely there must be many gods, not just one?

The packhorses moved in line ahead slowly but surely, pacing along the unmade road. On dried-up river beds small mushrooms of dust emanated from their hooves. Occasionally they jockeyed for position, but often they were content to go at their own measured pace. Very soon the rhythm of the caravan took hold of us and we settled down, as all caravans do. The sort of pace you could keep up for weeks on end.

In front was Fazal Din with the leading rein. He smoked cigarettes through a clenched fist. He took a deep breath every few paces and was almost in a trance. The other horseman, Jamal Din, at the rear, chewed *naswar*, Afghan snuff, and every so often exuded a long jet of green spittle that congealed in the dust.[17] In the Hindu Kush I had seen the effect of opium on porters. It delayed their progress by hours, even days, as they slowly lost track of time or where they were going. Every man has his poison.

I can still smell the caravan, an earthy, pungent smell that reeks of warm horse, sweat, leather and straining muscles. Even in sub-zero temperatures it had a certain *je ne sais quoi* – a musky stable odour of horse dung with a bit of hay and fodder thrown in for good measure. *Eau de cheval*. Wolves would have picked the scent up many miles away on the cold wind and licked their lips.

The packhorses stood patiently every morning, waiting to be loaded. Three were brown or bay – the fourth was black. They all had a white blaze on their foreheads, a makeshift bridle and leading rein. They say that Zangskari horses are some of the toughest in the world, second only to Yarkandi horses. They can carry loads and even people over the main Karakoram Pass at over 18,000ft, and the Indian army often used them for the resupply of troops at high altitude.

The relief of walking was enormous. And then out of the silence came the sound of a bell approaching us. Clear and insistent – a silver horse bell. The horse was ridden at a trot by a red lama. Over the saddle was an ornate Tibetan saddle rug with dragons and snow lions. An imposing man with a broad, bronzed face and good stirrups. A fine and inspiring sight. The lama passed without a word, but smiled and raised his hand. It was as if he were in meditation. These mountains have that effect on you without you even thinking.

The sound of the bell was so clear that it stayed with me for several hours. The pace of the horse and demeanour of the rider were so very different to ours. He was probably a monastery manager making his way back to Leh before the snows came. Just a silver horse bell, and yet the space within which it rang seemed so vast.

Parkachik glacier

Sleeping outside was positively parky, -15°C, sometimes -20°C. First night, a field beyond Parkachik. I sheltered behind the hampers. Making tea was not easy as water had to be gleaned from small streams that only flowed under the ice for a few hours a day. The ice axe came into its own.

All during that first night, as I lay on the frozen earth, I could hear the glacier creaking and groaning to itself as it slowly crept down the slopes of Nun Kun towards the cold green waters of the Suru river. The Parkachik glacier is over eight miles long and sounded like some wild animal turning over in its sleep, stretching and yawning. A wild beast that fed off avalanches. Its snout came right down into the water.

Day two. We set off before dawn. A crescent moon, pale amid the stars. I watched as a 100ft pinnacle of ice hovered, teetered and then toppled into the water in slow motion. Hardly a splash, just a ripple reaching out. The glacier once came right across the river. In the past this was the beginning of Buddhist territory and grazing rights. Somewhere nearby there was a rock inscription in Tibetan that demarcated the boundary of Rangdom. Invisible boundaries of influence and ideas. It was difficult to tell where autumn ended and winter began. Fluid frontiers.

The Suru river was clear, green and sedate. Ice floes from the glacier were joined by thousands of other smaller ones from upstream. A continuous process, and fascinating to watch. Ice in another dimension, like ice ferns but on a vast scale. The freezing-up of a large Himalayan river was a long and tedious process that took many months. Yet few people witnessed it. Sometimes great sheets of ice formed in the shallows and froze over. But the river level often changed. If the sun shone for a day or two, the glaciers would melt a bit and the river would rise, and if it was very cold the side streams froze up and the river level fell. The ice sheets would then collapse, break up and flow downstream. A continuous process of ice forming and breaking, ice being carried downstream. Hundreds of ice floes were on the move. A dignified procession. And the green of the river not dissimilar to the one green pane of glass in my room, only a slightly darker shade.

When there was deep, still water, the river froze right over and then you heard the eerie scraping noise as all the ice floes invisibly passed underneath, dragged along by the current. But it would be quite a while before you could walk on the ice. The river in winter was alive, organic and took its time to freeze.

In the upper reaches of the Suru valley I had the distinct feeling of being in no man's land, limbo, trapped between two very different worlds. A strange zone with few, if any, signs of habitation, as if passing from one country to another, from one language, belief system and philosophy to another more colourful, expansive world. This was like walking on thin air down a vast mountain corridor wracked with harsh, cold winds, low cloud and occasion snow flurries. Very occasionally peaks could be glimpsed. All unclimbed, apart from the twin summits of Nun Kun. All beckoning. Maybe the mountains talked to each other. Maybe the glaciers had a language of their own, crevasses their own code of practice. Humans were almost superfluous unless they meditated.

The more I walked, the more the mountain silence began to penetrate my bones and my way of thinking. If you looked carefully there were many different zones, all related to altitude, grazing and snowline. Near the villages were the zones of farmers, then the zones of shepherds and yak herders, and the more subtle Buddhist zones of monasteries, monks and nuns, where meditators spent weeks, even years, surveying the peaks and glaciers. It was this last zone that interested me most of all. Zangskar beckoned from afar.

As the path began to rise towards the yellowy light of dawn I caught sight of movement far below. Unusual … a figure, a man who crossed the river above a waterfall with a bundle of dried grass strapped to his back. Quite where he had come from I could not make out, or even where he was going, but he must have been out there all night.

And then he came up towards the road and I saw that our paths would cross. He was cheerful, despite being very cold, and had taken his rough homespun trousers off to cross the river. His legs were still bare and dripping; in his cummerbund, stowed away, a small sickle about six inches across. We greeted him warmly and I marvelled at his tenacity. I was put in mind of Matsuo Basho, the famous Japanese haiku poet, and his observations on Japanese peasants in his *Narrow Road to the Deep*

North.[18] I felt as if I were on my own narrow road, only I was going south and east not north. But our feelings about winter were the same. This unkempt but cheerful man was on a voyage all of his own. There were no villages up here and what he was doing was something of a mystery.

> Only an old man clutching a sickle –
> Drops of water – dried grass
> Silvery beneath the crescent moon
> His cloak covered in patches.
> Feet and legs bare
> Shades of things to come.

We passed like ships in the night. His greeting a handshake. His smile infectious. More than anything else this cheerful old man and his small parcel of fodder strapped to his back told me about the precariousness of their lives. Here every blade of dried grass counted. Maybe he was searching for an animal, like the famous ox-herding pictures used in Zen teachings, or returning from a trip over the other side of the mountains leading a yak or *dzo* for sale. You never knew how long winter was going to last. It was always a gamble.

Boundary of Buddhism

Sometimes where a stream crossed the road, it froze over into a great ice sheet maybe a hundred yards long. Each horse was gently coaxed across. We dug out frozen earth with a stick and scattered it on the ice so their hooves could get a grip. A broken leg up here would have been a disaster, for a horse could not survive the night. And if we lost one horse, the other three could not carry the extra load. Slowly I began to admire the horses' tenacity. They were bred in Zangskar, so in a sense they were going home.

Usually we stopped around midday for an hour. With three pieces of dried yak dung you can make a good fire set between three stones. If it was dry it broke with a crack. There was often no firewood, just scrub. Dried dung from the summer's grazing was essential. No fire – no warm food.

At one point we passed three small lakes that were so still they reflected the mountains perfectly. Half frozen over. Each line, like a ripple, led right round the pond, a night's frost creeping out from the shore, an inch, then six inches, then a foot, then several feet at a time, until, like the previous night, it covered half the lake, the contours in the ice like tree rings recording the frost's nocturnal advances. The following night it would freeze over completely. At one point I looked back at the Nun Kun peaks and saw a great rock face towering over the valley. Even from twenty miles it looked magnificent.

After the second day's long march I saw the first prayer flags. The boundary of Buddhism, a psychological, social, linguistic and religious frontier. This was where Zangskar really began. From now on I was in Buddhist territory and despite the cold wind it felt very different. I felt like I was coming home and repeated the odd mantra under my breath. I sensed a degree of protection, as if the local gods were now on my side. Buddhists left nothing to chance.

Scores of prayer flags were strung out from long, thin willow poles anchored into small cairns. They are usually found on the summits of passes or at other key points on the journey such as river crossings. It is where the spirit of the pass or the mountain or the village resides. A place of offering and worship.

These flags were faded and fluttered in the cold, dry wind, each colour symbolising a particular Buddhist idea or element. Yellow is earth, green is water, red is fire, white is wind and blue is outer space. Five elements instead of four. On each cotton flag there were mantras and Buddhist prayers. A wind horse is often printed in the centre, special horses (*lungta*) that carry the prayers galloping on the wind. In each corner there are mythological creatures: a Garuda bird – wisdom; the dragon – gentle power; the Tibetan snow lion – fearlessness and joy; the tiger – confidence. This was a complex spiritual world, a potent mixture of Tibetan Buddhism and shamanic, pre-Buddhist folk beliefs still very important in the mountains, particularly when the elements are unpredictable. Compassion and inner strength transmitted on the wind.

These prayer flags are often hand printed from old wood blocks that have seen many seasons. Flags are replaced at certain times of year by local villagers and they have a distinct psychological effect, as if harnessing the powers of nature. A powerful political and territorial statement, for although the path gets tougher and the altitude higher, at least you know that you are on Buddhist soil at long last.

You have entered the land of Buddha's teaching, where following the path to enlightenment is the aspiration of many. Indeed, the word for Buddhists is simply *nangpa* – the 'insiders'. It means they are inside the teaching, and that they are seeking the solutions to existence and philosophy and life's perplexing questions within the very nature of mind itself, a radical quest based on long experience of silence and inner common sense.

Nangpa is not to be confused with *nan pa*, which means bar-headed goose, the species that flies over the main Himalayan range twice a year on migration. They breed in Ladakh and the lakes of Tibet, then fly over the Himalaya to winter on the wetland areas of north India, reversing the journey in spring. They have been seen flying close to very high mountains – even over Everest – and are very strong flyers indeed. One Tibetan source says, 'You cannot see the summit from nearby, but you can see the summit from nine directions and a bird that flies as high as the summit goes blind.'[19] Maybe the geese are temporarily snowblind.

Geese are mentioned many times in Buddhist teachings to symbolise the mind's migration and the wisdom of non-attachment, as well as being a metaphor for enlightenment, which is 'like a goose arriving at a great lake'.

Mantra

Having passed the first prayer flags we camped for the second night beside the track, sleeping out rough as always. We had collected twigs and dried yak dung as we walked. To make lighting a fire easier, small pieces of dried horse dung were soaked in kerosene and then ignited. You knelt down and blew till the fire took. Another trick was not to camp anywhere near a village. All the firewood and scrub would have been collected and there would be little or no grazing at this time of year. The villagers needed every scrap of fuel they could find.

That second night we slept out in what must have been a summer grazing camp with low walls. Darkness came quickly to our shivering fingers. Lighting stoves and using matches became a major preoccupation. Tying bootlaces and doing up buttons became a chore. The stubbornness of numb fingers lingered in your mind, for without your fingers you can do nothing. Not even strike a match.

The stillness was remarkable. Only the odd noise of horses moving from foot to foot as they slept standing upright in among the rocks. Our breath froze. No one else was on the move in the mountains at this time of year. The snow was already a month late, so we were cutting it very fine indeed. The frosts were unbelievably hard.

Boiling point is always lower at high altitude – pressure cookers are useful when cooking rice, so long as they don't explode – and mountaineers use the boiling-point temperature as a guide to height. There were graphs that could be used to measure the altitude. Roughly speaking, at 13,000ft the boiling temperature would be about 87°C, which made tea less appetising and porridge a little gloopy, and you lost 1°C for every thousand feet you climbed. So at 20,000ft your tea would boil at roughly 80°C. A good rule of thumb. I had my own altimeter in a leather case and wore it round my neck. I consulted it every day. It was my compass, my lucky charm, my amulet.

On the third day I saw the first Buddhist monastery, perched on its lone rock far away in the distance. Here was something to aim for, a navigational aid, but in the end we took a short cut to one side. The main building was whitewashed but the Temple of the Guardian Deities (the *Gonkhang*) at the rear was red, which made a great contrast. This was Rangdom Gompa, a Gelugpa monastery, yellow-hat followers of Tsongkhapa, the great 14th-century sage.[20]

The valley opened out into a vast flood plain, barren in winter but with a great sense of freedom. Five valleys meant five winds and five rivers. The monastery stood alone on its great rock, a wonderful spectacle but also cold, desolate and dusty. There were two villages: Zhuldok, the nearer one, and Tashi Tanze, tucked away on the other side of the monastery.

In November you walk on borrowed time. In Zhuldok I counted about twenty houses, roofs all heavily laden with neatly stacked fodder and firewood, ready for a long winter. The houses were not crammed together but separate, about thirty yards apart. Windows were larger than those down in Suru. More wood, more glass, more windows, more prosperous, their main wealth coming from selling horses, cattle and yaks in the autumn.

There were also fewer people. Monkish celibacy and fraternal polyandry saw to that, although I was never quite sure how the women felt about it with two or even three husbands. But in the Buddhist world women can only inherit land if there are no brothers. They are then in a very strong position, and can even hire and fire husbands if they want. It often depended on the size of their landholding and how many workers they needed. Arrangements seemed to be very flexible. Some men had two wives. Some women had two husbands. Divorce was not uncommon. Then there were nuns. As a culture they had learnt to keep the population down. The land can only support so many, and in winter food becomes scarce. Who can predict how long a winter will last? Instinct, intuition and ancient customs have a way of keeping you on the straight and narrow.

ཨོཾ་མ་ཎི་པདྨེ་ཧཱུྂ༔ *Om mani padme hum*

In Zhuldok each house was daubed with the mantra *Om mani padme hum*, six syllables invoking wisdom and the inner path.[21] They also had a line of red dots along the wall at waist height to keep the ghosts and evil spirits away, and the odd red triangle daubed on the corners of the house – Buddhism and Central Asian shamanism in one convenient package. Even wooden windows were outlined in ochre and black to give them a greater presence. The windows were the eyes of the house.

Heady stuff early in the morning. *Om mani padme hum*. Not a bad mantra to be walking to, repeated softly under one's breath, each step a syllable.

Wind horse

Outside one house a woman leaned out wearing a *perag*, her headdress covered in rough-cut turquoise. She offered me a jug of yogurt that she had just made, saying, '*Dun, dun, dun*' ('Drink, drink, drink'). It was the old rule of travelling, a curious friendship that exists between those who are on a journey and those they pass. And yet I was a stranger in winter. I accepted the yogurt willingly. Such generosity.

The yogurt had a smoky flavour a bit like peat smoke, which gave it a fine edge. It was sharp. How they keep their yogurt cultures alive in the winter was remarkable. Yaks stood around the village loitering and were then driven off to some last patch of grazing by a young girl with a long willow wand.

All over Ladakh and Tibet the mantra *Om mani padme hum* is repeated thousands and thousands of times every day in monasteries, on prayer wheels, in private contemplation, fluttering on the prayer flags in the carved stones and in the murmured repetitions that accompany every walk of life. Then there are the 100,000 prostrations that can take several months to complete. In Phuktal Gompa I once saw an old but very fit man doing his prostrations on a wooden board. He had small white pebbles that he moved every time he completed ten, then a hundred, then a thousand. I think he did a thousand prostrations a day, so it would have taken him a hundred days. Sometimes pilgrims prostrated themselves full length along a road or path, mile upon mile. Humility itself.

There was also a small wind-driven *mani* wheel on the roof corner of the first house in Zhuldok, and later I saw small water-driven prayer wheels that went round and round, the Buddhist universe endlessly sending out good prayers and invocations. We would need many mantras to take us over the pass before the snow came down. It was still a very long way and the snowline crept ever lower on the mountainside.

When chanting *Om mani padme hum*, it was extraordinary to think that millions of people across the Tibetan Buddhist world were also chanting this simple 'prayer', invoking not only compassion but emptiness itself. It felt as if we were walking into the void. Form and emptiness, mountains and the feeling of infinite space. To hear the mantra chanted by a hundred monks in a monastery is extraordinary, the young boy monks very high, almost squeaky, and the old monks who have seen seventy winters or more, very deep, low and sonorous, their faces dark and gnarled like old walnuts. The internal rhythms take the mind into very calm regions, the repetition possessing a strange healing power that cannot easily be explained.

Then there were *chortens* dotted along the way, otherwise known as *stupas*, squat Buddhist structures in various phases of collapse, a bit like vast pawns from a chess set dotted about the landscape.[22] Whitewashed once a year, they also embody teaching in a symbolic way, sometimes containing the remains of holy men or small moulded clay Buddhas (*tsa tsa*) made with ash from cremations.

As I left Zhuldok I passed a group of three *chortens* representing the three Buddhas, past, present and future. Plenty of philosophy to chew upon. *Chortens* are quite complex – the square base represents earth, the dome represents water, the spire on top represents fire, which transforms life into ashes. Then on top of that a parasol and crescent moon which represent air and a sun which represents outer space, i.e. aether. Five elements instead of four. Some *chortens* are small, others large.

We then cut across old marshes that in summer were a haven for wildfowl, but the water table had sunk and what was left of the water remained as ice, frozen into small waves, an undulating silvery sheen of ice crystals. Maybe a quarter of a mile of silver-coated sand, like a shoal of small, silvery fish. The ice crystals crunched underfoot. The surface was ruffled and ruckled into small waves blown by the wind and frozen almost instantaneously. *Sastrugi.*[23] Windblown.

Cold and dry, with four valleys funnelling the winds towards us, Rangdom Gompa with its red and white walls sat sedately on top of its rock, commanding the whole valley. The morning light was not bad at all.

For some reason when I was walking behind the horses, a few jumbled lines from T. S. Eliot's *Waste Land* came to me, about shadows and red rocks, shelter, fear and handfuls of dust, which seemed appropriate, though I thought it unlikely Eliot would have ventured so deep into the mountains at this particular time of year … in this particular weather, with these particular horses. It was indeed a wasteland in winter, yet it had great power. Emptiness beckoned. Heavy-duty dust storms lurked round the corner.

An hour later on the right-hand side of the monastery I saw a remarkable sight. It must have been a mile away at first, but in the high-altitude air the light plays tricks and what looks near is often far away. A small dust cloud moving quite fast and then, as the cloud got closer, I saw a lone monk wearing a yellow hat and a red cloak riding fast out across the valley. He came towards us and passed within several hundred yards, but was intent on his own journey. I could again hear the silver horse bell ringing, a clear, insistent tone that carried far. The monk was strong and his horse seemed to understand the urgency of his mission. No one undertook such journeys at this time of year unless they were absolutely necessary. Here was a messenger with an important message.

The silver horse bell in that clear air was hypnotic in its intensity and the bell kept pace with the horse's hooves. This was no time to hang around. The horse moved at a fast trot, not a canter, a pace that the horse could keep up for hours on end. The monk cut across the valley with the wind behind him and rode up the steep cobbled path towards the monastery. As he did so the vast wooden gates of the monastery slowly opened and swallowed him whole. Here was a real live wind horse. The poetry was in the dust and the red rock from which he sought shelter.

I knew then that I had crossed a boundary, that the mind and the mountains were very closely linked. There was certainly no turning back now. The mountains were flexing their muscles. Snow beckoned.

Ice quartet

Sometimes we had to cross icy rivers barefoot, taking off boots, socks and trousers, wading in up to our thighs. No easy matter, but essential. Sharp stones cut my feet and after a while they went numb. I carried a towel in the top of my rucksack so that feet could be dried off and rubbed back into some form of circulation. Frostbite was never far away. Not all rivers freeze over, and if you do have to cross, choose a place where the water is shallow, take a strong stick and lean into the current.

The horses took the rivers in their stride but they often had problems getting out because of the ice on the far side. The freezing water drained off their coats and the tousled horsehair of their underbellies immediately formed as icicles. After a few minutes they jangled in the wind. With four horses like this it was not far off a syncopated rhythm, a strange eerie winter music – ice on ice – packhorse music, walking into the head of the valley. Equine gamelan, an ice quartet.

For half an hour the icicles made their strange, slow, melancholic music, an icy xylophone that chipped and chimed. It suited the cold isolation. Then the wind got up. In the distance I could see more dust storms and whirling dervishes sweeping along the valley, picking up dry dust, sand tamarisk scrub from dried-up river beds and marshes. Whirling dervishes reached upwards for hundreds of feet, then just as suddenly disappeared or danced off in a different direction.

As we turned a corner it was our turn to face into the wind. Sand tattooed my face. I drew the headscarf tight around my eyes, put my shoulder into the wind and looked down just enough to see the path. Horses' heads were also bowed as they knuckled under and sagged when the full force of the wind hit them. This was where they needed their thick coats and eyelashes to keep dust and grit out. We left them to their own devices following what path they could between the glacial deposits, rounded tumps known as drumlins. We drew our scarves even tighter but still the wind burrowed in. There was no respite.

The wind must have been at least 30 or 40 mph, a katabatic wind that dropped suddenly from the peaks.[24] Stopping was out of the question, so we plodded on, hunched up, bent double.

This was the beginning of the Pense La, where we rejoined the road. Long stretches had been cleared and boulders moved, but bridges still had to be built. There were many bends ahead and the altitude began to tell. The horses took it at their own pace, as did we.

Every so often we could see evidence of road engineers – yellow paint daubed on rocks telling us how far we were from Kargil. Here were culverts in the making, footings for bridges, piles of stones waiting to be used as hardcore, oil stains where compressors and drills had worked. It all seemed somehow alien. By Himalayan standards this pass was tame – the section leading up to its highest point had taken five years to construct because there were so many bends, but the far side was far steeper. Mountains do not give way easily.

The more height we gained, the slower our progress and the more time there was to look at the peaks and glaciers. When the clouds cleared the whole run of mountains was visible in a chain, massif after massif. But I was still very wary of the weather. I knew from Andrew Wilson's report of 1875 that six feet of snow fell overnight on the Pense La in September and that packhorses were left struggling up to their girth straps in snow. It was now mid-November and reaching Zangskar would be a close-run thing.

Pense La and Opus 133

You get used to sleeping on hard ground. No mat, no tent, no shelter, nothing. How I missed the foam-rubber mats that I had inadvertently left in a taxi down in Amritsar in the dark. So it was just a sleeping bag under the stars, but there weren't any stars. Only just before dawn could you spot them, like navigation beacons. The smell of yak dung burning was welcome, as was the salt tea.[25]

Was it the third or the fourth night since Panikar? In these mountains time loses all meaning. The gradient of the road was not too steep as it wound backwards and forwards. Sometimes we took short cuts, always climbing up.

We slept out on the track halfway up the pass. By chance I had with me a new Sony radio/cassette recorder that was destined for the *tehsildar* of Padum[26] – and I twiddled the knobs and was able to tune in to what turned out to be a rather clear signal. Radio Moscow – a late Beethoven string quartet eerily dancing its way through the mountain air. Opus 133, I think it was. *Grosse Fuge*. Great Fugue. Quiet then vibrant, almost demonic, like the whirling dervishes, the radio signal weaving in and out of the peaks. Trust the Russians. But then again radio reception would be pretty good. Central Asia was a stone's throw away and we were very high up. Opus 133 kept the wolves at bay that night. Later on during the winter, wolves followed me much more closely.

The competing tunes and fugues were exhilarating, wild and uncompromising. It was exhausting to listen to. Even at sea level. And yet up here in the Himalaya it felt very appropriate. It had its own magic. It mirrored the strength of the mountains. The string quartet cut insistently through the cold air, on edge, manically tugging my mind this way and that. An urgency that matched my own – and the weather's, which was hovering, as if the whole winter were condensed into those fifteen or sixteen hectic minutes. The Great Fugue, gyrating and pulling, plucking notes from the mountain air. A high-altitude concert. A brief respite – a final farewell – an invocation and offering to the spirits of the mountains as powerful as any that Buddhist monks could muster to keep the snow at bay. And then it was gone ... Sadly I would have to sell the radio when I got into the valley to help pay the balance that I owed the horsemen.

We slept on the road because there was nowhere else to sleep, and just when we thought we were alone we met two men from Tungri, whose horses were carrying timber for building. Timber is very scarce in Zangskar and this looked like sawn timber from Kashmir, four by two, bought in Kargil. The timber was 15ft long and dragged on the ground, an ungainly load for horses, particularly when swinging around bends.

It was comforting to meet other travellers going in the same direction. We had a small fire and they joined us. So five of us camped out on the Pense La. The Zangskaris started singing low, slightly mournful songs, no doubt about their village ... they sang well into the night. We slept by the embers of the fire. The stars shone very brightly between the clouds, a good sign because it meant that it would not snow.

The hour before dawn was always the coldest. The horsemen got up and went, bridles in hand, searching for the horses and put nosebags on them. They had not strayed far. No sooner had the horses chomped their way through the barley than the men sorted the loads. Four separate piles of luggage, odd-shaped hessian sacks that we knew by heart. With all three of us helping it only took about five minutes per horse to get them laden, the horses sensing the urgency as much as we did.

Loading in the half-light has its problems, and fingers were again very stubborn and clumsy. We soon left the men from Tungri behind. Their load kept slipping, and anyway they hadn't got to make a return journey. Once over the pass they were home and dry.

The further we got up the pass, the lower the cloud came down. The small lake was completely frozen and a lopsided sign read 'Pense La 14,500ft'. There was a *chorten*. The *lhato* was another pile of rocks, *mani* stones and quartz crystals with prayer flags and curved ibex horns.[27] Ibex, sure-footed wild goat of the mountains and inner spirit of every Zangskari. Here resided the spirit of the pass, and Buddhists would light incense as offerings, sometimes branches of juniper they had brought with them, recite mantras that would give thanks to the gods and pray for a safe journey. Every house in Zangskar has its own small *lhato*. Offerings of incense are made every morning.

The marmots had gone underground. I marvelled at the marmot's ability to hibernate for six or seven months.[28] They could stay in their burrows from October to May, more than half the year. Their alarm call is a whistle, almost a sharp shriek like a bird of prey that at first has you looking up in the skies. Then you look down and see three or four chubby marmots standing up on their hind legs looking intently at you. Then diving down into their burrows as you get closer. But the pass was silent. Marmots all asleep, fathoms down.

It was so cold on the Pense La that not even a lammergeier circled. Only prayer flags fluttered, torn ragged in the stiff breeze. I placed a stone on the cairn and offered up a Buddhist prayer for the safe return of myself, the two horsemen and their horses.

It was on the other side of the pass that I got my first view of Zangskar in winter on the scarp, a steep 1,000ft drop. The road zig-zagged as it descended. To the south, amid long lines of ragged peaks, was the Durung Drung glacier, over a mile wide and snaking off eight or ten miles into the distance – a magnificent sight. An elegant glacier, its meltwater powered the upper reaches of Zangskar. Despite the cold winds I was happy. I knew deep down that the gamble to get into the valley before the snows came down had paid off. But I also knew that I would have to cross this pass again on my own on skis in deep snow in late spring when conditions would be very different and much more forbidding.

My life in Zangskar was only just beginning. Winter was well on its way.

Home straight

That evening I watched the horsemen make the fire with dried dung. They blew carefully, mouths close to the earth, till the flame came and with it fragrant smoke that filled the valley like incense. We gathered firewood to see us through, for in Zangskar there is little. Here they do not so much as waste a twig. Life is very precious when in the balance.

In summer these open spaces were mountain pastures where herds of yak roamed. Villagers lived in low, black yak-hair tents like nomads, moving every few weeks to even higher pastures just below the snowline, then back down again – the ceaseless round of milking, making yogurt, butter churning, cheese making, dung collection, spinning and a little weaving, unchanged for thousands of years. And in autumn, after harvest, the animals returned to their villages carrying their own butter. Butter was currency and life itself, possessing high value and conferring status. Rents were paid in butter. Butter lamps burnt in monasteries, even though it left the paintings covered in a fine film of soot. Butter was used in every ceremony and had a high symbolic value. Offering butter was a gift from the gods. Butter was drunk in Tibetan salt tea and used for softening skins. It also warded off evil and disease. It was this butter that was traded down the *chadar*, the frozen river, in the depths of winter.

It was on the morning of the fifth day that I saw the first Zangskari village, Hagshu, on the other side of the river, a bleak spot in winter. Not even a dog barked. Up the side valley lay the Hagshu glacier and the Hagshu La, one of the highest routes over the Himalayan range, gaining you access to an array of fine peaks, all as yet unclimbed. It is from Hagshu La that the bears come over from Kishtwar. Himalayan brown bears. They are quite a nuisance and will even break into houses to find butter.

It was not till Abring that I saw houses on this side of the river. Three hamlets scattered amid the alluvial fan of a stream, where it was just possible to clear enough rocks to give the fields a chance. Borderline agriculture.

The fields looked bare. At 13,000ft they can only just grow barley and peas, while lower down they grow wheat at 12,000ft, some of the highest wheat in the world. These are remarkable agricultural settlements. Barley grows at 14,000ft. Crop genetics must play a part. Seed grain is exchanged between villages every few years. The lower villages have more fields and less livestock, the higher villages more livestock. Then there are nomads from the east who exchange salt and wool for grain. A complex and delicate trading system that has evolved over hundreds, possibly thousands of years. And there are still traces of the old hunting community as well, in the villagers' social life, carvings and diet.

It is remarkable that anything grows at all in such a short season from May to September, but it does. At these altitudes there is increased ultraviolet light, which may help. As we pass, people raise the odd hand but our passage is not remarked upon. They see horsemen all the year round.

It was near Phe that we spent the last night. We had made good progress. On the map I noticed all the glaciers that we had passed but were often unseen deep within the main Himalayan range. Most were named on the map: Haskira, Kange, then Hagshu, Sumche, Lechan and Mulung, the valley that led up to Dzongkhul monastery and the famous Umasi La. Then the Haftal glacier. All unseen yet crucial.

Dzongkhul monastery produced many fine scholars, including Nawang Tsering.[29] It is believed to have been the site of a cave used by the Indian mystic Naropa for meditation. Meditation is such a key part of Tibetan Buddhism that monks are often very reluctant to talk about it. To many monks, meditation is such a commonplace activity that they see no need to mention it; plus, they are often given special teachings and cannot divulge these teachings to the uninitiated. Talking about silence is immediately a contradiction.

For a thousand years or more Zangskar has been an ideal spot for such meditators and they will often find their own remote places in which to practise. That is until the arrival of the road. I was afraid that the valley would soon be filled with the noise of diesel engines. But trade was trade.

These monks will secrete themselves away in remote caves. Some will be walled up for three years, three months, three weeks and three days. Such advanced meditators are fed by local villagers and left to their own devices. Some are Tibetans who have been forced to flee their own country.

I regarded these meditating monks like glaciers, hidden away above the villages, often unseen, but their influence was vital. Great reservoirs of knowledge, powerful and solid. Without them, Zangskar would be infinitely poorer. Hopefully they would not melt away. Here time and space are held in mind. Each frozen waterfall is now silent, each cave a retreat, with its own echo and texture.

Explosives and chang

Day six. After Phe came the village of Rantaksha, where I met a group of men working on the road led by a young, energetic monk from Karsha monastery. He wore his yellow hat askew and was the local explosives expert. The introduction of explosives into the valley posed its own problems, which I discovered had quite a bit to do with certain people fishing ... getting the length of fuse right was crucial and knowing where to run to always helped.

They signalled to us to get down and we all ducked just in time behind a *mani* wall as a loud explosion sent fragments of rock sailing over our heads. The monk ran out to see the effects of his handiwork. They had no drill and no compressor, so there was no depth to the explosion. An obstinate boulder that took several days to remove.

Here the road was being constructed by the villagers themselves. The headman was the foreman, and his responsibility was to make up that section of road. Both men and women were employed with picks and shovels, the men paid 15 rupees a day and the women 12 rupees. The men were often old and worked more slowly, but the women often had young babies and stopped to breastfeed them. They joked and laughed. It was a family affair. Sometimes in the summer you could hear the air filled with wonderful lilting songs as a gang of young women shovelled away. They knew how to enjoy life and worked faster than the men.

Truth of the matter was that it was often difficult to get the men to work on the roads because they regarded working in the fields at harvest time as more important, or else they were off trading or on the high pastures. So it was often only the old men who were at home and able to work. Why did they need a road?

Were horses and yaks not good enough? Also, they had no real notion of what money was or understood its true value. Everything was exchanged in what was essentially a barter economy. Fair exchange is no robbery. Stocks and shares. Yaks and butter.

Bridges were major jobs, and government engineers were employed on their construction in summer. The road had to be finished up to that point to enable lorries to bring steel girders and joists. Traditional Zangskari bridges were constructed from birch twigs plaited together to make cables that were then strung across the roaring torrents to make suspension bridges, some as long as 200ft. There was one at Padum, another longer one at Zangla, and many others. Ancient technology, but it worked well and was sustainable.

The roadmen, pleased with their morning's work, sat down in a circle on old rugs and produced *chang*, the local homemade barley beer made without hops or malt, which they then proceeded to drink. This beer, always a bit murky, appeared from a large brass cauldron they had concealed behind a large rock. There was a brass ladle, and they filled up small wooden cups that they had secreted in their cloaks.

With all the earth moving and demolition of rocks, the natural order of things had been upset and the earth spirits had to be appeased. Even when ploughing took place the earth spirits had to be placated, but with the road building some older people felt that unseen forces were being disturbed that would later engulf the valley. Yet here no one seemed to mind very much. They had a job of work to do. The lords of the soil might very well be offended, but they bided their time.

The men chatted away and then offered me some more *chang*. I declined politely, saying I had to get to Padum. The horsemen had been careful not to engage anyone in conversation and were now almost out of sight. The road was one of the more exciting things to happen to Zangskar, another invasion of sorts. As one wise old man later said to me, 'Yes, the road will come. We cannot stop it. But when it comes we will lose our peace of mind.' The roadmen slipped into quiet, almost contemplative silence, and then ten minutes later went back to work refreshed. On the other side of the river lay the village of Ating, which was en route for Dzongkhul monastery.

Tungri, which means 'conch shell mountain', was where the two men carrying the long lengths of timber were from. The road crossed the river on a narrow bridge that was just large enough for horses. The river was completely frozen over. From this point we entered the great triangular plain of Padum, which extended for about ten miles. It was here that the two powerful rivers joined to make up the Zangskar river.

From Tungri to the next village of Sani was about two miles. I could already see the trees in the distance. Sani is a holy village with many old carvings and an ancient monastery. As I passed by I saw the holy lake – frozen over. It is the holiest village in Zangskar, dating back to the time of the great Kushana king Kanishka, and the spiritual nerve centre of Zangskar.

In the summer there are festivals and half of Zangskar gathers to read the Buddhist scriptures. As well as housing Naropa's shrine, Sani is also the site for the guardian deity of the valley, called Junu Tunglak.[30] They used to make animal sacrifices in his honour well within living memory. The shaman would go into a trance and give prophecies, even stick swords into himself. The name of Junu Tunglak is feared and respected, and the old rock carvings are smeared with butter as offerings.

After Sani we crossed the plain of Padum and passed long *mani* walls, old carvings and the odd *lhato*. It was getting towards afternoon and another dust storm blew up. In the distance it was just possible to make out the village of Padum clustered round the terminal moraine, the houses closely packed between the rocks.

When we approached I saw a strange sight. Horsemen by the score suddenly emerged from the village, maybe fifty or sixty of them galloping off in all directions, all in red cloaks. It seemed as if all the headmen of all the villages and all the head monks had gathered there for a conference or special meeting and were now returning home. It was a fantastic sight in the dust and the dusk. These men knew how to gallop. As we got nearer, many of them passed us, proud, almost warlike. It was like a raid, and some even carried rifles. They had probably served in the Ladakh Scouts. Buddhist, yes, but Zangskari first.

Arrival

At long last I had arrived, my journey from Panikar to Padum having taken six days, one day less than planned. The packhorses were unloaded, my luggage taken upstairs and dumped on the floor of the small room. The horses had been excellent. I could not have done without them. I went to the *tehsildar* and in his small cramped office, which was also his living room, I exchanged the radio/cassette recorder for 1,000 rupees. I then paid the horsemen their balance and gave them some extra clothing to stave off the cold on the way back.

From the small temple on top of the mound I heard the long, low, unmistakeable sound of monastic horns, like the lowing of cattle. It went on for most of the night, as it was the tenth day of the tenth month of the Fire Dragon year. The ceremony commemorated the arrival in Tibet of Guru Rinpoche, alias

Padmasambhava, after whom Padum was said to be named. Form and emptiness, skilful means, Middle Path and all that, the wisdom of the sword cutting through delusion. I felt that Buddhist Zangskar was at last beginning to flex its muscles.

I would miss the lilt of the packhorses, their pace and temperament, their silent loyalty and the steady click, click, click of their hooves, the smell of *eau de cheval*. One journey was over and another much longer journey was beginning. Surviving the winter was not just a physical challenge but like a *koan*, an unanswerable question, a riddle, a silent Buddhist paradox that had to be solved.

2

VILLAGE LIFE: PADUM

Late November 1976

Skis and snowshoes

Every morning in my room as I watched the sun touch the Buddhist monastery above the village of Padum I would light incense. The monastery was situated on an escarpment and called Stagrimo, which meant 'Hill of the Tigress'. The old seven-storey palace on a mound in the centre of the village had all but gone, but the monastery was still functioning. Stagrimo was a red-hat *Drukpa Kargyu* monastery linked to Bhutan. *Drukpa* meant 'dragon person' and *Kargyu* meant 'whispered' or 'oral' tradition. So it was a monastery of 'whispering dragons'. Padum's importance in Zangskar was due not only to the old palace and the monastery but to a fine suspension bridge made from birch twigs twisted and plaited into ropes and cables. Every few years the villagers would gather with vast piles of birch to replace the frayed cables. Ingenious local engineering.

When you have been walking every day for nearly a week your body wants to keep going, like perpetual motion. The rhythm of the caravan was infectious. The mind has to catch up with itself. So when I arrived in Padum it took a while to orientate myself. I slowly settled into the room, with its bed under the window. Well, there was no bed. Just the sleeping bag on a slightly undulating dusty earth floor with an old threadbare Persian carpet that I had picked up in Srinagar. It was better than sleeping on the road or in a field.

The feeling of having made it into the valley in the nick of time was extraordinary. I couldn't quite believe it. There was a warm glow deep inside me, despite the low temperatures. I was on my own and I loved it. I had been very lucky indeed.

My main problem was sorting out the vast higgledy-piggledy pile of luggage and accoutrements that now lay on the floor. It took several weeks to restore order, during which the two wicker hampers came into their own.

Preparing myself for such a long expedition in the Himalaya in only six weeks had been quite a challenge, but one that I relished. Solo expeditions have a particular flavour all of their own. For a start you have no one to talk to but yourself. No one else sets the agenda, so you make what you can of the world in front of you. You think you know your limits but you are keen to test the boundaries. As always with expeditions, it came down to food and equipment.

The long, graceful wooden touring skis from Telemark in Norway were lent to me by Kenneth Lumsden, a sprightly consultant radiologist in Oxford. During the 1930s Kenneth had been a butterfly collector in south-east Tibet with the plant hunters Ludlow and Sherriff. A framed selection of blue exotic butterflies lived at the bottom of his stairs in Yarnton, just outside Oxford, wonderful reminders of the mountains and just the same sort of magical blue that you find in Himalayan blue poppies, a deep blue shared with the mountain sky – blue the same colour as the Medicine Buddha, almost lapis lazuli.

His great friend was Major Peter Hailey, Bursar of St Antony's College at the university in Oxford. Hailey had been in Ladakh in 1939 and before that in Gyantse in Tibet as trade officer. He loved Tibet and had collected many Buddhist artefacts, including a large set of old *tangkas* that he had given to his college. They hang there to this day. He also lent me an important book on Ladakh by William Moorcroft and George Trebeck. They had both known the Hungarian linguist Csoma de Kőrös in the 1820s and had recommended that he go to Zangskar to study Tibetan. They also arranged a small stipend for Csoma. Peter Hailey was, I think, a Buddhist, and he once told me over a cup of tea that he wanted to be reincarnated as a racehorse.

I had two pairs of snowshoes, the first from Labrador in Canada – steamed birch and caribou gut with a 'beaver' tail, exquisitely made by the Nasqapi Inuit, now museum pieces. These had also been lent to me by a doctor, Peter Steele from Bristol, but he was now in the Yukon. The second pair were much more basic. Oblong and bamboo-framed, and were once used in blizzards by Yorkshire Electricity Board men to reach outlying farms when lines were down. Nothing flash. Just to be sure I also took a pair of Erbacher lightweight cross-country skis from West Germany.

Mountaineering gear lay on the floor: coiled yellow and red kernmantle climbing ropes, orange belay slings, a piton hammer useful for cracking apricot stones every morning, carabiners, ice axes, a snow shovel, snow saw and snow anchors, as well as hurricane lanterns, candles, matches, torches, batteries, the Primus stove, snow goggles, glacier cream, Dachstein mitts, sheepskin-lined flying boots, first aid kit, two max and min thermometers, a wind gauge, an altimeter in its leather pouch, a lightweight tent and a wide variety of clothing, gloves and other boots.

Added to this was a pressure cooker and army mess tins, invaluable for morning porridge, notebooks and sixteen packets of six candles. The ration – half a candle a night. That would last in theory 192 nights and take me into late April. I also had woodworking tools – spokeshave, bradawl, gimlet, chisel, awls – Vicks inhalers, medical kits, plasters, bandages, Dettol, syringes, pethidine, antibiotics and the makings of an Everest blunderbuss cocktail: tincture of morphine, kaolin diuretics, for high-altitude sickness, and laxatives. I even had a small shiny metal shaving mirror, but although I hung it up I decided not to shave. It saved time and water every morning, and warm water was at a premium. The Mirror. First law of expeditions.: keep an eye on yourself. Children loved it.

The long wooden Norwegian skis I used to keep the door shut, particularly when the wind was blowing hard and dogs were patrolling the rooftops.

Hints to Travellers

My real luxury, apart from the large bag of dried apricots, was a small library, a fathom of books, which lay beside one of the hampers. I dipped into them whenever I felt like it.

I took my own small green Everyman pocket edition of Henry Thoreau's *Walden*, an important lodestone, as well as his *A Week on the Concord and Merrimack Rivers*. In addition I had *The Story of My Heart* by Richard Jefferies, *Cottage Economy* by William Cobbett, *An Essay on the Principle of Population* by Thomas Malthus (I had grown up in his house at school), Herman Hesse's *The Glass Bead Game*, Dostoyevsky's *Crime and Punishment*,

Knut Hamsun's *Hunger*, *The Narrow Road to the Deep North* by Basho, several books on Buddhism, including Zen, *Notes and Queries on Anthropology*, *Ladakh the Chronicles* (very old Ladakhi texts first published in the *Journal of the Asiatic Society of Bengal* in 1910) plus a book on Tibetan paintings, as well as *Self-Sufficiency* by John Seymour. Food for thought.

The real jewel, however, was a small, blue, thickset volume called *Hints to Travellers* by the Royal Geographical Society. I had bought it at the Society for its pre-war price of 15/6, the very last copy they had. End of an era. It contained everything you needed to know about porters and coolies, dog sledging in Greenland, Bactrian camels, ration boxes, the behaviour of Primus stoves at high altitude, pemmican, dark glasses, sheep saddlebags, bell tents, Whymper tents, yak tents, seed collecting, camel racing, singing sands and typhoid, as well as first aid, vitamin C, sea sickness and snow blindness. There was even a paragraph on typhus. It said you went down on day twelve, which is exactly what happened to me in Afghanistan. And if you were lucky you resurfaced a few weeks later, which luckily I did.

My main concern in Zangskar, however, was frostbite ... the invisible enemy that dogs every mountaineer and polar explorer, and not easy to detect till it is too late. *Hints to Travellers* had this to say:

Cold brings on a spasm of the minute arteries carrying blood to the skin, which, as the blood supply is cut off begins to die. More dangerous when the oxygen pressure is low, at high altitude. The fingers, toes, ears and nose are particularly affected. The parts become numbed and then lose all sensation. The skin is white and cold and a condition of death, or incipient death of the tissues, results. As the

circulation is restored the parts become blue and congested
with agonising pain.

To avoid frostbite wear suitable clothing, particularly
round the ears and face; and boots big enough to allow free
movement of the toes; tight boots are dangerous. If sensation
in the toes is failing, call a halt, remove the boots and
massage the toes. Never postpone this for lack of time.

Defrosting yourself was obviously an art. Mountaineering litera-
ture was littered with references to fingers and toes that went
black and gangrenous, and either fell off or were amputated with
a penknife. A friend of mine's great-uncle, Henry Morshead, had
lost several fingers at 25,000ft on Everest back in 1922. Sobering
stuff. I had been warned.

At the back of *Hints to Travellers* were adverts for expedition
equipment from the 1930s. I loved these. Tweed jackets and
Burberrys, Primus stoves, prismatic compasses, telescopes – sport-
ing and lightweight pocket models – tents, sleeping bags, rucksacks and awnings, Crosse and Blackwell tinned food. Everything
you needed for 'explorers, travellers and dwellers overseas'. One
advert simply said: 'KEEP GOING ON BOVRIL.' Alas, I had no
Bovril … or even Marmite. At altitude your taste buds veer either
to sweet or savoury. Mine were definitely savoury.

Apart from my trip to the RGS library, I had also been to the
Alpine Club in South Audley Street. There, lurking on a top shelf
at the back of the library, was a large, dusty tome entitled *Ladak*,
written by Alexander Cunningham, an army officer turned
archaeologist.[31] His book had been published in 1854, the same
year as the Charge of the Light Brigade. I had tried to open it but
without success. Its pages had not even been cut. In those days
Ladakh was quite literally a closed book. I asked the librarian for

a ruler with a bevelled edge and began to cut the pages one by one ... and a world of coloured plates and drawings slowly began to unfold. Cunningham had been on a boundary commission to demarcate the border between Ladakh and Tibet, and later founded the Archaeological Survey of India and identified many of the key Buddhist sites in India.

Reading in bed by candlelight was about the only thing you could do at night. Books kept the mind ticking over, and it was often too cold to hold a pencil and make notes. Ink, of course, froze, so you saved your thoughts till the sun appeared. Frost bit.

Maps

Every traveller needs good maps indicating safe ports of call, bridges, passes, villages, mountains, whirlpools and watering holes. Maps are strange beasts. They have a life of their own and can lead you into danger or out of danger. Even the possession of maps in military zones can be dangerous.

The Survey of India maps that I used had been smuggled out of the basement of the Ministry of Defence by my father in his briefcase. I was simply told to cut the tops and bottoms off the maps and not let on how I had come by them. A senior staff officer had helped him. What the navy were doing with maps of Ladakh and the Northwest Frontier was a mystery to me, but I never questioned it. Those maps were invaluable.

I carried my Survey of India maps wrapped around a ladies' greenheart fly fishing rod, but they had been stolen in Srinagar bus station late at night. Luckily I had taken photocopies. The surveyors' work had not been in vain.

Before I left England, I went to the RGS and met Eric Shipton in the map room. As a mountain explorer and map maker, Eric had been everywhere: Everest, the Nanda Devi basin, Shaksgam, Snow Lake and the Karakoram.

I showed Eric where I wanted to go and traced with my finger the route of the Zangskar river down though the Zangskar gorge until it reached the Indus. He looked at the maps in silence, then after a few minutes looked up and said with a twinkle in his blue eyes, 'We had no idea that valley was there ... In those days we always looked north to the Karakoram.'

Eric was fascinated. He scanned the maps and looked more closely at the terrain, the peaks and the dotted contours, which were slightly disjointed. After another minute or so he raised a bushy eyebrow. 'Those heights are only spot heights. The peaks are much higher and all unclimbed ...'

There was a distant, almost wistful, look in his eyes, as if he were back again in the 1930s. It was a wonderful, magical moment that lasted only a few minutes, but the whole spirit of his way of exploring came to life. I sensed his quiet determination, the feeling of optimism, hope and adventure. You learn by osmosis.

Eric had a great love of Tibetan Buddhism, Primus stoves and *tsampa* – the ground-down roasted barley that they had eaten on early Everest expeditions. He loved exploration for its own sake. He was, as they say, 'his own man'.

When he walked from Leh over the Karakoram Pass to reach Kashgar – a journey of 650 miles or so – it took him about seven weeks. Eric was a great admirer of Buddhism. The fact that he gave my small solo expedition his blessing and encouraged me to take his two-man, lightweight expedition philosophy to its logical conclusion of a one-man expedition, was just what I needed. I met him several times before I left. I was very lucky indeed to have his support and approval. The last time I saw him he was packing his scant belongings for a trip to Bhutan. I never saw him again. Within six months he had died of cancer. Impermanence. C'est la vie.

Hill of the Tigress

At the monastery of Stagrimo, the Whispering Dragons had an air of authority looking down over the village. The Dragons were both magicians who had mastered the 'black' arts, invoking spirits and driving out demons, and yogins who liked to meditate and drink *chang*. Yet they had razor-sharp minds and had undertaken many years of hard training down in Lahoul.

The monastery was a place where specialised teachings were passed on from master to disciple – *Dzogchen*, the Great Perfection, an intimate process involving acres of silence and years of hard training. A handful of monks tracing their lineages right back to Guru Rinpoche, the Tantric wild man of Tibetan Buddhism who came from Swat in Uddiyana in the heart of old Gandhara. In those days most of north India and Afghanistan was Buddhist, as well as large parts of Central Asia. Guru Rinpoche was a big hero in Tibet and Ladakh, the master magician who had introduced Tantric Buddhism into Tibet in the 8th century CE.[32]

There were many statues and paintings of Guru Rinpoche in the monastery. He looks wild and carries a trident, the sort of person you want on your side both physically and psychologically. In his right hand a Tantric thunderbolt and in his left a skull cup.

His mantra *Om ah hum vajra guru padma siddhi hum* (pronounced 'Om ah hung benza guru pema siddhi hung') was often repeated by Zangskaris when going down the frozen river.

It had great power, conferring protection and good luck, and inspiring confidence in the most dangerous of situations.

I used to recite it to myself when the ice got thin, and discovered that it generated its own energy and a sense of commitment, even freedom, together with clarity and inner calm, concentrating the mind till it was itself crystal clear. I found that the power of the mantra was very effective.

Guru Rinpoche also had his wise and beautiful female consorts, which implied that he had mastered enlightenment through sexual energy and bliss, one reason why he was so popular with Tibetans. His principal consort was Yeshe Tsogyal, one of the five wives of the famous Tibetan king Trisong Detsen. Religion, sex, power and Buddhist enlightenment all interlinked at the highest level, just the sort of thing Tibetans and Ladakhis liked. Life would be very dull without a consort.

As I looked up each morning I could see the sun hit the Hill of the Tigress. The ice crystals under my fingernails were unbelievably cold. Winter was now flexing its muscles. I had much to learn.

So I made the most of the last days before the real snow came down. I went for short walks and inspected the ancient carvings down by the river, early images of the Buddha carved on a vast boulder. From the small slots cut into the rock for timbers I assumed this must have been the site of an old temple. In a grove of willow there were more rock carvings close to a cave, possibly pre-Tibetan, 8th and 9th century CE.

I inspected the river, which was already frozen in many parts. This was my future. I had to get to know the river, I had to acquaint myself with the ice, to test it to see where its strengths lay. It was tough and yet fragile. The river had frozen over first where the water was deepest and slowest down by the bridge.

They said it froze over at the time of the monastery festival back in October – an auspicious sign, ready for the monks dancing in the courtyard of what was once the old palace. Sometimes if it was a fine day I would go down to the cave well wrapped up to keep warm and watch the ice floes pass one by one. A safe location to meditate. Occasionally a goat strayed and kept me company.

Stenzin Namgyal

Not long after I had arrived in Padum there was a knock on my door just as it was becoming dark. I opened the door and was greeted by a well-dressed young boy in a maroon cloak called Stenzin, who handed me a note. He was about eight years old and very self-possessed.

The note simply said, 'Mr James. Please come with the bearer for some *chang*. Phuntsok Dawa, teacher.' It was written in blue ink on a half-page of lined paper torn from a child's exercise book. Although *chang* was beer, it was actually more like green scrumpy and had a certain edge to it that you learnt to appreciate. An acquired taste. How could I refuse such an invitation?

Phuntsok Dawa was from Padum but worked as a teacher in Karsha. His father was Tashi Namgyal, *Gyalpo* or King of Padum, also known as 'Rajah', and was connected via the kings of Heniskut to the old kings of Ladakh and thus to old Tibet. Phuntsok Dawa meant 'Excellent Moon' in Tibetan.

Stenzin waited patiently as I brought the hurricane lamp and put on my sheepskin-lined boots, originally designed for use in cold stores back in the UK. I pulled my balaclava down, put my mitts on and felt my way down the rocky stairs with one hand. I

held the lamp up and edged past cattle and horses in the stable.
I then slid the small wooden bar back into the recess that held
the door in place and ventured out into the village. There was by
now a glimmer of moonlight on the peaks above.

Once in the open there was silence. It was too cold, and the
villagers were far too sensible to waste their energy outside after
dark. Animals were gathered inside just after the sun went down
and fed hay and straw. If they were lucky they were also given
spent grains of barley from beer making. The animals knew which
houses they belonged to and patiently stood outside, waiting to
be let in. In the early stages of winter, sheep and goats were taken
back across the frozen river by young girls to get the last of the
grazing. The girls always returned with wicker baskets on their
shoulders full of dried dung or tamarisk scrub, sometimes singing
songs with wonderful melodies as they came across the frozen
river or down the mountain. Never a moment wasted. Every
piece of dried dung counted, because if winter was a month
longer than normal, there were real problems – a fine line
between survival and starvation.

I followed Stenzin carefully round the village. Sometimes
there were dogs on chains that lunged at you. Occasionally I
saw lights in single-pane windows, small tins filled with kerosene
and lit with homemade woollen wicks. Some were butter lamps
and some mustard oil, giving a pleasing yellow light. There was
no glass in the village at ground level because it was easily
broken by yak's horns and children. Sometimes the space
between two houses was only three or four feet wide, just
enough room for a laden animal or two yaks. I passed five or six
houses, then turned left into an alleyway and was soon outside
the rajah's house. It was much like everybody else's but slightly
larger. It had a low wall outside for keeping animals in during

the daytime and tethering horses. On top of the house were great piles of fodder and firewood, as well as faded prayer flags. Inside was a small courtyard where the *tehsildar* would sit and hold court. This was Stenzin's home, in which three generations lived together. His grandfather, the king, wanted to meet me to find out why I wanted to come to his valley and how far it was to my home.

I went into the house and crept through the dark stable. It had low ceilings, so you kept your head down. Phuntsok Dawa's family, like everyone else, lived upstairs in the summer and at the end of September moved down below, where they lived in winter quarters with the animals till about May, mirroring the migration between summer and winter pastures. In the stable I met the family horse and *dzo*, as well as sheep and goats. *Dzos* are half-bred yaks and more valuable. Females were called *dzomos* and gave more milk than their yak counterparts.[33] Animals in Zangskar were very placid, and their links with the Zangskaris were strong. They depended utterly on one another. Animals were your friends or relatives reincarnated, to be treated like family. Even monastery dogs were sometimes regarded as old monks who had not passed their exams and needed another shot at life on earth.

Stenzin took me by the hand and we went through two stables. I found a door by touch, like finding the inner sanctuary, trimmed my lamp and then blew it out. I had a torch but it used up valuable batteries whose life in such cold was short-lived. As I went into the room my eyes slowly adjusted to the semi-darkness. It was warm. Two sides of the room were bare rock – they lived half underground. It felt like a cave. There was a stove in the centre and dried dung and scrub for fuel, just as we had on the move. Economy and necessity.

This was a microcosm of Zangskari life. The whole family was there for the whole winter. Survival and partial hibernation. Maybe they learnt from the marmots. Phuntsok got up to meet me and said, '*Juley*,' the customary, all-purpose Ladakhi greeting. He smiled, then shook my hand and motioned me to sit down beside his father, Tashi Namgyal, the rajah. This was an honour.

Tashi Namgyal – rajah

Tashi Namgyal was seated on the other side of the stove wearing two slightly threadbare magenta cloaks one on top of the other, which is the custom in winter, and was chanting his daily *puja*. He had dark raven locks of tousled hair and a fine wrinkled face. On his brow was a piece of black fur about six inches long that came from eastern Tibet via the head lama of Bardan Gompa. I was told it came from a black and white bear. Not a panda but possibly a rare blue Tibetan bear, which also has white on its chest and is sometimes known as the snow bear – Tibetan Buddhism and Central Asian shamanism hand in hand. The bear-skin was held onto his brow with a leather strap, lending him a regal aura. It gave him inner strength, as if he were summoning up the spirits of his ancestors to help fight the winter and the dark forces that lurked all around. In fact he was making an invocation to the Buddhist goddess Tara to protect him.

Tara was a firm favourite with Tibetans, a confident goddess who has several forms: White Tara, Green Tara and Red Tara. Always lively and often depicted sitting slightly off centre with one leg down as if she were about to get up and dance, her ten-syllable mantra *Om tare tuttare ture svaha* is often repeated hundreds of times like a lullaby. Reciting her mantra was often part of a healing practice, a liberator from suffering. She is a fine antidote to monastic austerity, a female bodhisattva[34] whose inner qualities are used to help the practitioner to develop compassion, loving kindness and emptiness.

Slowly I began to realise that being a Buddhist was not only multi-layered and multi-dimensional, but that advanced Buddhist philosophy and teaching percolated into all levels of the village. Daily practice was woven into their every action, their lives sandwiched between monasteries and fields, wall paintings and yak dung, family life and Buddhist ritual.

Beside the fire was Phuntsok's wife Dolma, who had been brought up in Karsha. Her brother was Sonam Wangchuk, the Lonpo of Karsha, who came from an ancient line of leaders and ministers. He was also an *amchi*, a herbal doctor, and an *onpo*, an astrologer, whom I would see later.

Phuntsok's mother sat at the back holding a baby, the latest addition. Phuntsok had three children: a son, Stenzin, who had collected me, a daughter, Padma Dechen, a year or two older, and a young baby girl. There was another son, but he had died two or three years ago of measles, which came every seven years or so, like locusts.

Phuntsok was making bread and his wife was blowing on the fire to make the embers glow. The stove was made from Indian army jerrycans and the chimney from biscuit tins – a little bit Heath Robinson, held together with string, but just the job. Smoke is one of the main causes of eye and chest problems, so using a makeshift chimney is an advantage. The pipe also heats up and keeps the room warm. Living conditions were basic, but it was warm and friendly. Yak dung, cow dung, horse dung, sheep dung, goat dung all had their place in the home fuel economy. Occasionally they used a small kerosene stove to make a quick cup of tea or boil rice. There was a pressure cooker, their pride and joy, which Phuntsok Dawa had bought down in Srinagar when he had completed his teacher training.

This invitation to supper was a chance to talk about Zangskar. Although linked distantly to the royal family, Tashi Namgyal had fallen on hard times. He could trace his ancestry right back to the ancient line of Tibetan kings that had fled to Ladakh in the time of Langdarma, a thousand years ago. Langdarma was a rebel who had reverted to the old Bon religion and persecuted Buddhists. He was famously assassinated by a monk at a time when the Tibetan nation was very warlike and caused many problems for the Chinese. In the early days it was the Tibetans and not the Mongols who were the 'barbarians' on the border.

Tashi Namgyal was the head Buddhist in the village, and as a scribe and mediator he wrote applications to the *tehsildar* in Urdu on behalf of his villagers. He had once trained as an *amchi* and an *onpo* under a monk at Bardan. But he was not the only king in Zangskar. There was another king at Zangla: Sonam Thondup Namgyal. His son Nima Norbu had been a monk but then left the monastery to get married.

Over the winter months Phuntsok Dawa became not just an interpreter but a translator of his culture and a very good friend. It was through his eyes that I really came to know and understand the valley from a Buddhist perspective. I now felt that winter had really begun. A time for marriages, storytelling, ritual ceremonies and festivities.

Phuntsok was a gifted and kind man who spoke Urdu, Ladakhi and English. His brother-in-law was Sonam Wangchuk, and he lived in Karsha. It was Sonam Wangchuk's great-great-uncle on his mother's side, Sangye Phuntsok, who was Csoma da Kőrös's teacher. Scholarship was greatly revered in the valley.

Phuntsok also told me that after Partition in 1947, when

British India was split up into India and Pakistan, they had lost everything. When Pakistani soldiers came from Kargil, they barely had time to leave and fled down over the Shingo La to Lahoul with their own horse and over the Rohtang La to Manali, a journey of two or three weeks. They escaped with Khushok Bakula and Stagna Rinpoche, who then went back to Leh. When the family returned a year later the house had been gutted and all their possessions auctioned off. That was thirty years ago.

The downstairs living room in the rajah's house was very basic. There was no real window, only an opening or two with wooden boards that were removed if the smoke got too much. Everybody lived and slept and ate in this room in winter. It was cheek by jowl. I was offered red salt tea, and then some *chang*. Teshi Namgyal was a good brewer and a good distiller of *arak*, a moon-shine-like poteen. He proudly gave me some in a small silver cup, and very good it was too. *Arak* helped them to survive the winter. Without the spirit of *arak*, the spirit of Buddhism and the spirit of yaks, life in Zangskar in winter would be very hard indeed.

Phuntsok Dawa – teacher

In the corner of the room by the stove, Phuntsok Dawa was wrestling with his pressure cooker, trying to get it apart. There was a slight hiss of steam. Given the altitude, having a pressure cooker made good sense as cooking often took much longer than at sea level and used more fuel. The pressure cooker was also a status symbol. The hissing noises were very reassuring, meaning that supper was not far away. Often they left it to cook on for fifteen minutes before taking the weights off.

As well as rice and dahl I was given some *sabzi*, green vegetables like dried nettles or rough spinach collected in the summer and left to dry. There was a small bit of mutton that was placed on top of the rice. Meat is a rarity, but this was the time of year they killed most animals for the winter. Sometimes a family would kill a yak and share it out among relatives, and this would be reciprocated later in the following year. Royalty would only eat yak, not the crossbred animals.

Meat was often stored by air-drying it in the cold. It froze quickly and was hermetically sealed. Dried meat was shoved in the rafters out of the range of dogs or cut very thin, dark and slightly smoky. A delicacy.

It was very generous of them to offer me a meal as I had no real way of repaying them. Phuntsok's family all huddled round the stove for warmth and ate together. The younger children had already gone to bed and were lying on a sheepskin, wrapped up in their cloaks. It was not uncommon for three or four children to sleep in a row, all tucked up. Washing was optional but not unknown. Water was at a premium.

Extended families were often large, so survival depended on cooperation and closeness. Even sleeping was a communal affair, all in the same room. Zangskaris used sloping wooden head-boards as pillows, placed four feet away from a wall, and slept on their front with their knees in a crouched position, meaning that only their knees, shins, toes and foreheads touched the ground. This is the foetal position, and babies would often sleep like this in the first few months of life.

Ladakhis were also cremated in the same foetal position, which signifies rebirth. I preferred to sleep lying flat out. This lost more heat, but I had my Everest sleeping bag filled with Scandinavian eiderdown. Thank you, eider.

Such habits when on the move in a harsh climate made all the difference. Women could sleep like this in the open fields when overworked by breastfeeding and weeding. Phuntsok's wife Dolma had given birth the summer before out in the open, in the fields below the monastery. She worked right up until the last minute and did not seem any the worse for wear. There was a strict two- or three-week taboo on the women doing any work once the child was born, which was just as well. Breast milk was highly prized in winter. Many families had often lost a child or two – infant mortality was about 20 to 25 per cent, in some of the higher villages possibly more. Life was precious, and at these altitudes a long life was a rare gift and greatly valued.

In Zangskar there were men and women well into their nineties, and this from a small population of about 10,000. If you survived the first five years in Zangskar you did pretty well. So long as an avalanche didn't get you or the ice on a frozen river gave way. Excess *chang* or *arak* was another potential hazard.

Tashi Namgyal could even remember the raids of the Tibetan nomads from the east, who would ride down onto the plain after harvest and take grain before returning to western Tibet. So much for Buddhist values. Shoot first, ask questions later. They were supposed to repeat the mantra *Om mani padme hum* as they pulled the trigger. It was this shield of warlike nomads that used to keep Tibet safe, but even they were no match for the Chinese army in 1959. It is remarkable that Ladakh is still in Indian hands, as it could so easily be part of Pakistan or Chinese-occupied Tibet. It was saved by the bravery and ingenuity of the Indian army. Tashi Namyal also remembered Tibetans coming on pilgrimage and making their full-length prostrations for a mile or two as they approached the old Kanishka *chorten* at Sani.

Ladakh was a time warp, a quirk of nature and politics, in some ways more Tibetan than Tibet itself, where Chinese communism had taken its toll. Many of the large Tibetan monasteries had been destroyed and their monks dispersed, although the full horror of what had happened in the country was only just emerging. Many Tibetans ended up in Dharamsala with His Holiness the Dalai Lama, and many perished in the 1959 uprising or on their way out of Tibet. Others were shot or died in camps. Back in Scotland after an army winter-survival course I had seen Akong Rinpoche. Out of his group of three hundred trying to escape, only thirteen survived. Akong was so hungry that he had to eat his boots. The artist lama monk Sherab had been shot in the arm.

Ever practical, Phuntsok suggested that if I needed a stove, Ringzin the blacksmith was the man. All I had to do was to acquire two Indian army jerrycans and some firewood. Firewood was arranged to come from Shila. It turned out that the rajah's wife was from there and her brother was a well-known meditator. Ringzin lived under the big rock below the old Padum palace. Phuntsok also said that there was to be a wedding. Thubsten's daughter was getting married to a man from Kumig, a village high up on the other side of the river from Padum. Thubsten was a neighbour of mine. Generous and humorous.

With my hurricane lamp I found my way back to my house. I slipped my hand inside the hole next to the front door and slid the wooden bar back into its socket. The reassuring smell of animals exuded some kind of warmth. This really was a stable economy. I went upstairs, looked at the stars from the open roof, surveyed the peaks covered in snow and then crawled back into my sleeping bag, hardly taking any clothes off. At least I remembered to put the Norwegian skis against the door. I once found a dog in the room rootling around, and after I chased it out the dog ran along the rooftops. But dogs weren't too bad. Young boys were more problematic.

Sadly in those early days tragedy struck. I lost nine kilos of dried apricots. The bag just disappeared from my room when I was out one day, lock, stock and barrel. Stolen. That was a very bitter blow. I was looking forward to taking them on winter journeys. Apricots were unobtainable in Padum and I only had a few in reserve. The apricot theft was a great mystery that I never solved.

The lamp spluttered and then blew out. The wind dropped a little and it started to snow, just a light dusting. Winter was teasing us. The village knew what was in store.

Daily bread and nomads

Every morning I drank salt tea and ate two small round loaves of fresh bread, each like a small discus, maybe four inches across and half an inch thick. The Buddhists use the dregs from beer making, which contain just enough yeast to give the bread some lift and flavour, a slight nuttiness. I provided the *atta*. The flour was stored in five-kilo canvas sacks. The bread was cooked on a flat hot stone over the embers of the fire. I would slice the breads down the middle and fill them with jam or Amul cheese. If warm they were beautiful, an excellent way to start the day. Very useful when out and about in the mountains as they had structural integrity.

I also heated up porridge in an old army mess tin on the Primus stove and mixed in what was left of the apricots soaked overnight. One kilo had been in a smaller bag that survived the great apricot theft. Old habits die hard. A warm breakfast is essential in those temperatures. I used my piton hammer to crack the apricot stones. A real luxury and a bullseye every time as bits of nut flew off in all directions. The kernels were delicious, slightly sharp and of course nutty. The shells were used for lighting fires. Nothing was ever wasted in Zangskar.

If the weather was fine I would take breakfast on the rooftop and look across the valley towards Karsha and its large monastery. The walls were whitewashed, an important task that took place in spring when the villagers moved from their winter to their summer quarters. Whitewashing cleansed the house from evil spirits of the preceding year. Old and new. Equinox – day and night. The whitewash was applied with a rag on a long stick dipped into a tub, the painter often covered from head to toe in white splodges.

The only work being undertaken in the village apart from the ceaseless round of spinning and weaving was to clear out the last of the night soil before winter set in. Well-composted dry soil is shovelled out from the latrines into pannier baskets and carried by patient donkeys to the fields. Here it is tipped out into mounds that resemble large molehills maybe three feet high. These mounds play an important part in the spring ritual, when the earth is scattered onto the surface of the snow. This induces the snow to melt more quickly, which not only moistens the soil to ensure the germination of the seed but gains as much as a week. A clever trick. An endless cycle of taking from the land what is needed and returning what is not.

Wind erosion was a major problem, and some fields were left with barley roots to stabilise the soil. In others, the roots were taken out and used as fodder during the winter. If a female animal did not survive the winter to reproduce and give milk the next summer it was a disaster. At the same time male animals, the crossbreeds of yak and cow, the *dzos* and *dzomos*, were needed for ploughing. The female yak was called a *brimo* or *demo*. The phrase 'yak butter' was therefore an oxymoron, which itself sounded like yet another crossbreed.

At the end of autumn, grain was distributed to monks and

monasteries. Rents and debts were paid, then the Buddhists started a ceaseless round of brewing up *chang*. Wheat for bread, barley for *tsampa* and beer. And as they now had access to subsidised government rations of rice and flour it meant that there was even more barley for *chang*. So they had large parties, often at night, with the whole village sitting outside on long yak-hair blankets under the stars. They certainly knew how to enjoy themselves.

The Changpa, the nomads from Rupchu in the east, had by now gone back, leaving salt and wool in exchange for grain and peas. They formed great caravans of a thousand sheep and goats, all carrying small saddlebags with about four kilos in each bag. So with a thousand goats and sheep, that was four thousand kilos on the move, nearly ten tonnes of wheat and peas. The salt was dug up from salt lakes near the Tibetan border. An extraordinary sight, seeing so many sheep on the move laden with small saddlebags. The nomads came not once but twice a year, each journey taking them about a month, grazing as they went. The long-staple wool was clipped when they got to Zangskar and was a vital ingredient when weaving their homespun cloaks, which were later dyed red or maroon.

The Changpa spent the winter not in houses but in black tents made from yak hair, which sheltered behind low rock walls. Occasionally the nomads intermarried with villagers from Shun and Shadey, which were also at 14,000ft, a sensible arrangement of interdependence. The nomads were reticent, careful to preserve their independence and integrity. Perhaps they realised how fragile their trading way of life was, now that the road was in the offing.

One Changpa asked me how far away my country was. He had camped with his pile of salt saddlebags piled up on a grassy knoll next to Stagrimo monastery and was shearing sheep. The sheep had their legs tied, then were laid on their sides and sheared one at a time, a slow but quiet process. The sheep did not seem to be stressed at all as they were handled every day.

The man's face was like wrinkled leather, from spending many years outside. The front part of his head was shaved, with a long pigtail down the back of his neck and gold earrings. He came from the land of wild yak, wild asses and black-necked cranes. The Changpa also kept pashmina goats for their fine wool, which was sent down to Kashmir to make Kashmir shawls. Half a bag of salt equalled a bag of grain – a hard life, if ever there was one. They needed these slender, tenuous trade routes as much as the local villagers in Padum, yet these economically fragile routes were already under threat from the road. The trade routes were kept alive through kinship and family links – a time-honoured tradition – and the nomads spent most of their life walking, no bad thing in summer.

The Changpa sheep were strong and healthy, so it was a serious question, 'How far is it to your country?' In other words, 'How many days will it take me to reach there with a flock of sheep?' I knew that the distance was about five thousand miles as the crow flies, so I did a quick mental calculation. His sheep travelled about ten miles a day as they had to be grazed, loaded, watered, unloaded and even milked along the way, which meant five hundred days, but they would not have travelled every day and rarely in a straight line. So I said, 'About two years.'

He looked away, thought for a while, then turned back and asked if there were sheep there. I said yes, there were. And grazing? Yes, plenty of that too. He seemed satisfied and went back to shearing the wool from his sheep with a pair of old metal shears. For the nomad, walking was a natural way of life. Many Zangskaris could walk, spin and carry on a conversation at the same time. Not a minute was wasted. Walking meditation.

The mountains were a sophisticated series of trade routes which spread out like a spider's web. Each village had its own links, its own patterns, its own paths. And when the nomads came to Zangskar en masse they would arrive in Padum, then spread out and go to their respective villages where they had trading links.

Once the grain had been exchanged, the balance was put aside for use in the winter and as seed corn. It was stored in special chests or coffers in a storeroom made from mud bricks and lined with mud to make them smooth. These were sealed, each family having its own wooden seal, which was stamped on top, well out of range of rats and mice. These wooden seals were very old and had wonderful designs on them. Grain was important and storing it in a dry, safe place was vital. Grain would keep the family going for twelve months or more.

The really busy time was after harvest, when small, water-powered corn mills operated day and night before the streams froze over. On a good stream there would often be four or five mills using the same water, one after the other. Millers were important people and they had to keep the mills in order. Their craft was crucial to the local economy, as were blacksmiths. It was time I got my stove made up and fixed.

Ringzin the blacksmith

First, catch your hare ... I bought two old army jerrycans and took along old biscuit tins and milk-powder tins that I had collected. Tins had a value in Zangskar far beyond their contents. Even small apricot jam tins were used to protect young trees and saplings from the ravages of goats. It was simple, and all you needed was a pair of tin snips. You cut the top and bottom off, then sliced down one side of the tin so that it could be slipped round the young tree like a collar. Maybe half a dozen tins were needed per tree. It stopped the goats from stripping the bark and as the tree grew the collars expanded. By the time the tree was five or six years old the tins had rusted and fallen off. Unsightly, but an ingenious solution. It gave young lads a job and bamboozled the goats.

Ringzin the blacksmith offered to make me a box stove, a *bukhari*. He eyed up the two metal jerrycans that I had specially bought for the purpose and started right away. He sat down beside the fire and drew his box of tools towards him, selecting a cold chisel and a hammer. Off came the handle in two clean sweeps, then the seams were deftly split open from top to bottom. Jerrycans were ubiquitous, an idea nicked from the Germans in the Western Desert, hence their name. Made from pressed steel, the Indian army loved them. They contained four gallons (or twenty litres for continentals), so weren't too heavy to carry. In Padum jerrycans were used to bring water up from the river in winter. A gallon weighs ten pounds, so a full jerrycan weighs forty pounds plus the can. Young girls were therefore carrying forty-five to fifty pounds up from the river, with a rope over their shoulders, zig-zagging three hundred feet up winding paths. The boys who helped were very laddish and used the empty jerrycans as toboggans, riding down on them to the river and taking the curves as competently as any bobsleigh champion in Zermatt. It made what was a chore into a game. But that was the easy bit.

They filled the jerrycans using a small tin can, which took ages. They first had to break the ice at the waterhole every morning with stones, as the main ice of the river was by now two feet thick on either side. They balanced carefully so as not to fall in. To miss a single day breaking the watering hole was fatal as the ice became too thick and hard to break. The children's fingers were often chapped and cracks ran deep. Water was needed for tea, cooking and for animals. In summer it often had mica in it from the glaciers, so it was tipped into a large copper pot and the mica sank to the bottom.

After a few minutes the two halves of the jerrycan stood side by side like identical twins, albeit the reverse image of each other. Ringzin took one, put the corner over the small stone that acted as his anvil and smashed it out, the metal fraying. He did the same until all eight corners were squashed. He then had two sheets of more or less flat metal to play with. He knew what he was doing.

He did the same with the other jerrycan, cutting it with a punch and finishing off with tin snips. Basic but effective. The sides of the stove were measured out. An end, a bottom and a top, with a stoke hole in front. Out of his pocket came horseshoe nails. Meanwhile a young lamb poked its head out of an unused oven door, so he closed it – the warmest place for the time being. The nails were beaten out and became rivets, then he cut two circles in the top plate. The biscuit tins he attacked with the tin snips, bending each piece over and then jointing them on a double flange. After two hours I had a stove. And very fine it was too.

Triumphantly I carried it back to my room and proceeded to install it with the help of the landlord's son. We cut a hole in the outside mud brick wall for the stovepipe and tried it for size. Up came a large, flat stone upon which the stove would sit. The box stove fitted well. The joints were 'cemented' in with mud, then a small hearth was made and rounded out to receive ash, and the biscuit-tin pipe thrust through the hole in the wall into the outside world. Battered tins made the pipe longer on the outside, to try to get it to draw better. I then brought wood down from the roof. A local man had carried a load – a *maund*, roughly eighty pounds – on his back all the way from Shila on the other side of the river, for which I paid him 80 rupees. A *maund* was an old measure used throughout India: one *maund* was forty *seers* and a *seer* was two pounds, although weights and measures varied from state to state, town to town.

Matches were hard to find. Once located, the kindling burnt well with the door open, but when I closed it the room filled with smoke within ten minutes. After that I used to have a small wood fire for about an hour every other day. Just long enough to cook some soup or dahl and a little rice. I gave up using the blue petrol stove when I had to throw it out of the room into the snow. Blazing, it sizzled. Farewell, petrol. Mountaineering stoves were wonderful things. I loved pumping them up, but this one had sprung a leak and I did not want it to explode. Life is short enough.

The jerrycan stove lifted the temperature of the room above freezing every other day. That in itself was luxury. I was in effect camping in a mud-brick bothy. Every night I made sure I took the plastic water container down to the stable so that it would not freeze. One night I forgot and it froze solid. You only do that once. It took me two or three days to get it to melt, even when left on the roof in the sunshine. A long, tedious process that involved banging the container and poking it with a stick to break the ice up. The animals gave much-needed heat in winter, and I now understood what it must have been like living in a medieval longhouse. Animals were essential for the family's wellbeing, and vice versa.

Sometimes I would go on the roof and watch the smoke coming out of the stovepipe. My firewood was stacked there, odd tangled bits of birch, willow and poplar. I had to make the firewood last all winter; to get any more would be impossible once the snow fell. 'Home economy', as William Cobbett would say.

Late autumn was a time for celebration and weddings, bringing families and villages together. Here in Zangskar weddings lasted for three days. The drumming had already started for Thubsten's daughter's wedding.

Ringzin the drummer

For a while I could not tell where the drumming was coming from. All I could hear was the long, low drumming that seemed to be coming from the moraine below the old palace. After a while I went to look for the drummer and climbed up a ladder on the side of a house nestling under an enormous boulder. I found two men sheltering from the wind behind a great stack of wood and hay. One of them was Ringzin. They played for two days. To one side was his small hearth and a goatskin bellows that he used for small jobs like making jewellery and necklaces – silver baubles from melted-down silver rupees from Queen Victoria's time. Or else repairing ploughs and teapots.

The blacksmiths were of a lower social and economic standing that the other farmers. They owned a little land, but after harvest or at festivals and weddings they were paid in grain and money. So they doubled up as musicians, and that was how they survived. The more skilled the blacksmith, the more jobs and thus the more grain they received. Some blacksmiths were very skilled and held in high regard, and people would travel great distances to obtain their work. In one village called Chiling, down the

Zangskar river, they specialised in copper and brasswork. We would pass it on the *chadar*.

One possible derivation of the name 'Zangskar' is from the words *zangs*, meaning copper, and *kar*, which means 'white' or 'abundance'. Occasionally nuggets of pure river copper have been found in Ladakh. In Tibetan mythology, there is a copper-coloured mountain. Western Tibet was also known for its alluvial gold, but this was regarded as the Buddha's metal and never exploited, although the monasteries had rights to the gold panning in the sand in the bends of the river nearest to them. As always, the geologists and the military had the best maps. Good modern maps are very rare in India particularly close to a border or war zone. So it was only Indian geologists and military who had good large-scale maps. If you were lucky you could look at them. Photographs not allowed. Minerals were important. Zangskar had another suggested meaning: Zan-mKhar" (food palace), 'abundance of grain' (i.e. a granary). Grain grew very well in the central valley and crop yields were very good. Irrigation was very reliable.

The blacksmiths had two drums each, about eighteen inches in diameter with goatskin stretched across them and a rope between them so that the drums could be slung over their shoulders or played when walking or riding a horse, a bit like small kettle drums. Weddings were good for them as they were paid well in cash and grain. They performed at most public occasions, and did so with great skill and gusto. Their drumsticks were wooden and about a foot long.

Ringzin, who had an earring in one ear, also owned a small lock-up shop alongside his house. He was a strong man and wanted to get on in the world. I respected him for that. Being at everyone's beck and call can't be easy. There were only three

Buddhist shops and Ringzin's was one of the first. His shop was a lock-up stall six feet wide with wooden shutters, and he sold items such as biscuits, torches, batteries, candles, sweets, cooking oil and ink. In summer there was a tent wallah who came up from Manali. He had an ex-army bell tent and kept things like dried yeast, cloth, brocades, tea, jewellery, sewing thread, dyes, sweets, all manner of spices, soap, horseshoes and even Primus stoves. He camped just outside Padum for two or three months and must have done quite well. He was an ex-monk who had been defrocked for having an affair with a local woman. Nothing new in that, he was just unlucky to be caught. In a red-hat Drugpa monastery such as Stagrimo in Padum it would not have been so much of a problem.

Thubsten's younger daughter supplied Ringzin with endless cups of tea and his hands obviously got very cold. Every so often he would put the drumsticks under his arm and shove his hands up each sleeve of his cloak. It must have been at least -10°C, but that did not deter him. Every so often he would spit on the palms of his hands to get a better grip and start again. The skins of the drum would be tightened in front of a fire each night to give just the right note. Ringzin wore a hat a bit like a deerstalker but made from lambswool. When it got really cold he would pull the flaps down to cover his ears. He wasn't going to let a bit of drumming and blacksmithing get in the way of making some money.

Later on, Ringzin started to let out rooms, but that was in summer. He was working a bit like an indentured labourer. For him the road stood for hope, a possible way out of his social and economic trap. Tied to a job that was hard work, there was no real escape either for him or his children.

From a Ladakhi point of view, handling metals was a danger-ous occupation and it was best left to those that had the skills to do so. The earth spirits were vengeful, and working with metal and smelting was a dark art. Disturbing the earth was risky. Even ploughing was potentially dangerous – and as for road building, that remained to be seen.

Two days is quite a long time to be playing the drums sitting cross-legged. The drumming was magnificent – playing in and out of each other's rhythms, experimenting with different patterns – and the rocks echoed to their detonations. Then word came towards the end of the second day that the horsemen from Kumig were approaching.

The ringing of the silver horse bells carried far across the plain as the men rode up to the village. The cavalcade had its own rhythm, half a dozen or more horses at a fast trot. There was something ancient about these sounds mingling, as if drumming, the sound of hooves rising and falling and the clear pitch of horse bells cast their own magical spell over the village. A pageant, a play, a ceremony with many actors was about to unfold, as one of their own was about to be captured and spirited away to another village. Drumming up custom.

Horsemen from Kumig

From a distance the horsemen looked magnificent, dressed in orange cloaks and sashes of orange silk the colour of mandarins. They wore ornate headdresses, a bit like willow lampshades covered in tinsel with rabbitskin caps underneath. This was the bridegroom's party. They had come for the bride. The groom was left at home. It was a pre-arranged 'bride by capture' party. Specially chosen men from Kumig would have to sing and answer many questions before they were allowed anywhere near the bride's house.

On their arrival, Ringzin picked up his drum, tucked the drumsticks into his pinkish cummerbund and went down the ladder with the drums slung over his shoulders. He wound his way between the giant boulders that still bore the smooth swirls and eddy marks of the lake that once lay there. The existence of a lake is recorded in the history books of the monasteries, so Phuntsok Dawa tells me. Sometimes glacial lakes are held back by moraines or landslides further downstream until they eventually burst. Geological time is very similar in extent and scope to Buddhist time, where the unit of time is measured in *kalpas* or cycles of 100,000 years. Sixteen million years is just another estimation of a *kalpa*. In other words, a very long time. One Ladakhi's lifetime is therefore just a twinkling in a yak's eye or a flick of his tail. Time, like the mountains, is always on the move, as if Buddhist time has several different versions of itself running consecutively. Now it was the time for weddings.

When he was on the ground, Ringzin put the short rope around his neck and continued drumming in short bursts as he walked towards the open fields where the horsemen of Kumig had gathered. He was a key player, and people quite literally danced to his tune.

The field belonged to Thubsten. Stones were set out and the men from the bridegroom's party dismounted. It would soon be very cold indeed. Each family had its own *phaspun*, the close circle of friends who always helped each other out at births, weddings and deaths. They worshipped the same *lha* or spirits.

Dogs, then children, then villagers came out to greet the men from Kumig with slow handshakes and a lifetime's mark of friendship and recognition. This was part of the ritual. The horsemen were from a village with little meltwater on the other side of the river and up a side valley, and had crossed the river lower down where it was shallow but not frozen over. It was about six miles away or two hours' walk if you were swift. One thing about walking in Zangskar was that there were often resting places between villages, either small *mani* walls or stone seats just at the right spot. It had taken many years to perfect the art of travelling. These connections between villages were invisible bonds of kinship that could be slewed by a new economy focused on the road.

There was something superhuman and godlike about the men. This was old Zangskar. They all had pigtails and looked like warriors who had come on a raid, only it was women and household goods they were after, and one woman in particular. But this was all staged and agreed in advance. A drama to be acted out with much singing and dancing and drinking.

The saddles with silver pommels were lifted off, as were the fine Tibetan riding rugs. These rugs were old and probably came from Yarkand, Khotan or even Mongolia. They were piled up on the ground and the horses allowed to rest. The men shoved their silver-tipped riding whips into their cummerbunds, along with an array of knives and heavy pen cases, all the accoutrements of a nobleman. They stood still and silent as if on parade, unused as much to all this attention as to the ceremony and rich clothes. They seemed as if in a trance. Truth was they had probably drunk quite a bit of *chang* before they left and were more than a little drowsy.

Only the breath of the horses and the sweating flanks made it real. The sound of the silver bells strapped around the horses' necks had reached far across the plain. From the roofs of the houses prayer flags fluttered and people now streamed out as if in a deluge, doors creaking as they pushed past the animals. They did not want to miss the party.

Weddings were often arranged six or seven years in advance and a series of gifts had to be exchanged: *chang* and the white ceremonial scarves called *khataks*, even jewellery. A good family with a daughter aged say twelve or thirteen might receive as many as half a dozen offers, particularly if she was a good worker. In Zangskar women not only did farm work but had to raise children, run a home and cook, as well as making butter, cheese and yogurt. Negotiation might take several years, giving time for reflection about the proposed match and the relative social status of the two families.

In Zangskar jobs that were traditionally men's were often shared with women, but men now had government jobs, joined the army or went trading. On the whole, women in Zangskar seemed strong, independent and very much in control of their homes. There were several different types of marriage, and this struck me as eminently sensible and flexible. Almost every system of relationship imaginable was possible, from polygamy, monogamy, fraternal polyandry and serial monogamy to the avowed celibacy of both monks and nuns.

And yet for a young woman marriage must still have seemed very daunting. Sometimes she had never been to the bridegroom's village, indeed she may not have even met the bridegroom for very long. So on their marriage day she was faced with the prospect of leaving not only her family home and the protection of the household god, but also her village, friends and animals, to go and live in another village with a man who might or might not treat her well. It was an upheaval both psychological and emotional for the parents as well. They were losing a key worker on their small farm. Divorce was always possible but took quite a bit of negotiation. There were good divorces and bad divorces. Girls usually stayed with their mothers and boys with their fathers.

The horsemen from Kumig were kept out of the main village for several hours after dusk. They sat on the ground, were plied with more *chang* and made to dance and sing – ancient rituals and riddles that harked back to the old days when Ladakh and western Tibet were rivals to central Tibet itself. (After an unsuccessful war Ladakh lost control of western Tibet with the treaty of Tingmosgang in 1684.)

The horsemen brought with them the 'best man' dressed in white, the *teshispa*, the auspicious one, as well as their own drummers and musicians. The men were greeted and given ceremonial *chang*. They produced from the folds of their gowns small silver cups for drinking. The lady giving the *chang* sat on the ground with her copper bowl and ladle, and offered them the liquor with the words '*Dun, dun, dun,*' – 'Drink, drink, drink.' And they did. Speeches were made, oratory was admired.

The best man, whose job it was to bring the bride back to their village, was dressed in a white *gonche* or cloak, and had ornate riding boots and hat. He carried a bow and arrow, which harked back to the old hunting days and warfare. The arrow was used for divination, for picking out the bride as a token of good luck. A symbol of office. The groom was left back in his village, contemplating his future and his family obligations.

The dancing and singing outside went on for about three hours as the temperature plummeted to about -15°C, but no one minded. And then at a certain point the revellers got up and walked towards the village. Simultaneously a shout came up from Thubsten's house, and another group of dancers, followed by a bevy of young girls, the bride's friends, came out and the two groups collided. Both had been drinking and the exchanges were then very humorous. These were the bride's party, and they were not letting the others in till they had proved themselves as competent singers.

There began yet another bout of singing and dancing, but this time the singing was very focused. It was led by a man called the *nerfon*, whose job it was to ask questions through riddles in couplets, question and answer, as the bride's family questioned the groom's family. They were singing excerpts from the ancient *Gesar* epic – the old ballad of Tibet and Ladakh – a poem akin to *Beowulf*, running to thousands of verses.[35] It was a central part of their culture that reached back to pre-Buddhist times. Tales of miraculous births, horse races, long journeys, battles, brides, kings, queens, ogres, demons, kidnapping and feasting. The singers were surrounded by the whole village and after each song the bride's family yielded a little more ground. Only a yard or two to start, then as much as ten yards as they got nearer to the house, till after an hour or so they arrived at Thubsten's front door.

But still they were not let in, and a third complicated singing contest took place amid much raucous laughter from the village. Small clay or *tsampa* models were held up and exchanged, and there was much ribald laughter of a very sexual nature. Suggestive comments were *de rigueur* concerning animals, bows and arrows, male and female private parts etc, etc, the raunchier the better. Shoes and boots were dangled from the rooftops with string and sticks like fishing rods.

At long last, and only after they had guessed what rare delicacy the mother of the house had cooked, the bridegroom's party were let near the house. Even then they were kept on the doorstep till they were offered a special soup. When they entered the house the whole village piled in. They then ate, drank and danced till first light, just like a Saturday night back home when the home team has won.

The men in robes urinated discreetly outside the stables – the *chang* had begun to take effect. They were also drinking *arak*, and this no doubt helped to fend off the cold. Inside, the men were glad to sit down and formed a row at the head of the room. Everyone had their place and there was a strict hierarchy determining where people sat.

The women all huddled together wearing jewellery, goatskin shawls and their headdresses, turquoise-laden *perags*. The *perag* is a wedding gift from mother to daughter and they are very valuable indeed, new stones being added with each wedding. They are symbolic of the family's wealth and social standing. Some stones will be very old, and when backed onto felt and coloured cloth made the *perag* look a bit like a cobra's hood that flowed down the backs of the women. The bride is kept out of sight for the first night's festivities.

It was so dark and cramped inside it could easily have been a cave. Small kerosene lamps were strapped to the pillars of the house. There was an intense feeling of closeness, as if the herd had come together. People drank and sang, but of the bride there was no sign. She was biding her time in the family storeroom and she could not look at her family god, in limbo until she was under the protection of her husband's family god. Such things were very important.

Everyone slept in a heap wherever they lay down. The *chang* had certainly taken effect. There was no turning back now. The groom was on his own and so was the bride. Time to ponder the joys and responsibilities of married life and take advice from his family. A lifetime of commitment binding two families together like the suspension bridge made of birch twigs. Subtle but strong, with a bit of give in it and well anchored on either side.

The bride

The bride appeared late the following morning and wore her finest *perag*, with side flaps made from black lamb's wool sewn into strands of her plaited hair. A gift from her mother. They said that the side flaps were introduced many years ago by a queen of Ladakh who came from the Kulu–Manali side, and she designed them to keep the cold winds off her cheeks in winter. The height of fashion. Very often *perags* were remade for each wedding. The bride's mother's stones had been sewn onto the felt backing, new stones and red coral beads were added, and rough-cut turquoise or lapis lazuli had holes drilled through them so that they could be sewn on easily. Some of the *perags* were very heavy and represented centuries of accumulated wealth. No one sold *perags* directly in shops. They were passed down and remade at each wedding, with the mother then wearing a lesser *perag*. The only problem occurred if there were no girls to inherit the *perag*. In such cases the *perag* was given to the monastery, who might well auction it off to local Zangskaris. Usually it would go to a cousin or be kept within the family for another generation. What was unusual about *perags* in Zangskar was that the women still wore them every day, even when working in the fields. To see such wealth and beauty in the landscape was a reminder of the close connection between the agricultural land and the high status of women.

The bride could not be seen because she had a white cloth over her head that she drew across her face like a veil, from behind which she occasionally peered. Her head was often down. She was sitting in her father's house at the head of the room where the men had been the night before. She seemed very uncertain, almost faint, and crying as was the custom. Even if she was pleased to be leaving home, it was important that she put on a show of remorse and sadness to be leaving her village. It was a moment of great uncertainty, even trauma. She was not allowed to enter the shrine room. Next to her was the best man, the *teshispa*, who looked bleary eyed. His arrow had chosen her, the auspicious moment connecting the marriage to divination, warfare and hunting. The divine bow and arrow. Food, prophecy and fertility.

Half a dozen monks were now in attendance. They had also drunk quite a lot the night before, and were now reciting sutras and mantras on the rooftop. They had their own musical instruments: cymbals, shawm and a reedy clarinet called a *surna*, so there were monastic musicians as well as the blacksmiths.

Phuntsok Dawa explained that the reason the bride wore a veil was that she must not see the family god, the *lhato* who lived on the rooftop in among the juniper and ibex horns. She was leaving his protection. By now the bride was in the main room, sitting with her head down. She was supported on one side by her aunt and on the other by the *teshispa*, who was half asleep. As was the custom, the bride's aunt would ride with her to Kumig and stay a few days to reassure her about the wedding night, acting as her confidante and support. Advice was vital. The aunt would only return when the bride was settled.

Other very important matters took place around midday. All the dowry was sorted out, written down and recorded: cloth and dishes, bowls, spoons, cups. The exchange of wealth was for all to see, and it was passed up through the central hole in the kitchen to the roof outside and then down a precarious stepladder to be collected later. Even animals were exchanged. Weddings were planned many years ahead and a family might have to make a number of trips down the *chadar* to trade butter to pay for it or

sell large animals like *dzos* and yaks. The rich tapestry of recipro-
cal gifts was honoured, and one's standing in the community was
visible for all to see. This was an expression of an ancient and
semi-nomadic way of life. Animal wealth. Status. Security.

Towards late afternoon the drumming intensified. The men
from Kumig, now somewhat drunk, came out of Thubsten's
house, followed five or ten minutes later by the bride and her
helpers. Ringzin and the other blacksmith sat cross-legged in the
dust, drumming for all they were worth. Staring straight ahead
as if in a trance, Ringzin spat on his hands to get a better grip of
the drumsticks. The tempo increased, and then just as the bride
was about to leave she ran back to the house and was fetched
back by her helpers. She ran to her mother and was by this time
genuinely crying. Her mother said something to calm her down,
and then everyone sat down and started drinking again. The
amount of *chang* drunk must have been prodigious – hundreds
of gallons – and took weeks to prepare. This time they were
drinking *arak* to fortify them on their journey back across the
river to Kumig.

Another hour passed as the bride sat down weeping on the
ground. Someone then lifted her onto the best man's horse and
tied her to him with a long scarf around her waist to keep her
from falling off. This really was bride by capture. Her aunt was
similarly mounted on another horse. The drummer from Kumig
mounted his horse and drummed incessantly while his horse
circled, keen to get going, then he charged up and down, raising
the tempo. The pounding of hooves added to the sense of
occasion.

Eventually they all left and rode off at a full gallop in a great
cloud of dust like a war party, following the winding paths across
the fields. The sound of silver horse bells rang out loud and clear.

The bride, still veiled in a white scarf, clasped the waist of her best man for dear life, and her aunt rode ahead of her. Two women destined for another village.

The whole village of Padum stood on the rooftops and watched in silence as the cavalcade made off. They had lost one of their number, one of their own, and they would not see much of her again. She would be tied to another house, another family, another household god, and have her own children. Silently they went back to their own homes, tired and subdued, wrapped up in their own cloaks and their own thoughts.

Thubsten, a good, solid man, stood in the middle of the field talking to them all as each passed, shaking hands and inviting them back to his house. But the whole village was exhausted, drunk and hungover, all in the same breath. They slept for a day and half, and then the first snow fell so quietly no one seemed to notice.

3

SNOW AND
NEW YEAR

December 1976

Unexpected visitors

It was five days after Thubsten's daughter's wedding that the police jeeps came. Some said they crossed over the frozen river, others that they squeezed through the narrow wooden bridge at Tungri. They were the very first vehicles ever to reach Padum and they took everybody by surprise. The Superintendent of Police back in Leh had made the decision to act. The authorities were concerned about the recent trouble – a few headstrong Muslim officials had rebelled and their women had attacked the senior government officers in Padum – and they had to nip things in the bud. Mrs Gandhi's Emergency was in full swing. But what had actually happened in Padum was very difficult to say. This was a very quiet backwater, far from Delhi, the episode a remote storm in a Himalayan teacup.

It was late afternoon. Most of the villagers were taking earth from their stables out into the fields. The donkeys stood silently outside the houses, not even flicking their tails. The *tehsildar*, Ved

Prakash Gupta, the chief government official of Zangskar, was sitting outside on a chair in the rajah's courtyard. He now had the radio/cassette recorder and was listening to the mellifluous tones of the well-known singer Lata Mangeshkar. He was in heaven, in a trance, in love with Lata. He missed his family.

Then I heard some excited voices calling to one another across the rooftops. Something unusual was going on. It seemed as if the whole village was standing on the rooftops and looking towards Sani, from where a small dust cloud was clearly visible and moving towards us. Was this another whirling dervish, another band of horsemen, a raiding party from Tibet on their way home? Or was it the army in scout cars? My antennae were alerted. I thought that the truck in Suru would be the last I would see until leaving Zangskar, but I heard the all-too-familiar noise of engines whining like persistent bees. Where had they come from? The road was not yet completed – and why here of all places, at this time of year?

The clerk and the assistant cooperative manager climbed up the rickety ladder and got onto the roof, from where they saw two jeeps slowly weaving their way across the fields and around the dusty piles of night soil, the engine noise rising and falling as they negotiated rocks, small walls and dried-up irrigation ditches. The whole village stopped work. Everyone except Gupta was intrigued. He was still in love with Lata Mangeshkar, his head swaying slowly from side to side in time with the music and his hands moving as if he were dancing.

Then I realised what it was. The mountains had yet another small trick up their sleeve. The engine noise grated against my soul as people rushed out to see what was happening. For them it might as well have been an aeroplane or a spaceship, but I sensed deep down that it did not bode well. The clerk and the assistant cooperative manager knew exactly why these jeeps had come – and that there was nowhere to run.

These two green police jeeps covered in dust did not come to the main village but made a beeline for a low white building standing all on its own several hundred yards away, down by the river beside the old Buddhist carvings on the great boulder. The building had been built as an orphanage but the police had taken it over. Orphans usually ended up in the monasteries.

Here the police radio operator had just finished shaving and was cleaning his teeth with his finger, vigorously rubbing his gums and then spitting the water out. He wore the green woollen tunic of the JKP, the Jammu and Kashmir Police. He held the communications of Zangskar in his fingertips, being in charge of the only radio in the whole valley, and every day he reported back to police headquarters in Leh. It was this radio that the Muslim government officials had seized on 6 November after their small riot, and they had not allowed him to summon help. In a back room there were packing cases and batteries, and the radio antennae stretched out of the window across the rear of the hut. One or two rifles were lying around. This was holy ground for Buddhists. Prayer flags fluttered.

More policemen hurried out to see the arrival of the jeeps. The police radio operator slowly buttoned up his tunic and combed his hair. It was not every day that jeeps arrived in Padum. In fact they had never come before. He had to look smart.

The last two hundred yards were rock-strewn and very bumpy, so the villagers helped clear the path. Engines revved and the jeeps swayed from side to side. Finally, a three-point turn. They backed up to the police hut and jubilantly switched the engines off. The small flag of the Jammu and Kashmir government on the bonnet fluttered in the breeze and then went limp.

The Deputy Superintendent of Police (DSP) climbed out, followed by Jamyang Dorje, his trusty lieutenant and right-hand man, who was Special Branch – CID, to be precise. The Sikh, the *sardaji*, who was supposed to be in charge of the police in Padum, was still missing, just as he had been at the time of the trouble. He was 'not well', absent without leave, visiting his family. The loneliness and the thought of another winter were too much for him.

The policemen waved to the villagers and went inside the building. They needed *chai*, as it had been a very long journey. A little oil dripped from a gearbox onto the ground and congealed in the dust. The jeeps had done well to get here in the first place and their tyres looked very battered. This was it, the very first vehicles in Zangskar, so I photographed them. A historic moment.

'The bridge at Tungri, you see. We only had an inch either side, and Haftal Nallah, that was frozen over. We were lucky.'

Jamyang Dorje had previously served for two years in Zangskar. A few years back he had gone over the Umasi La to get wood specially for the bridge at Tungri. He probably knew more about Zangskar than any other police officer, which was why he was chosen for the job. I rather liked him.

A shortlist of names was put forward and then whittled down to three. The DSP stood around in the blue duvet jacket that he had bought from a foreigner the summer before. He was keen to get back over the Pense La before the snow came down. In the end he took several men away with him to Kargil for investigation. What had actually gone on I wasn't sure, as no one talked about it. There were mutterings about a riot and rifles on the rooftops and men about to shoot into a Buddhist crowd. Revolt was not the best move in Mrs Gandhi's Emergency, when so many miscreants and journalists were locked up and the key thrown away. But these were minor Muslim government officials blotting their copy books. The *teshsildar* returned to Lata Mangeshkar. He had been beaten up by Muslim women wielding sticks and chair legs. He still bore the bruises. As did the SDM – the Sub Divisional Magistrate from Kargil. Rajah Tashi Namgyal had escaped though their earth latrine. Dirty but safe. Egos bruised.

Each of the local men under arrest had a bundle of clothes with them, as they would be gone for a minimum of six months, maybe longer. Their wives and families came down to see them off, letters were exchanged, bread stuffed into cloaks. Some Buddhists showed up to see what was happening, but not in great numbers. Most watched from the rooftops. One of the drivers proudly polished the bonnet of his faithful jeep.

Jamyang Dorje and the two police constables would stay for the winter down by the old Buddhist carvings. The DSP smoked a last cigarette. Then the jeeps drove off, weaving this way and that through the piles of night soil and bumping across dry irrigation ditches.

No one waved this time.

Snow falling

When the first heavy fall of snow arrived it closed the valley off from the outside world as decisively as if someone had pulled the blinds down and wound the drawbridge up. Winter laid siege to Zangskar. Not just this valley but every other valley in every direction. The village battened down and no one went anywhere. All the passes were now impassable, every mountain locked tight, every village on its own, every glacier snow-covered from head to toe. Even getting between villages was very difficult. It was as if all the inhabitants of the whole valley – men, women, children, artists, blacksmiths, weavers, musicians, soothsayers, monks and nuns – were in a closed order, as if we had taken a vow of inner silence and contemplation. Introspection was the order of the day. Looking out and looking in. Silent retreat. The meaning of life, basic and simple. A communal sense of survival and time for celebration. And to combat cold and darkness, a great sense of humour was essential. Silence was traded with silence. Body language. A firm handshake. An invisible bond. A certain look in the eye. Half their lives were spent in these winter conditions, so it formed a major part of their psychology. Not just one winter, but many winters.

Even the yaks were resigned to winter, the cold season for which they were amply equipped with their long, shaggy designer coats. They could only dream of summer pastures. What went on inside a yak's mind, I often wondered. *Bos grunniens*, the grunting ox, descended from the wild yaks that are nearly twice their size. If wild yaks charge, watch out. They weigh about a tonne.

Yaks can be black, brown or even white. They do not eat grain, only grass and hay. Maybe they think of other yaks or imagine what it would be like if they were truly wild again. Maybe they are grateful that man has chosen to domesticate them and feed them over the long winter months. Maybe they are reincarnated soldier-monks who in a previous life had not passed their Buddhist philosophy exams with flying colours. Horns are essential, curved and useful. Tails end up as fly whisks or on top of tall poles in monastery courtyards. Their hair is clipped to make tents and mats, bags and ropes. Totemic and useful, even after death. The all-purpose yak. Symbolic. Given as a token of gratitude or a standard carried into battle. Solid, reliable, trustworthy and remarkably nimble. No wonder they are worshipped as gods.

It was strange being trapped in Zangskar – yet with that entrapment came a degree of freedom, quiet resignation, surrender to the natural world, but no sense of giving in. A fine balance. No foreboding, no fear or trepidation as in a real siege; everyone knew that winter would last six or seven months. You marked time. Spring would come and the passes would eventually open one by one. The Zangskaris' cautious optimism was tinged with an acute awareness of the need to conserve not just energy and heat, but food supplies, firewood and fodder. The bitter cold could still take you unawares if you were caught out in deep snow, or if the winter went on too long and supplies ran out.

Hunger was a problem, and animals might well have to be killed if the fodder stocks were low. Phuntsok Dawa told me that in 1956 over two thousand horses and animals died, and many old people as well. It took years to recover. They'd had very heavy snow that year in September that ruined their harvest. Some lost all their livestock and in the following spring men had to pull their own ploughs.

Avalanches were a major problem, and unpredictable. In one village, Shila near Padum, a whole family of nine people, their sheep and goats, were all wiped out in a single night. People sometimes died when visiting relatives in the next village or going to a festival. Avalanches were feared.

Clouds edged down the mountain, and the feeling of snow in the offing and the sense of winter biting at our heels had been coming for weeks. After Thubsten's daughter's wedding we all knew that winter was the next player on the stage. Time was running out. Thubsten's daughter would be spending winter in another village, with another view and another family. She would be sleeping with her new husband and working in another house, in another kitchen. That is how life progresses. She would be giving herself, her labour and indeed her young, strong body to another family. That is the endless cycle of *samsara*, the wandering world unfolding itself, of cyclical change, birth and rebirth, sex, death and marriage, but not necessarily in that order. We are only here on this earth for a very short time indeed, a mere twinkling, so why not enjoy it? Enlightenment – an interesting notion. Emptiness was maybe genetic after all, or was it just endemic in winter? Maybe it is coded into their Ladakhi DNA.

I remember seeing large snowflakes coming down at night. I was so intrigued by this fast-heavy fall of snow that I donned my grubby orange anorak over my magenta Ladakhi cloak and ventured onto the roof. I held up my hurricane lantern and stared at the continual display of snowflakes falling for what seemed like hours on end. I was mesmerised. Complete silence. The flakes were large and very still. Not a breath of wind. The only sound was the occasional hiss as a snowflake landed on top of the hurricane lamp and melted in an instant with a slight spat. There was something theatrical about it all, as if the village were the stage set for the winter scene of a rural opera. But this was for real. Each flake its own destiny, gyrating silently, swirling in its own wake. A swift intensity – closing in on itself. Large flurries – pale night – winter's passport.

For ten days the snow fell. Nothing moved. No one was about. No animals stirred, only the faint smell of musty dung drifting up from the stables down below. Everybody was fast asleep, as if the village was deserted. No sign of life anywhere. Everyone had worked so hard during the summer months and the autumn gathering in fodder, herding animals, weeding crops, harvesting. Then there was butter making for the trip down the *chadar*, or collecting firewood and dung in vast baskets. Only now did they have time to recover their sense of equilibrium. Time to draw in and gather their energy once more. Time to relax and sing songs, to tell stories and drink *chang*. Winter was a time of wellbeing, of having time with the family. Snow and ice bound them even closer.

Stretching for hundreds of miles in every direction, this snow formed a deep Himalayan blanket that wrapped itself like a cloak around the valley. We felt safe. Cocooned. Hermetically sealed. Virtuous. As if under the guardianship of the mountains. The spirit of winter clothed us in silence and made us feel at home. We passed the time of day in contemplation. A hard-earned luxury. Quietening down. Acceptance. Gratitude. Deep knowledge.

Metamorphosis

The falling snow had a deceptively innocent quality to it, each snowflake having its own complex hexagonal pattern, its serial number that gave it a unique identity. But when several feet thick, the snow could easily wreak havoc. And because of the low temperature it could stay as powder snow for days, weeks, even months on end. This was fine on the fields, but on mountains it led to powder-snow avalanches. A seemingly innocent slope of about 40° was the most dangerous. Avalanches also needed a trigger. Snow has a life of its own and can take several very different paths. Snow is also very heavy. One inch of rain is roughly equivalent to twelve inches of snow. It just depends on the rate of deposition and temperature. Slow compaction. Crystal world. Complex structure. Then fragility sets in.

For villagers there was a more pressing problem; as snow built up on their flat roofs, its weight soon became a real headache. In mountain villages on the southern side of the Himalaya, say the Kulu–Manali side where they had even deeper snowfalls, the houses had steep, pitched, alpine-style roofs because there was an abundance of timber. The snow eventually slid off the roofs under its own weight, a menace only to those immediately below. But here, if the snow was allowed to build up to a depth of several feet, the weight would eventually break the roof. If the snow started to melt, the roof would disintegrate as it was only made from earth, mud and brushwood.

So while it was falling, villagers would sweep the snow on their roofs into large piles with a homemade birch-twig broom and then let it rest for a few hours. As it went through its meta-morphosis, the snow became more solid, more compacted, like 'snowball' snow, easier to handle, in a process known as sintering. Fine, delicate crystals break down and realign themselves into larger, flatter patterns, which then refreeze; the snow shrinks and locks together as air is excluded. Villagers would then shovel the snow off the roof onto the ground below with a flat wooden shovel. These wooden shovels came from the other side of the Himalaya – the Kishtwar side – and had to be carried over the Umasi La, a high pass with glaciers.

Getting the snow off the roof was a good job for the children, and they loved it. Sintering also occurs with strong winds, and this was very useful when I was seeking shelter out in the open – even in the valley you would carve out blocks of snow and build a snow shelter. It could save your life.

Over winter the alleyways between houses became lethal as snow turned to solid ice, and you had to make sure that you were not walking underneath when they were shovelling snow off the roof. These alleyways had just enough room for two yaks with horns to pass. If a yak started from one end of an alleyway it was just as well to stand aside and let it come through before you started on your way.

After heavy snow there was complete silence, the dim morning light reflected back onto the red and green floral cloth suspended under the ceiling. It wasn't until well past midday that I heard more brushing and scraping noises. There was a quiet rhythm to it, then a thud and a thump a few hours later as the snow was chucked off the roof into the alleyways.

I went for a stroll around the village and heard monks performing a *puja* in an upstairs room of a house in the middle of the village. There was a candle and a yellow glow at the window, which seemed inviting through the snowflakes. They chanted for hours on end, and at the climax of their ritual the monks played cymbals and drums full pelt, blew their horns and thighbone trumpets, and rattled their pellet drums. It was as if they were summoning the snowfall themselves to celebrate the beginning of winter.

Later on, at the end of the winter, I saw monks in Karsha perform a special *puja* to bring more snow, and sure enough more snow came down. Without snow in winter there would be no glaciers, and without glaciers there would be no meltwater in summer and no irrigation for crops. No food. Buddhist ritual and weather were not unconnected. Ladakhi symbiosis.

Over the next ten days snow fell continuously. One night a very strong wind blew powder snow into my room. Here, there and everywhere fine particles of snow managed to squeeze through every crack and cranny by the window and by the door. But it was a very civilised ten days. Everything quietened down. In the daytime, yaks and one or two other animals were turned out to get a bit of fresh air. They stood around nonchalantly, letting snow gather on their backs as they chewed some hay. Apart from that, nothing happened.

This winter silence was addictive. Muffled by snow, the whole village fell silent. The silence kept us whole, it kept us fresh, it kept us alive, and we fed on the silence as if it were an essential part of our diet, a rare commodity that is traded in the mountains, more precious than gold, silence that had evolved within their culture, a silence that the Buddhists deeply respected. Mountain silence. A very particular silence that was clearly under threat from road building.

For ten days I could not even see Stagrimo monastery. So I stayed put in my small room and had time to ponder what exactly it was that had brought me to this remote Tibetan Buddhist valley. The inner path had many twists and turns, and I mulled over all the interesting people who had helped me along the way. It humbled me.

Maybe I was also undergoing a kind of metamorphosis, but what the end result would be was still open to question. To think like a Zangskari was no easy matter. You had to be very tough indeed, resilient and patient. I had plenty of books. You kept warm and turned the pages. At night you lit candles, half a candle a night. Being a hermit wasn't so bad. Peasant academic.

Rajah's moonshine

Life in Padum had its own quiet, measured pace, interspersed with communal drinking sessions that involved quite a bit of singing and dancing and the telling of jokes and stories. There was a rota system for Buddhist prayers that worked every four weeks, which was about how long it took to brew the next batch of *chang* and reflected the cycles of the moon. Families would meet up in each other's houses, usually on certain days of the month like the 15th, which was always full moon in the Tibetan calendar. The 8th and 10th were also auspicious days set by the calendar. Religious observations had to be kept. The cycle of *chang* was endless. No wonder they liked the winter. Time to relax.

During the day when the sun shone, most villagers were out on their rooftops to sit down out of the wind next to piles of fodder and firewood. The women worked, spinning, plying, carding wool, talking, chatting, telling stories, even grinding grain by hand in simple querns. Women liked to work together in each other's houses and often sang as they worked. These were important winter activities, just as milking, herding and butter making were important in the summer. The men did weaving and carpentry, building work, brewing and reading old Buddhist texts. Men also knitted and spun as they walked and talked. No time was ever wasted. Children were taught to spin very young. Such skills were vital for survival. In winter Zangskaris thought about summer, and in summer they pondered the necessities of winter. Each season had its own charms and dynamic imperative.

One day when I went to see Phuntsok Dawa there was a strange fragrance in the air coming from the storeroom and I knew that Rajah Tashi Namgyal was up to something. Men who brewed *chang* also periodically practised the art of distilling *arak*, and Tashi Namgyal was no exception. He was a dab hand at moonshining. The process was simple. You steeped barley for a day or two and then put the wetted grain into a sack, which was then shoved into a haystack or placed in a storeroom. When this first stage of germination was complete, the grain was heated up slowly in a large copper and allowed to ferment with dried yeast acquired from the Lahouli tent wallah, then stored in a small open barrel. You could strain it and drink it as *chang*, or, as the rajah did, carry on and distil it.

To do this distilling you had a circular metal or clay pot in which you held the mash. Above it was a pot of cold water and cleverly suspended below that on strings inside the whole device there was another smaller dish that collected the condensed alcohol. Ingenious. It required great skill to get the fire burning at just the right temperature and speed, and yak dung was ideal for this controlled slow burn. The temperature was regulated by raking embers in and out, and the cold water in the upper pot had to be replaced every so often to keep the temperature coefficient even. Alcohol comes off at about 78°C, though it may be slightly lower at high altitude. If the heat is too great, good spirit is lost as vapour to the gods – the angels' share – or, in Ladakh, to the *dakinis*, the sky dancers so beloved by Tibetan Buddhists.

As an experiment I did some brewing of my own with the help of Phuntsok Dawa. We roasted the grain to malt it, but alas there were no hops. The end result was pretty good. I steeped some of the rajah's *arak* for four weeks with a tin of apricot jam to make an apricot liqueur – an experiment well worth attempting. It was very good. He rather liked it. It just needed more apricots and acres of patience. A small artisanal business opportunity.

Without *arak* many Ladakhis could not survive the winter and in some monasteries there was even a penchant for army rum. Tashi Namgyal was a dab hand at distilling and offered me some in a beautiful small silver cup. It tasted good and the inner warmth was very welcome. When Jammu and Kashmir went 'dry', the Ladakhis were given special dispensation to keep distilling as it was an essential part of their life. Certainly the Indian army could not survive in Ladakh without XXX rum or Indian Scotch in the Leh officers' mess. Tashi Namgyal's moonshine was practical. Zangskaris took great pride in their secret skill. Spirit of the gods.

Losar – New Year

A week or two after the first heavy fall of snow I received another note from Phuntsok Dawa, again brought by his son Stenzin Namgyal. It simply said: 'Mr James. Please come with bearer for some more *chang*. It is *Losar*.'

At the bottom it said 'Phuntsok Dawa, Teacher'. His name 'Excellent Moon' meant that he was born on a Monday. *Losar*, Zangskari New Year, was equivalent to winter solstice, roughly 21 December. The Buddhists operate on the lunar calendar, starting with the new moon, and have a cycle of twelve years. Each year has its own animal: Rat, Ox, Leopard, Hare, Dragon, Snake, Horse, Sheep, Monkey, Rooster, Dog, Pig. Teshi Namgyal explained that five elements were attached to these animals: fire, earth, iron, water and wood, which gave a cycle of sixty years. 1976 was the Fire Dragon year, which was followed by the Fire Snake year. I preferred dragons to snakes.

Technically, *Losar* was held for six days and six evenings starting on the last day of the tenth month of the Dragon year. In other parts of Tibet, New Year was the end of the twelfth month, usually in late February. Apparently the King of Ladakh once undertook a military expedition against his neighbours, and allowed his troops to celebrate New Year in advance to give them good luck and boost morale. Ever since then, the Ladakhi New Year has been celebrated in December rather than in the spring, as in Tibet. It's called Farmer's New Year, while the spring New Year is called King's New Year.

It was now mid-winter. Deep inside Tashi Namgyal's house, in the lower room beyond all the animals in the stable, his extended family gathered. The rajah sat to one side, once again put on his black bearskin fringe over his forehead and started saying his prayers. He clicked his fingers three times as if summoning up local spirits to a feast and recited the mantra, the repetitive prayer that churned over in his mind a thousand times. An awesome performance.

The mantra on his lips, *Om mani padme hum*, so beloved by Buddhists all round the world, had been in their bloodstream for over a thousand years. Even before they were born, the reassuring sounds of the mantra would have reached them in the womb. Soothing and reflective, mantras go very deep indeed and work on many levels. Translating many of them into English is not so easy. I had a Tibetan grammar book written by Herbert Bruce Hannah QC (1862–1930), a barrister in Calcutta, published in 1912. He roughly equated the phrase to: 'The source of all speech, vitality and thrilling consciousness, the wish-granting jewel, I am, the omnipresent life principle.'

A slightly fuller translation may be rendered thus: *Om* invokes not only the practitioner's impure mind but the pure mind of the Buddha, and tries to close the gap; this is essentially encouraged by adopting the Buddhist Middle Path, where *mani* the jewel of enlightened altruism and compassion is joined at the hip with *padme* – lotus wisdom – and they both come together to produce *hum*, an indivisible state of pure mind in which method and wisdom are one. The mantra 'O jewel in the lotus' also has other inner Tantric, even sexual, meanings that are often acted out in monastic wall paintings.

Profound everyday wisdom, high-altitude philosophy. Sounds easy, but takes years to achieve – not bad for six o'clock in the evening. *Om mani padme hum* is everywhere: carved on stones all over Ladakh – often on the top of *mani* walls – written on prayer flags, painted on rocks by the roadside, a byword for Buddhist practice and deeply embedded in Ladakhi consciousness.

Prisoners not only built these impressive walls, which were maybe half a mile long, but also had to carve the mantra to make up for their misdemeanours. The mantra is firmly embedded into the quadrangle of the mind, into the niches of monasteries and even on the backs of *tangkas* to bring them to life.[36] To activate the *tangkas* the eyes are finally painted in and the *tangka* blessed by a high lama. Buddhist psychology whittled down to these few words and ideas. I loved the Tibetan script. Freedom and flow. It was brought from India and adapted in the 7th century CE by Thonmi Sambhota, who had been sent by the King of Tibet.

Om mani padme hum. So simple and beautiful, and yet so complex. Almost musical, the hypnotic pattern of sounds reverberated round the room like a magician casting a spell. The mind resonated and the rhythm brought people together. These were sounds they had heard since before birth. It was their cultural signature, a password that opened doors of perception.

Tashi Namgyal was reciting the words to his family while they were cooking, and to all the animals. Winter solstice was a dangerous time, when the sun was lowest in the sky, the daylight shortest and the nights coldest. But ritual has its own power. He then continued with his ritual to Tara and made a mandala offering. The soft Tara mantra also sounded rather beautiful, like a lullaby – *Om tare tuttare tore soha*, which, when repeated hundreds of times, had a hypnotic effect.

On the shelf above where the rajah was sitting were eight small dough figures of animals that he had made, about the size of small toys. They had tufts of wool for coats or skin. Here were yak, deer, ibex, sheep, goat, horse, donkey and cat. In front, four small butter lamps burned.

The figures, the rajah explained, were 'to remind children to be kind to animals'. They also invoked fertility, particularly the ibex, a key connection with the mountains. Ibex were still very important, and if someone was ill they would make an offering of miniature ibex modelled out of *tsampa* dough to the local monastery. Barley and ibex. Key ingredients for living, hunting and gathering.

The small bit of bearskin that Tashi Namgyal was wearing around his head was to keep evil spirits away and helped him to concentrate. The head lama in Karsha also had one. It empowered him, hovering above his eyes and giving him a shamanic appearance as if he were well and truly communicating with the ancient spirits of central Tibet. As always, pre-Buddhist beliefs lay only just beneath the surface in Zangskar, strong forces that the powers of Buddhism had a hard job keeping under control.

Om mani padme hum with a black bearskin covered the options both ways. Being pragmatic, villagers often hedged their bets both ways, particularly at crucial times like New Year. You couldn't be too careful in the mountains. One hundred and eight recitations as per the beads – the *mala* – that you often saw in people's hands or wrapped around their wrists.

When Tashi Namgyal had finished his *puja* he took the bearskin off and smiled. At sixty-six, Tashi was still very sprightly. He had been born in 1910 and was much respected in the Buddhist community. The top button of his *gonche*, his cloak, hung open, this silver bauble had a small swastika on it. His hair was black like a horse's mane.

Stenzin Namgyal, the boy who had brought the note, leaned over a small desk trying to read the Buddhist scriptures, which he could do well. He was very bright. The rajah put away his *puja* instruments, bells, *dorjes* (thunderbolts) and a copper bowl or two. He made a mandala offering in the morning with rice, barley and dried flowers, a ritual offering that can be interpreted on many levels, an offering of the universe with the mythical mountain Mount Meru at its centre. One accumulates merit as well as focusing and calming the mind. Tantric visualisation was the key. Worlds within words.

Tashi then offered me tea, taking a glass from off the shelf and wiping it carefully. When he was sitting at his *puja*, the rajah wore spectacles from Kashmir. He showed me where they had broken over the bridge and how they were held together with Sellotape. Had I got any glue? Glue they had in the valley was made from boiled-up horse's hooves, but it was not very strong. Mixed with soot it made ink. They also made paper in the valley from the middle section of a root, and very fine paper it was too. The inks and paints were also made in the valley for the monastery so that they could make religious books and commentaries. Monasteries were in effect publishing houses.

Araldite. Yes, I had some Araldite glue in a tube and I promised to bring some the next day. 'AH RAAAL DITE,' the rajah said, and seemed very pleased. He had a good sense of humour. 'AH RAAAL DITE' had become yet another mantra. Even the children thought it was funny. *Om mani padme hum* 'AH RAAAL DITE'.

The tea was sweet, not butter or salt tea, but with cardamom and cinnamon. 'Lipton tea,' he said, and produced the red and yellow packet. It was indeed Lipton tea, grown in the part of Assam known as NEFA, the North-East Frontier Agency. Like the North-West Frontier, but NEFA wasn't a bed of roses. The Chinese army were always breathing down their necks and had invaded in 1962, just as they had done in Ladakh.[37] There was also an insurgency problem.

The braid on the rajah's collar and down the side of his cloak was worn, and the cloak showed signs of repair at the shoulder. It was said that when he was a dashing young man he would go round the village with a ladder, chasing young women with some of his friends, notably Sonam Raftan. The women would let them in if they knocked at the right window. The rajah always looked as if he had been feeding his own animals with odd bits of hay and straw lying around. More often than not he had a quizzical half-smile on his lips. He was very down to earth. I rather liked him.

The rajah's nose was also slightly red, probably from drinking *arak*. His cheekbones were high and his beard unusually thick for a Ladakhi but not long. He looked regal. Just right for a *gyalpo* or rajah.

Young butter lamps

On the other side of the room the children made butter lamps out of *tsampa* dough and Tashi Namgyal explained that another ceremony was about to take place outside in the square. The ritual had deep meaning. Warding off disease and mishap was very important, as disaster was always only just round the corner. Stenzin's younger brother had died of measles two or three years earlier. It swept through the valley every seven years or so, so they needed to ward off evil. Life was hazardous, and that was long before you stepped onto the ice.

Phuntsok Dawa's younger brother Thinley Dawa was there with his wife and children.[38] *Thinley* meant 'enlightened activity'. They lived next door in a smaller house, all crammed up along one wall.

Not far from the rajah's house was the great *chorten* of Padum, built by one of the old kings. It had a square base and a rounded top graced with a tall wooden pole, and through its middle a passageway that would take a yak or two. If you looked up, in the centre under the top there was a mandala on the ceiling and the paint slightly peeling.

All the children of the village had gathered under the mandala, waiting for the rajah. This was the longest, darkest, coldest night. Everyone carried their small butter lamps slowly in procession from the rajah's house, the small wicks made out of two twists of spun wool already lit. The rajah carefully took each lamp from each child and placed it inside the *chorten* in small cracks between the stones till the inside was a mass of small, guttering flames. Shadows danced, and the old mandala high above came alive. A fitting ceremony for such an evening. A festival of light on the shortest day and longest night. Dark forces that have to be kept at bay. An ancient ritual designed to create security and confidence. A feeling of wellbeing and shared responsibility. Winter solstice.

Then, when the butter lamps had all been placed inside the *chorten*, two larger figures appeared wearing wooden masks – Abe and Meme, grandmother and grandfather. They had large walking sticks and long sheepskin cloaks, and had come all the way from India and Lahoul bringing the Buddhist message, good tidings and long life. Meme had a wispy goat-hair beard, and Abe the grandmother wore outrageous oversized wooden jewellery and cowrie shells. Buddhist bling. Holding the masks close to their faces, they pretended they were very old.

Then two younger boys appeared, both about twelve years old. One, the *teshispa*, the auspicious one, had a bow strung across his back and a quiver of arrows. He wore a white cloak and a ceremonial hat similar to those worn by the horsemen from Kumig. The other was the crow-headed work leader known as Legon Charok Donchen, a protective diety linked to Mahakala. The boy had a wooden crow's beak on his head with three eyes, the third eye for divination and augury. The King of Bhutan had a gold one of these as a crown, though there it was a raven, an ancient symbol of royalty connecting kings with the sky and the ancestors, as ravens often picked the bones clean in sky burials. Corvids connecting the earth to the sky. The kings descended from above. Divine flight. In his belt the *teshispa* also had a small horsewhip as a symbol of status.

Abe and Meme both carried large sticks and had already consumed quite a bit of *chang*. They brought good luck and greetings: '*Likim Kar*' ('Happy New Year'); 'May you have a long life'; 'We bring presents from India'; 'Long life and good luck'; 'May your yaks prosper.'

Another six boys, the *bakpa* (mask people), wore old-style Ladakhi hats, like nightcaps folded down one side and tucked into the rim. They were black with a blue lining and tassels down the back. The girls wore flat-topped caps and shawls from Lahoul, with red and green cloth on the outside and sheepskin on the inside. Very warm by the look of it. They stood around looking at each other as if it were a fashion parade.

It is said in the old chronicles of Ladakh that Zangskaris came from Guge, a kingdom near Spiti, whose capitals were at Tholing and Tsaparang, now in western Tibet. The children danced an old Lahouli dance, a history lesson. After the ceremonies the men drank *arak* and returned to the rajah's house. Young butter lamps still burnt, illuminating the mandala. The dough to make them came from barley and the wicks from sheep's wool, the annual cycle in one fell swoop – the festival of light, and light returning. An offering, a gift from the mountains, a chance to redeem the unfortunate happenings of the previous year, and look forward to a prosperous and healthy New Year. *Likim Kar*.

The dragon

As it was cold and dark we returned to Tashi Namgyal's lower room. The rajah's wife had not ventured outside. She was seventy-two and had a towel round her head to keep her warm. There were no windows, just a small wooden board that could be opened if there was too much smoke. Luckily there was a chimney for the stove.

To one side of the stove was a *dongmo*, a wooden tea cylinder about three feet high with a piston that was moved up and down. Sometimes made from bamboo, it was used for mixing butter tea: *gur gur char*. Dolma, Phuntsok Dawa's wife, was sitting by the fire. She put a good dollop of butter into the mouth of the *dongmo* and poured the steaming red liquid into it from a kettle on the stove. This red Tibetan salt tea was known as *namkin char*.

She stood up, grasped the piston of the *dongmo* and put some rough *changpa* salt in as well. She put her foot through the rifle-sling strap of the *dongmo*, checked the level of the liquid was right, then pumped the piston up and down for about three or four minutes. The cylinder gurgled, and when it was ready she poured the tea, now pink, into the kettle and served it in small cups.

Dolma had a young baby that her mother-in-law was looking after. The rajah sat down again and started to make a model of a dragon out of *tsampa* dough. Having rolled out several lengths of dough, he began constructing the dragon. It was the end of the Dragon year. Ladakhis like dragons as much as they like snow lions. The rajah made a long, S-shaped serpent, supported by twigs and matchsticks, as dragons were not known for their structural integrity, then he did the head and the tail. The dragon kept falling over, maybe because it had drunk too much *chang*, but it was *Losar* and an excuse for a party.

Eventually the dragon sobered up and the rajah shaped the head, gave it eyes, large ears, dragon whiskers, horns, fangs and teeth. Finally he made a man with a round hat, colouring the hat with blue ink he obtained by dipping his finger into an ink pot. He tied a white scarf around the man's head and in front of it made a bowl of incense. The children loved it.

At one point the twigs on the model yak caught fire from the butter lamp in front of it. Phuntsok Dawa got up to extinguish the flames, the yak looking none the worse for its ordeal. These miniature animals were a real treasury, a bestiary, a reminder of their flocks and herds and their reliance on animals for survival. The dragon sat in pride of place. First the festival of light in the old *chorten*, now the fire and dragon offering. Reproduction, food, farming, fertility and the returning of the light. Keeping the good spirits on side. Hedging your bets in a precarious spirit world. Seasonal good cheer.

Likim Kar

The New Year celebrations had only just begun. They would go on for six days, mostly in the evenings. The *bakpa*, the young lads with old Ladakhi caps, sauntered back into Tashi Namgyal's house with a bit of a swagger, knowing they were centre stage. They were followed by Abe and Meme, who still wore large wooden masks and carried their stout walking sticks. They threw barley flour everywhere and smeared people on their brows with butter as an auspicious sign. They brought good luck and New Year's greetings, a bit like first-footing.

Meme, the 'grandfather', was raunchy and often approached women in a slightly provocative way, aware that he could get away with it. Crude songs were also sung, a celebration of life forces and procreation. Daubed on the wall were the words *Likim Kar*, as well as sun and moon motifs to ward off evil. The pillars and book-shelves were also daubed with white dots. The boy dressed in a white cloak and headdress touched the beer barrel with his sacred arrow, a bow and quiver over his shoulder. He was the auspicious one capable of divination. Another boy to one side was wearing a bird mask on top of his head. They were the important young men for *Losar* and kept turning up, as if to reinforce the ancient pre-Buddhist order of things that still lived beneath the surface. Every house now had a dragon. It was a village of dragons.

A fire was then lit on the open hearth and a small branch of juniper set alight, the rajah put his bearskin back on again and bells clanged; *tsampa*, barley, *chang*, water – all were thrown through the air to the gods, very dramatic as flames leapt to the ceiling and the previous year's evil was induced to enter the dragon. Real hocus pocus. Purification wizard. The beer barrel stood full and had white butter marks around its rim for good luck, and everyone's faces were lit up by the brushwood fire. Flour was thrown around until people were covered in it. Everyone laughed. When the rajah gave the sign, the children took the dragon out on the plate, cymbals were hit and Ringzin drummed. The dragon was carried aloft by the rajah out through the courtyard up a rickety ladder onto the roof and thrown down to the ground outside to the fields below. You could hear the shout of victory often uttered when they crossed a pass: *'Kyi kyi so so, lha rgyalo'* ('Victory to the gods').

The poor old dragon only lasted a few hours and was then devoured by the village dogs. The dogs did very well on winter solstice. If each Buddhist house chucked out a dragon, that was a lot of dragons to bite the dust in one evening. The rajah sat back. Another year's evil had been taken out of the house.

Phuntsok Dawa's family then fed half the village. Young boys and girls danced, the *chang* flowed. Some women went back to their houses and brought more jugs of beer with them, and these were poured into the barrel. A communal drinking session. In fact, in Padum they had drinking sessions every fortnight or so, and there was a regular circuit. These sessions provided a chance to discuss all sorts of matters and were staged on religious days as well.

Everyone was fed one at a time, in order of age and seniority. And then, one by one, as they were sitting in order of rank, merit and age, the men got up in turn, some unsteadily, and announced *Likim Kar* again and again. It was also everyone's birthday, because in Zangskar you are zero when you are born, you are one at the first New Year and then everyone added a year at New Year. Very sensible. People knew when they were born, which day of the week and in which year, under which stars and which planets. How many summer pastures have you seen? How many winters have you seen? How many ibex? How many snow leopards?

I was overwhelmed by the Zangskari sense of hospitality, sharing an abundance of barley in the form of *chang*, which had ritual status. With the arrival of rations and government *atta*, the Buddhists had more fields for *chang*, so in a good year the valley was overflowing. Large parties were common.

The New Year drinking session went on long into the night. They told more stories, sang more songs, fell asleep. What else was there to do?

Ibex and wild monks

Losar went on for five more nights, with all events happening after dark in about -20°C in the light of one or two lanterns. The people needed to placate the forces of nature so that the sun would return.

The village would gather in the late afternoon in the village square by the flagpole with the yak's tail on top. Young boys would dance and re-enact scenes from Tibetan history, six girls dressed up in green and red cloaks from Lahoul, and one or two villagers were got up as monks. My next-door neighbour Mr Tashi Tantar had a bedraggled cloak and a yak-hair mask. He beat his drum with unabashed ferocity, then he danced around in circles, imitating the monks. The villagers roared with laughter. Making fun of the monks was always a good laugh once a year. It was the villagers, after all, who kept them fed and clothed. But some of the monks were serious meditators.

There were two in particular. One rather wild one with long tousled hair was known as Gonpo, the other as Nochungtse; he was uncle to Sonam Raftan. Nochungtse had not been down to the village for about ten years, but Gonpo was a regular fixture and liked his *chang*. Their teachers were descended from the founder of their monastery, Dorje Zinpa. They had meditated down in Lahoul, where they had learnt *Dzogchen*, the secret teachings. There was far more to these monasteries than met the eye. These practitioners of *Dzogchen* were hardcore meditators. Wisdom came from deep within. Wild monks.

Villagers also re-enacted scenes from the plague, when many died and Guru Rinpoche brought them back to life. Measles still swept through the valley periodically and young children often died. Disease was never far away.

Then there were deer and yak dances, with masks like those in the monastery festivals. Two men dressed up as women and took it very seriously, wearing fine *perags* with turquoise, and even scarves and sunglasses. On another evening there was a jolly hunter, together with two men dressed as ibex. There was much cavorting as one ibex tried to mount the other. Fertility was an important part of *Losar*. They all lived close to their animals, close to the land, close to each other. Girls had to be tough to survive and needed a strong, earthy sense of humour. Some chose marriage, others the nunnery. The only escape outside the valley was in Leh or Manali.

Everyone looked up to ibex. The villagers' hunting instinct lay only just beneath the skin. There were old rock carvings of ibex being hunted by men with bows and arrows. *Losar* was a time for the local gods, a time when everything came together. New Year was a vital part of their identity. Occasionally ibex were caught in avalanches and later dug out. Ibex meant food and survival.

On the last day lamas crowded into a house close to Phuntsok Dawa's. All sorts of elaborate dough offerings were made, decorated with red butter. They made a frightening figure called Barmah, who looked like Mahakali.

All day the lamas read sutras and recited mantras. Then at a certain point, just as the sun went down behind the peaks, they blew their trumpets and their horns, banged their drums and cymbals ferociously and rattled their *damarus*, the skull-pellet drums, all in a crescendo. The head lama sat in the corner wearing a fine red hat not dissimilar to a bishop's mitre, his scarf drawn down over his chin like a handkerchief, his glasses resting on the end of his nose, tilted down to read the prayers. His red hat showed many years of use.

The cymbals clashed and the silver- and gold-encrusted pipes piped, then there was a reed-quivering moment, the pipers' cheeks bulging as they managed to do their double breathing, much needed for the long cattle horns. The precise time for throwing all the figures and spirit catchers into the river had been chosen by the astrologer. Then, at the critical point, the head lama put on all his ceremonial robes.

The trumpets sounded, at which point the lamas got up and made their way slowly down to the river. There was the crunch on snow and ice as they paraded around the village, then in single file they went down the slippery path to the bridge three hundred feet below, where they took up a rather precarious position on the ice. There was an ominous open patch of swirling water, the access point to reach the *klu*, the water spirits who had to be kept happy. The peaks looked icy. It was damned cold.

The head lama made sure that the various sacrificial objects, including the beast named Barmah, were all placed on the ice. The dish rested on an ibex head with horns, linking the ceremony to the local *lha*. The head lama slowly started a ritual ceremonial dance as he would in his monastery, but here it was on the frozen river. In his hand was a piece of what looked very like human bone, no doubt a powerful relic from a famous lama. Round and round on the ice, faster and faster till he was in a frenzy, then at the right moment he rushed up to Barmah, picked up the round dish and threw all the accumulated evils into the river, one after the other in quick succession. Drums were beaten and horns blown, while the village dogs looked on sadly as they realised that all the dough figures that might very well have been their supper had ended up being thrown to the fishes under the ice.

Evil had been averted for another year and the river placated. The water spirits were now appeased, which would augur well for a safe journey down the frozen river. The lamas had interceded for us. It was primitive magic but it worked on several levels: the Buddhist level, the pre-Buddhist level, the village level. It aimed to help with a good harvest, to avert diseases and to protect all those undertaking dangerous journeys.

The monks had earned their keep. The sun could now return and be welcomed back. It was around this time that Phuntsok Dawa made discreet enquiries about who was planning to go down the frozen river and whether I could join them. The *chadar* beckoned, but the ice was still very precarious. We would have to wait for a month or more. A faint smell of incense lingered in the cold air.

4

CHADAR – THE RIVER FROZEN

February 1977

Astrology

Zangskaris always consult the astrologer before they go on a long journey or get married. The *onpo* reads the stars and consults learned tomes about the compatibility of colours, planets and conjunctions. The heavens still control their lives through the yearly cycles, local spirits have to be appeased and offerings are made to the household god with *khatags* and incense.

The auspicious days of each Tibetan month are the 8th, 10th, 15th, 25th and 30th. On the 8th we weren't quite ready. On the 10th we were. These are Tibetan months, pre-set with a lunar calendar: the 1st is a new moon, the 15th a full moon. The astrologer, also called the *tsispa*, the 'calendar man', said that we must leave in the afternoon. It seemed common for journeys in Zangskar to start in the afternoon. Many of the festivals started after dusk, even weddings. The astrologer works things out with books and a table of sand, with a large wooden tray upon which he can work out his calculations. It is all about stars and timing.

The days of the week are taken from planets. Sunday is *Nyima* – the Sun; Monday is *Dawa* – the moon; Tuesday is *Mikmar* – Mars; Wednesday is *Lhakpar* – Mercury; Thursday is *Phurbu* – Jupiter; Friday is *Pasang* – Venus; and Saturday is *Penba* – Saturn. The day itself is divided into twelve *khyims*, which are further divided into five *chutshods*, the time it takes for salt tea to boil – about twelve minutes. Buddhist teatime.

Some days are better than others. Saturday, Sunday and Tuesday are bad for travelling; Monday is doubtful, but favourable for going south; Thursday unfavourable for going west; Friday unfavourable for going south and west. We were going north. In the end we left on Wednesday afternoon. Distances are measured in one day's journey – about fifteen miles if the going is good. A mile – the time it takes to get tired with a load on one's back.

Incense comes from small juniper branches, dried fronds or pine needles brought from the south scattered on a small dish with live charcoal and blown gently till the smoke fills the air. Incense placates the *tsen*, *nyen* and *klu*. *Tsen* are earth spirits, spirits of the soil that have to be placated when ploughing. *Nyen* are elemental spirits, the demons that float around, and *klu* are water spirits with a human head and a snake's body that live in the water and cause rain and maladies. It is a complex spiritual world, one that you enter at your peril without making offerings or taking precautions. Invisible danger made manifest.

I am not normally superstitious, but the journey down the frozen river was so important and perilous that I consulted the *I Ching*, the ancient Chinese soothsaying book, by throwing three coins three times and looking at the way they fell.[39] Heads and tails.

It came up with hexagram 59 – *Huan* – 'Dispersion sandwiched between joyous lake and limitation'. Images were of scattering, which is what we were doing on the ice. 'It pays to go over the water. Smooth progress. It is instrumental in crossing a great river.' That figured.

Ice floes, solidity, and then when the ice melts, a great river flows. The judgement was interesting. 'Success: the king approaches his temple. It furthers one to cross the great water. Perseverance furthers.' All good signs of going on a long journey to central Ladakh where the king, or rather the queen, lives. 'It is advantageous to cross the great river.' That was good enough for me.

'Dispersion, Dissolution, Overcoming Dissension, Scattering, Reuniting, Evaporation, Catharsis. Persistence in a righteous course brings reward. Wind blowing across the face of the waters. Flowing water. A man at the mouth of a cave, looking around with a stick in his hands.' Not bad for a first shot.

Be prepared

Since New Year I had made a new friend, Sonam Stopgyas, whose family lived next door to Tashi Namgyal. Sonam had not been down the frozen river before but his uncle Dorje Tsering had made the journey many times. They would be carrying butter. Phuntsok Dawa had arranged for me to travel with them. Luckily Sonam spoke good English and was a bit of a lad.

'Ready? Six days ... six nights ... not far down the river ... sometimes the ice cracks. The astrologer said it would be all right if we go tomorrow. Your boots? Smooth almost underneath.

Need some grip. Just enough. Too much and you don't slide. Boots must be flexible. Don't want frostbite? What are these? Gaiters? Very good for deep snow. There's a bag of *tsampa* and here that's another one, half roasted for soup, *tukpa*, and this is a leg of yak, well, part of a leg, dried – frozen. Put it on top. Never know when we need it. Got a pan, a mug, a spoon? OK, you'll be all right. How heavy is your pack? Twenty kilos? That's light! We carry butter as well. Got a stick? You'll need a stick. A good stout, reliable stick. You'll need to test the ice, for balance, tap-tapping, all the way to Leh. Gloves, good. Goggles, got a spare pair? Socks, you must have a spare pair. Four? Four pairs! You'll be all right. We only have straw. Lend us a pair.

'Stay the night here in our house. We go tomorrow. Uncle is coming – Dorje Tsering. That's my father's brother – maybe he's my father as well. We call him uncle, he lives in the same house. They are married to the same woman. Dolma. She's in charge. Then there's my sister – she's nineteen, you'll have to be careful. My father's looking for a husband for her. My elder sister, she's already married. She's on the other side of the valley at Hongshet. There's a very learned man who lives there. Been to Lhasa. Studied in Tibet. Nawang Tharpa. You'll meet him one day.

'Then there's Mr Tashi. He's your next-door neighbour. He's quite a laugh. We go off down to Leh, then I join the SSB – Special Security Branch. Going for training. My father wants me to marry a girl in Ruberak. I went to see her yesterday. She wouldn't look at me ...'

I had spent Christmas in my room reading Knut Hamsun's *Hunger*. It snowed and so I celebrated the festival, which is after all a version of winter solstice, with a tin of defrosted tuna, some pineapple cubes and a Christmas pudding. The Dundee cake made by my mother had long disappeared.

I now packed all my kit: spare socks, mittens, even an ice axe, unsure whether I would need it. We managed somehow to get ready, then lined up outside the house for a photograph, leaning on our sticks. Special prayers were being said upstairs for our safety. Incense floated down. We had a small sip of *chang* and offered drops to the spirits in the four directions. There was a great feeling of occasion and ceremony. Making preparations for a long journey was nothing new. Sonam's grandfather had walked to Lhasa and back twice, a journey of at least three months each way. On his last visit to Lhasa, Sonam's grandfather bought the Kangyur to bring back on yaks, but he fled without it when the Chinese suddenly invaded.[40]

As it was Sonam's first trip down the *chadar* his father brought out red, green and blue tassels, and spiritually equipped us for the journey. I also had the Union Jack sticking out of my rucksack, which they thought was very amusing. Strange how allegiance to one's country can overtake your mind at certain moments. The foolishness of youth – or was it just bravado?

Unbeknownst to me they made offerings to the local god who lived in a shrine at the side of the main temple and whose name was Junu Tunglak. But the god further down the valley – and real god of the *chadar* – was Sharshok. Most people never saw these gods. It was not strictly Buddhist but Bon, the old pre-Buddhist belief system still prevalent in Zangskar. They believed in spirits of house, mountain, river, irrigation channels and soil. We hoped that the local gods would look favourably on our journey. We would be gone about three weeks. Life was short. Sharshok would have to look after us.

Sonam was one of the lads, a blade, no less, and one of the most eligible young men in Padum, but he had caused a little local trouble. He refused to marry the woman his father had chosen for him; no doubt they would come to some arrangement. The times they were a-changing. Three years ago, three young lamas ran away from the monastery and joined the Ladakh Scouts. Like them, Sonam was defying convention, but maybe it was always thus.

As to the butter? How many high pastures have you seen? Strength and beauty. Dancing in the mountains. Under the stars quite a lot can happen. Making butter is a ritual. The milk is heated, buttermilk or yogurt is added and the mixture poured into an open tub. Then it is churned with a vertical wooden paddle and a leather strop that girls pull backwards and forwards until butter settles out. It's hard work. And as the young women work they sing beautiful counting songs. They make cheese from the buttermilk. Dried, hard, off-white, it keeps forever.

Much of the butter ends up as smoke in the monasteries. Butter lamps – an offering to Buddha, a symbolic gesture giving back to the mountains some of its own light. Butter protects the skin and women like it on their faces. Rouge, no less. Women make butter, men trade it.

Some men had five kilos of butter, others ten, fifteen, even twenty kilos. They were from the higher villages, with more yaks and better grazing. They discussed how much they would get for their butter. Around 40 to 45 rupees per kilo seemed to be the going rate.

Sonam's sister Dolma I had seen many times. She was making soup for me. She always seemed to meet me in odd places, ask me where I was going and where I had come from. She only had one word of English, and that was 'Yers'.

River crossing

Day one. It was mid-afternoon when we left Padum, but we only had to go to Karsha, about six miles. We would wait there for others to join us. No one seemed in a hurry. When the time was right we would go. Everything had to be in order. Safety in numbers.

News was eagerly awaited from those who had come through from Leh itself. No one wanted to be the first and get stuck, or, worse still, be cut off and stranded. Each year was slightly different. No news yet, but in Karsha we might hear more. Men who knew the river had their own language. They understood the ice. The language of caution.

We walked down out of the village and across snow-laden fields. A few people pressed letters onto us to take to Leh. These letters would have a strange journey. Tashi Namgyal had asked me to bring back some Lipton *char* with a red and yellow label, to which I willingly agreed. They had been so generous, it was the very least I could do. Red Tibetan tea now came from Palampur and was pressed into cones like small weights. The older men remembered hard black Tibetan tea rather like the *pu erh* traded in Central Asia; it was pressed into blocks about eight inches square that could then be broken up into smaller sections – oblong, about the same size and shape as dominoes, and used as currency as they lasted forever in the dry climate.

The first hamlet we came to was Kisserak, a huddle of about eight houses where we waited for another man to join us. Inside the house a lama was quietly painting a *tangka*, a Tibetan Buddhist scroll painting. Elements of gold. Ground-down rocks for colours. Painting gods. Belief poised on the end of a paint-brush. He could so easily have been Andrei Rublev ... the famous

Russian icon painter immortalised by the film maker Andrei Tarkovsky.

The *tangka* was of Milarepa, the wild man of Tibetan Buddhism, with his hand cupped to his ear listening to the silence of the void. Painted on cotton and stretched on a frame, the figures had been sketched out and the lama was painstakingly painting the scenes. It could take three or four months. He could only paint in the sunshine as the water and glue mix would otherwise soon freeze. The rules of proportions had been worked out in advance. Buddhist geometry. As we waited we talked about food, which would soon become a central part of our lives and thinking.

Talking was not easy when we were all strung out in line – the snow either side was two or three feet deep and powdery – so we talked when we stopped. But silence is golden. Silence is Buddhist. It can be weighed and treasured. Sometimes we were afraid to disturb the peace and quiet, the air cold and crystal clear. The journey already has its own inner momentum and purpose.

When we walked there was a slight chafing of packs, the sound of sticks, muffled in the snow, leather on ice as boots tramped, low breathing, and then Tashi's kettle, which was tied to the top of his pack, rattling like a sheep bell. You could hear Tashi a mile off. It was a cheerful note, just like himself. Every man had his rhythm. We learnt each other's pace and unconsciously meas- ured ourselves against each other so we fitted in. The group had its own routine, which took account of the snow and ice.

From Kisserak we made for Pipiting, the largest *chorten* in Zangskar, white and about forty feet high. It stood on top of a big mound overlooking the river and there was a small temple inside. We passed by, heading for Upti.

We were still on the central plain with the mountains all around, snow-laden, majestic, dormant. On the right was Kumig, where Thubsten's daughter now lived. What a wedding that was. 'Why, they got through a hundred gallons of *chang* easily and the *arak* as well,' said Thubsten, drawing on a cigarette wistfully. He was the only Buddhist in Padum I met who smoked. He wanted a pair of rubber boots in Leh.

Upti was the last village in the triangle. There was a crumbling Dogra mud-brick fort, a rocky plain and old river deltas. Irrigation channels came all the way from Haftal Nallah, and close to harvest there were often disputes about water. It was a cold wind that came from that *nallah*, cold and biting. A mile or two downstream the two rivers joined. The further we went, the more peaks we could see over our shoulders, razor-sharp peaks like an enormous cross-cut saw, row upon row of jagged, fluted giants waiting to be climbed.

From Upti it was a laborious slog, and an unpleasant surprise lay in store. The river was far from frozen, the water running clear and swift like a deer, with sheets of ice on either side. The river was over fifty yards across and two or three feet deep, and small ice floes were coming down fresh from the valley of the Durung Drung glacier. Very fast and very cold.

Tashi, always the optimist, whistled as he took off first his boots, then his trousers and hitched up his homespun cloak. Bare feet on the snow seemed to matter little, and without more ado he plunged into the water, which came halfway up his thighs, took hold of his stick and marched off into the freezing water still whistling.

Wading through the ice-cold water you could feel each sharp rock jutting into the soles of your feet, prompting a numbed rush towards the other side, all the time trying to keep upright with your stick, facing half upstream so as not to be knocked over, climbing back onto the ice sheet and only just getting out in time. Then the wind – *merde*. It cut right through you.

Speed was essential, and before long I found that my feet were numb. Not a good sign. Tashi and the others thought nothing of this crossing. They clambered out onto the ice and ran around a bit to get warm. We danced around half in pain, half in jest, to get some feeling back into the feet.

During the winter I crossed that river thirty times and got used to it. Cold, I discovered, was in the mind, though I must admit I always carried a towel and a pair of dry socks in the top of my rucksack. Mittens were essential, and these were tethered to a small harness that went over my shoulders and chest. It meant that I could take them off, leave them dangling while I attended to something else and I didn't lose them.

I sat down on my rucksack and rubbed some warmth back into my feet. Every minute counted, but the Zangskaris just laughed. They simply kept on walking barefoot and, when dry, put their trousers back on again. With my socks back on there was some relief. Four pairs of socks and then the Norwegian ski shoes. Even getting my snow gaiters back on was difficult, as ice had formed on the zips and they stiffened up. Keep moving. Keep moving.

Karsha

From the river bank to Karsha took half an hour, steadily climbing uphill through the scattered village of Yalung, then following the line of *chortens* and *mani* walls, leaving them on your right – you always went round *chortens* clockwise. Those who still practised Bon always went round the other way, anticlockwise. Counter-intuitive.

In Karsha there were stories of wolves and snow leopards. Wolves had taken a donkey a week before, but a man tailed the wolf, found a nest of cubs, killed them and received a reward. In the monastery there was a stuffed bear hanging up. They said bears came over from Kishtwar when they got hungry. There was a story of a man having a fight with one with his bare hands at Hagsho, and another story at Phe of a bear taking a goat on a chain, and simply walking off with it on its back still alive and kicking.

Two years earlier a snow leopard had come down into Karsha, close to the nunnery and the old temple belonging to Sonam Wangchuk's family. A lama living there kept six sheep in a stable below a *chorten* with very old paintings inside. One night he heard a noise and went to investigate, and found a snow leopard had got into the stable, killed the sheep and was drinking their blood. The lama closed the door and went to find someone with a rifle. They shot the snow leopard and sold the skin for 1,000 rupees down in Kashmir. Snow leopards and wolves were always preying upon people's minds.[41]

When we arrived at Karsha, Sonam Stopgyas and Dorje Tsering went into one of the first houses on the left. I followed, while Tashi and Thubsten went elsewhere. It was here we spent the first night of our journey. The owner was away serving in the Ladakh Scouts and had left behind his two wives, who were first cousins and seemed to get on very well – one looked after the house, the other the fields. A good arrangement. Sometimes their sisters shared the work. Their husband was away earning good money, the women came from the same village, the eldest was in her forties and had no children, so the arrangement made sense. The opposite of polyandry – and why not? With so many men being monks, many women needed a home. Either that, becoming a nun or marrying outside the valley. Zangskari women often used their rights and personality to maintain law and order. It was often the women who held the keys to various padlocks that led to the storerooms and trunks. Home economy.

Karsha was a large village and the monastery had over a hundred monks. Some were young boys, others were out in villages, on pilgrimage or away trading. We waited there for one more night, our numbers having risen from five to twenty, with a few more possibly to pick up. The men got on very well and formed small family or village groups for cooking. We would depart very early the next morning. We needed good luck, but no one travelled alone. The bonds of friendship, kinship and village were strong down the frozen river.

Tashi smells of horse

Day two. When Tashi and his mates had quite finished drinking *chang*, we set off from Karsha, heading for the village of Rinam and then Bishu, a journey of twelve miles. It felt very cold and the wind from Haftal Nallah was strong. We said nothing for the first hour or so, our teeth chattering. Tashi smelled of horse – you could smell it downwind very clearly – so we had no idea what he had really been up to. Maybe he had slept in someone's stable; it would certainly have been warmer there. But there was no way you could take a horse on the *chadar*.

Urgency was written into the men's faces. We were committed to the journey. There were now twenty-five in our party, which was good, about the right number, and even a few monks were coming with us from Dzongkhul monastery. They carried butter, which would buy their monastery what they wanted, and of course they got their share. Hardened meditators by the look of it.

We turned a corner and left the central valley behind as we were slowly but surely drawn deeper and deeper into the Zangskar range. The peaks were now different, even more jagged. It was a long haul, and when we arrived in Bishu it was freezing hard. As the valley narrowed, the hours of sunlight decreased. Each extra hour without sun meant the snow froze even harder into ice and less melted each day. The temperature plummeted. We stood around, waiting for someone to take us in or at least give us access to an outhouse. About half a mile away was the nunnery.

I ask Tashi how long a cloak lasted. Two years, normally – but *his* cloak lasted four or even five years. He was a connoisseur of old cloaks. I could see why. Patches everywhere. Women could spin six feet a minute if they were going well and the wool was neatly prepared with many hours of patient carding. But it took most of the winter to spin up enough wool to weave a cloak. Each cloak was a work of art. Tashi always lent a hand, as he knitted as well – a man of many parts, clown being one of them. He was a real entertainer, lifting our spirits. A good weaver could weave enough cloth for a cloak in a week and in return would get a big sack of barley. Not a bad arrangement. Some could weave enough cloth in a day.

In Bishu we found a billet in an outhouse, crowded in and lit a fire. The smoke was appalling. There was no stove. In the roof of the outhouse there was a wooden butter churner and in the latrine a wooden plough, important tools of the trade. Dorje Tsering made tea and *tukpa*, the Ladakhi soup. We felt really hungry for the first time. The cold was beginning to bite. *Tsampa* was poured into cups or bowls and prodded with a forefinger. Slowly it mixed with the salt tea. This was an exact art. Too little *tsampa* – it stayed mushy; too much – it stayed dry and crumbly.

First one finger prodded the small cone of *tsampa*, then two fingers, then all four. Before long the bowl was spun around, held in the crook of the hand and balanced in the palm of the other hand – a dextrous movement, but once mastered, quick and easy. With a little sugar this was called *kolag*, a dough ball. It tasted excellent. You couldn't get enough of it; the roasted barley flour had a nutty edge to it and the black flecks were dried peas ground down. We were saving our bread and rock buns for emergencies or when we didn't have a fire. This was a basic meal, quick, warm and nutritious. What more did you need? On this venture, every calorie counted, particularly when you carried food for the return journey, as well as butter. This was indeed a remarkable trade route.

Sleeping on your knees

The journey had already taken on a spiritual dimension. The moment we left I felt a very strong bond between these men. Our lives depended on each other, something that I had not experienced in Zangskar before. For the first time I was roughly on an equal footing to them – I was carrying my own load and I was part of their system, part of their village, family and tribe. The jokes between us were our own. The river ice, the long nights ahead to be spent in caves dancing round the fire, collecting chunks of ice for tea and scraps of firewood, cold fingers, agony in the feet; these we all shared.

Rock walls, the reverberation of our songs, the exchange of smiles, the silent agreement to rest. Such things made the journey a landmark, a way of being. Learning to survive where one false move could easily mean death by drowning. You had to have your wits about you at all times, and not just for the ice. Avalanches were common, and in a gorge you were trapped with no escape, like being in a gully. Eyes watched us silently as we made our progress, a stealthy procession. Then we found a place for the night.

Sleeping on your knees could be awkward if you were not used to it. I tried and failed, but the Ladakhis never got out of the habit of sleeping like this.

They would sleep in a long line and the last one in put the cloaks over everyone so they got the benefit of several layers, while keeping their trousers and undergarments on. Communal sleeping brought them closer together. A way of life. Safety in numbers. A close-knit clan.

Freezing mist

Day three. Next morning the river was so cold that a thick, freezing mist enclosed us for about two hours till the sun cut through, a mist that made our hair sparkle. Even the Zangskaris pulled their balaclavas down. You could not really see the river, and I lost all sense of direction within the mist, barely seeing the man in front. You heard ice floes scraping under the ice as they made their way downstream – eerie, otherworldly. The coldest morning of the whole trip was -30°C at least. Suddenly things became very urgent and we were aware of the need to get going.

Dark we rise before dawn –
Up and away in a matter of minutes
No time even for tea. Stars
Fingers numb – mind clear.
We grasp sticks firmly –
Head off into the freezing fog
Listen out for the river
Even Tashi is quiet – very quiet,
Shoves straw back into his boots
Pulls down his balaclava – fingers rebel.

As the Zansgkaris dressed each morning drawstrings on their homespun trousers and the tops of their boots had to be pulled tight. Blowing on your fingers helped a little, but your toes got cold. If you went too fast you sweated and if you stopped too long the sweat froze; the wind knifed us, but mornings were usually still. My breath froze on my beard and balaclava. Icicles formed, hoar frost was rampant, rime on rime, slender grasses became tapered in ice, any clothing that was slightly damp went as stiff as a board, socks became rock hard, like salt cod, and teeth chattered. You became frightened to take a deep breath in case your lungs froze. Something told me it was closer to -40°C. The hour before dawn. We each retreated into our own world.

Mist, the freezing fog, was coming off the river. Dense and silvery. We struggled through, breathing in with little gasps. There was frost in the air, which condensed on our clothing and hair, and we all soon had a metallic glaze, a pale pallor. Ears and nose one rubbed. We followed the river bank up and down watercourses. Hands were so cold and numb and clumsy that holding the stick for balance and tapping the ice was not easy. We lived half an hour at a time. The pace was fast, very fast – it had to be – and as we walked small needles of ice condensed all over us like white fur. Our feet and hands moved mechanically, and for all we knew we would be inside this silver shroud for hours on end. We stopped for a minute or so, then on again. Leaning against sticks, we rested on a small, rocky outcrop, the snowy ledge of a *mani* wall.

Underfoot the snow creaked, brittle ice moved and cracked. On a skyline way above us we momentarily glimpsed a thin finger of light, but then it was gone, fog swirling like steam, opaque, blurred. We were enveloped in its clutches as if a wild animal surrounded us. Eerie, almost frightening, it seemed that if one of us dropped behind we would never see them again. Ten feet, and you were gone. Each one of us a ghostly shape. Ahead of us – a shuffle, a blur. Sticks tapping. No one sang. No one talked. Silent travellers in our own parallel universe. To one side we heard the river, we sensed it, we felt its invisible presence. Moving and yet still. Scraping of ice on ice. Under wraps, underwater rasping, delicate, meandering. Obediently we followed in its wake.

One by one we slithered down the bank and made connection with the ice, one foot at a time. Communion, gingerly at first, then with more confidence. The wonder of it was that it held. To gain confidence we tapped our sticks against its hide. But still there was deep snow upon its face. We followed in the wake of others, a silent slipstream of frozen footsteps.

We all shared the cold, we shared the dawn and the first footing onto the river. Once we set sail there was no turning back. We were committed to the ice, to the canyon, to the gorge and whatever the Zangskar river had to throw at us. We lived on ice as if the Arctic were tucked into our back pockets. The sense of danger was palpable, but no one said a word. This was the *chadar*.

Savouring ice

If there was a band of ice six feet wide, a strip, a corridor, a passage between bank and river, you were all right. If it was two feet wide, the going became decidedly more dangerous. Your life depended on the thickness of the ice underneath your feet, which you could only guess at.

One foot was OK. If it was only six inches you had to be careful. In places it was two feet, even three feet thick. Then you were fine. The ice was often smooth as glass and wrinkled. There were also air pockets, which made wonderful oval patterns, bubbles trapped, as if there were a diver down below – some bubbles large, some small. Ice was always changing. We moved cautiously at first, till we got the measure of it. Occasionally in the mist we heard voices ahead and a pack on someone's back would suddenly loom up as we got closer to them. We could only see about three yards ahead.

As the morning progressed, the mist began to lift like a veil, pale and ghostly. Lift, and then fall again. The only noise, our muffled, creaking tread and the ice floes rasping underneath. We moved in curves, just as the river did, sinuous and winding.

Our eyes were forever on the ice, the world reduced to a few paces either side. And if there was any doubt we started tapping, using our ears as much as our eyes. Sometimes holding the stick as if it were a divining rod or out horizontal just for balance, like Blondin. The stick gave you confidence, and was useful getting on and off the ice.

We learnt to listen to the ice and watched how it moved. At night it sometimes detonated like artillery rounds, echoing up and down the canyon. At other times if there was an ominous creak, we would withdraw slowly, one step at a time, and make for the sides in a diagonal line. The narrower the gorge, the better the ice, except where it had mounded up and broken like pack ice, riding up over itself time and time again. Then there was the occasional noise of ice chafing against the rocky sides of the canyon. Ice sheets were vast.

Once in the mist we lost contact with the outside world – we were flying blind and couldn't see it. The mist embraced us. The only thing that mattered was the fact that we had to keep moving. We became part of it, our moods changing as the ice changed. Instinctively we learnt to read the ice, to know when to go fast and safely, when to be cautious, how far apart to walk, whom to follow, whose steps were the right distance apart.

Sometimes the faults in the ice would catch us unawares and we would retreat to the bank or rock wall. Sometimes alternative paths were available. Sometimes it involved climbing, quite serious climbing, and traversing along thin ledges.

You always had the man in front of you in mind, as invariably we travelled in single file. If you were too close you might both go under; if you were too far apart and the ice gave way, there might be no one to help you. Their packs were made from bent willow held together with ropes, which could be used in an emergency. Yak-hair and goat-hair ropes, homemade but pretty strong. Hair of the yak. If you went under it would be pretty quick. The flow of the river would see to that. And with a pack on your back that drags you down, you would sink like a stone or be carried under the ice before you could get out. Even if you could swim a little you would be too cold to climb out. Your fingers, hands and arms would seize up. It wasn't something we talked about, but it was always there in the back of our minds. In some places the river would be ten or twelve feet deep. The only consolation was that where the river was deepest, the river would flow slowest and the ice would be at its thickest, although it did not always work out like that. The frozen river had many tricks up its sleeve.

Then there were old avalanche cones from snowfields high above. And after a heavy fall of powder snow the gorge could become a death trap, the gullies channelling avalanches down onto the frozen river, the force and weight of the snow breaking the ice. Several times we had to climb over large mounds of avalanche debris and thanked our lucky stars that the avalanche had not come down while we were travelling.

Beyond Pidmu

In the thick mist we passed Zangla without realising it, as the village lies quite a way above the river. It was in Zangla that the other King of Zangskar lived. He was well known and well respected, having given most of his land to his villagers after land reform at independence.

The relief at leaving the freezing mist was palpable. The sun was now warm on our backs and it was a pleasure to be moving. We stopped for two hours in the shelter of a wall, a midday break, a fire in the open and a meal. Sheer luxury. Some villagers gave us a little of their precious firewood, for which we were grateful.

Behind Pidmu the cliffs rose suddenly and there was a steep ravine. A dangerous spot. Two years later twenty people were lost in an avalanche, and several houses swept away. In Lahoul that same winter – March 1979 – three villages were completely wiped out and around 250 people killed.

Avalanches are always dangerous, particularly in narrow confines. The powder snow builds up on a bed of old snow, smooth and fractured, crystals change and become brittle, slippage occurs. The slightest trigger, then the whole slope shears and comes down, gathering speed, sweeping all before it. It can be a horizontal crack, a stray rock or boulder falling, a rifle shot, or in the Alps even a lone skier or mountaineer. In our case it could be a herd of ibex dislodging stones.

Occasionally we saw ibex high above, and the Zangskaris yelled 'skin': Zangskari for ibex and pronounced 'skeen'. The ibex are very sure-footed, have long, curving horns and featured on the cap badge of the Ladakh Scouts worn by many Zangskaris. They identify with ibex. The animals are still hunted and appear on ancient rock carvings. Hunting ibex is part of their mid-winter festival. Symbolic links with fertility, hunting and mating. Survival and continuity. What ibex find to live off high up in winter is a bit of a mystery, but they are preyed upon by snow leopards and wolves – 'nature red in tooth and claw.' Even in Padum, herds of ibex are sometimes spotted on the mountainside opposite, and if they get caught by an avalanche they are dug out later on, ready frozen.

After the very last hamlet of Hanamur, the gorge narrowed down considerably and we left Zangskar behind. We were on our own and it felt good. From now on we lived entirely on the ice. We had entered another world, and were constantly aware that survival depended upon good luck and intuition.

Sometimes we sent a man out in front, testing with his stick, tap-tapping. If the echo wavered or there were crackly distortions, it meant that the ice was thin or there were flaws and fractures. The sounds gave the texture away. Sometimes there were hidden fault lines. Uneasy, uncertain, we listened for further cracks on the other side, and always at the back of our minds was the thought that the whole river could collapse. If the echo was solid and sharp, we were OK. If it was dissipated, then we became very careful. Sometimes they sent me out in front first as I had the lightest pack, and I would slide gently forward, wondering anxiously if the ice would give way. Then you really are on your own.

Sometimes the ice was clear; then you could see the bottom of the river and small, wavering currents in the flowing water, stones clearly visible maybe twelve feet below. Sometimes we moved singly, sometimes en masse. There was always an optimum distance between people, though this varied from place to place. Instinct played a very large part, as it does in mountaineering. We were not roped up. Yet there was an invisible bond.

Occasionally the ice gave out and cold water swirled around our feet, dangerously near. Our packs were heavy, and if you fell there would be no time to loosen them. The swift water would carry you under instantly. It would be quick.

Sometimes the snow on top of the ice melted under our continual tread and our feet started to freeze. It was dangerous, slippery. It all depended on who had made the steps, whether they were long or short strides, and which worked best – alternate steps or every third step leap-frogging or just struggling along, the stick on standby in the hand, balancing, twisting, turning, sliding, testing tap, tap, tap – tap, tap, tap, like an ancient woodpecker. Down one side, then retreat. Wet boots, wet socks – a nightmare. Tap, tap, tap, then down the other side of the river, always looking for a way through and trying not to climb the rocks or cliffs, but sometimes having to shuffle and teeter along ledges seventy or a hundred feet above the river. This we called progress, although at times we only gained ten feet an hour.

The river lived within us.

The gorge

As the gorge narrowed, so did the hours of sunlight. Time became elastic. You lost the normal mechanisms for judging its passage. Your parameters had altered. Your internal clock had no means of gauging the time except at midday, when, if you were lucky, a place could be found to rest in the sun, on one side or the other. In a dangerous spot, even two minutes can seem like a lifetime.

With the gorge twisting and turning, you also lost all sense of north and south. At times the river would almost take a right-angled bend. It all depended on geology and faults. We had entered another world. Almost subterranean. A world without prayer flags, a world that seemed indifferent to our progress and survival.

But our minds were on the river and the ice, unless we were climbing. We learnt to read the river's idiosyncrasies – its history, its character both above and below. In some places it was always changing, always shifting. Footprints of those that had gone before – maybe only a week earlier – ended up in a pool or disappeared completely without trace. This was disconcerting, to say the least. Ghostly. You had to be careful whose prints you followed and where they were going. I did not know how many Zangskaris could swim, but in those temperatures it would make little difference. Trying to swim in a long, sodden woollen cloak would be very difficult.

Occasionally there were tracks of snow leopard padding along, fellow travellers who used the river as a corridor, a bridge to get from one side of the mountains to the other. We moved as one body, like a long snake winding round the cliffs and abutments. Slipping over on the ice with smooth-soled leather boots was *de rigueur*. When Tashi fell over it was accompanied by hoots and gales of laughter as we helped him to his feet again, steadying him and retrieving his stick. Life was one long joke and the absurdity of our predicament on the ice well worth the laughter. The Zangskar gorge certainly had the measure of us, but did we have the capacity and stamina to traverse its length both ways?

First cave

On the evening of the third day we slept at Kilima Bao – Kilima Cave. Caves vary. Each cave has a name and history. Most are high up from the river on bends and must have been formed thousands of years ago. Some have a low lip under which you almost have to crawl, others are large. Some have low walls at the entrance to shelter you from the wind and to make cooking easier. But just as at the Zangskaris' homes, smoke was always a problem, and many of the ceilings were caked in soot and tar. Caves were for shelter, and that was just what we needed. Tashi spotted yet another herd of ibex on the other side and pointed enthusiastically. He would have made a good hunter.

Occasionally we looked at the mountains. The rock varied in colour from grey to orange to an almost mauve purple, red, pink, yellow and white with black streaks. The landscape was laid bare but the geology was difficult to read, as it was often tipped on its head. Most of it was sedimentary, limestones and dolomites laid down millions of years ago under a sea known by geologists as the Tethys Sea at the time of Gondwanaland. In Greek mythology, Oceanus consorted with his sister Tethys and gave birth to an ocean of nymphs as well as all the rivers, fountains and lakes. Fair enough, but why no Gandharan Sea? Then there were metamorphic rocks, shales, igneous intrusions, granites, gneiss and micas, as well as pockets of softer deposits and alluvial river pebbles that formed into conglomerates. It would take geologists years to work all this out. Their bread and butter. We admire its beauty and then pass on. Earth's crust. Our lives a mere whisper, a faint passing shadow.

Sometimes the rock rippled, twisted and contorted into fantastic shapes, buckling and tipping this way and that. We came across a vertical section maybe 5,000ft in one hit, the sharp end of plate tectonics where the Indian subcontinent with all its elephants, camels and cobras had collided with Central Asia. This was how it happened. Layers laid down were thrust into the air with the steeper side of the mountains on the northern side, and here the river cut its way through a fault. We were left marvelling at the scale and grandeur of geology stripped bare.

But what was most important to us was getting water and firewood before the light receded. When the sun sank below the mountains we felt the temperature suddenly drop, 1°C per minute for forty minutes. That was swift.

Below the cave there were large boulders and we struggled to carry firewood up. Willow grew in some abundance. The cave was larger than it seemed and we all managed to get inside it. Pots were balanced on three stones carefully placed, with the fire in the middle. We had first to melt snow before boiling it, a tedious business that took time – because of the altitude, water boiled at a lower temperature. If we were lucky there would be a small stream nearby that could be tapped into by breaking the ice. There would nearly always be water running somewhere. Occasionally there were 'warm' springs, but they were a menace if they were near the river, making the ice perilously thin.

We had to make several journeys for ice blocks and wood; green willow does not burn well at the best of times, but it was better than nothing. It was when you stopped that the cold really got to you, seeking out any gap, any part of your body that was not properly protected, like a knife piercing your armour.

When the others caught up and entered the cave they were greeted like long-lost brothers, although they had only been absent for an hour or two. Some were police returning to Leh after leave – they had better clothes, boots, jackets and parkas, as well as sleeping bags and rifles. One was a major, very good and quick. Ladakhis took all hardships cheerfully in their stride.

Here in Kilima Bao it was sheer luxury because we had half an hour of daylight left in which to prepare our food and tea. Each party had its own fire and so the cave became smoky; the ceiling was darkened and I wondered how many people used this cave. Maybe three hundred each year, going in both directions, some twice a year, so probably many tens of thousands over the centuries. Storytelling. Home from home.

Our feet were bare, with our boots left in pairs beside the fire to dry off, steaming gently. The straw in them was extracted and dried, and occasionally some was used as tinder or mixed with the kindling. Some of the men had matches that they kept dry. Others still had leather pouches with steel and flint to make sparks, using dry moss as tinder. It worked well once the moss was glowing red and carefully blown in their hand till it set the rest alight. Ancient technology. Ice age survival. They slept on yak skins.

Half an hour later, when the water was boiling, they made salt tea followed by *tukpa*, Zangskari soup with some meat and small dumplings. Despite being more commonly eaten at the midday break, they produced great lumps of steaming dough – *phak phe* – the size of cannonballs. We were issued with one dough ball each, and that was it. We sank our fingers into the ball, eating as much as we wanted and leaving the rest for another time. Simple but effective. There was also *churpey*, rock-hard dried-buttermilk cheese, but once in soup it had a pleasant aroma and a texture close to chicken. *Churpey* was a luxury, dried on rocks in the summer months in the high pastures. The main problem was keeping ravens and choughs from stealing it as it dried.

Flames from various fires danced and shadows began to run in waves across the wall of the cave. It seemed for a moment that we were hunters from another age, and I began to sense the importance of rock carvings and the *lhato*, the men with bows and arrows, the sense of sanctity and hunting, antiquity and necessity. Then again I thought of the herd of ibex on the other side and the way in which snow leopards would bring down the weaker ones. Not just ibex but *bharal* or blue sheep. Biological fitness. Maybe it applied to Zangskaris as well. High altitude is its own determinant. Niche marketing. Butter trading.

We were now off piste, free range, a law unto ourselves, not trapped but on the crest of a wave, enjoying a strange sense of freedom, letting go of the rest of the world. We were almost flying. The men danced and sang to keep warm, expressing their joy at being alive, and shared stories. Hardships hardly seemed to matter and no one talked about butter. They were all very humorous, and Tashi was good at shadow puppets. Ibex featured quite a bit, and he got cruder as the evening progressed. That was Tashi for you.

A camp fire at such a time of year seemed a remarkable thing. We looked at one another as our fingers were held out to the dying flames of the fire, the embers aglow. Although we said nothing, we understood the importance of our venture, the importance of each other and the magnitude of the mountains. We were part of an event that was far larger than ourselves. Our fingers clasped warm cups of tea and we stole glances into the night, just wondering what the next day would bring.

Slowly, one by one, fed and satisfied, the Zangskaris bedded down on the rocks, kneeling on tough old yak skins that had probably been up and down the river many times. Black and crinkly, tough as old boots. A yak is a useful animal both dead and alive. Yak is strong. Yak is powerful. Yak is beautiful.

Going to bed was a ritual for Zangskaris, as if they were paying homage to the world at large. They quietly said their prayers as they undressed, 108 *Om mani padme hums* usually doing the trick. Each one had an amulet or a charm strung around their neck or sewn into their hats, mantras that had been blessed by a lama and then sewn up in a small leather pouch, or they had some beads wrapped around their wrists. They took religion more seriously than they would admit. They were on a perilous journey, not asking for forgiveness or trying to placate a wrathful god. But quietly, under their cold breath, they extolled the virtues of compassion and the path to purity and enlightenment. 'Oh jewel in the lotus' is only a very rough translation. In fact the mantra works on many levels, purifying mind and speech from the dangers of jealousy, pride, ego, anger, passion, greed, ignorance, aggression, hatred – indeed a whole string of daily woes – and in their place aims to sow the seeds of generosity, ethics, patience and wisdom. Compassion laced with bliss, equanimity and wisdom. Not bad for six syllables.

When two or three Zangskaris quietly said their mantras, dynamic overtones and undertones crept in and a harmonic was set up, almost as if we were in a monastery. The cave echoed as the shadows disappeared and men crawled in under their cloaks. The last one in checked the cloaks were straight and no one had been left out. There were thirty of us now, jammed like sardines under this rock. A single star was just visible between two peaks. The world as far as we knew it had come to rest.

Frozen beauty

Day four. Living in a canyon was an unusual experience. After Kilima Bao we lived on borrowed time in the narrow, twisting corridor of rock. Every bend opened up new possibilities. At one point there was a hundred-foot waterfall frozen solid with cylindrical organ pipes of ice, fluted and beautiful, and a lone juniper tree clung to the side of the gorge on its left-hand side. The ice danced in front of us, then reared up once more, slabs three feet thick riding this way and that, twisted and frozen again. Chaos and harmony. Solidity in slow motion, like the mountains themselves.

More avalanche cones, and then one enormous one that we had to climb over like a cornice. It took time, one after another. Then another rock ledge along which we shuffled, fifty then a hundred feet up, after which back down to ice. A roller coaster. Ridge by ridge the mountains unfolded. Even when we stopped for five minutes we were still moving, although we leant on sticks. Our minds kept going. Then off again, body and mind synchronised.

The rock became a friend – we clung on, we clambered, we rested our packs against it, we slept under it, we marvelled at its changes in colour. Under boulders we found twigs and small branches trapped like driftwood from summer's meltwater. We resorted to feeling under the rocks to extricate these precious, weathered gems that were gathered and piled together to make a fire. Within half an hour we had a good supply.

The real rest was at midday when the sun shone and briefly touched our backs. To stop in the shade would be almost unthinkable but at times it had to happen. And when the fire was lit and lunch was ready, the warm steaming dough balls looked inviting because of their size, although they rested heavily on the stomach. Energy for the next few hours.

In some places the ice was completely clear and transparent like plate glass. This was rather alarming, for despite being thick and safe, it seemed as though we were walking on water. The bottom of the river, ten or fifteen feet beneath us, was as clear as the river with a slight pale green tinge, and we could pick out the individual stones.

Sometimes the ice was solid for a mile or more, flat, pale, opaque and fast. We got up quite a speed, like ice hockey players. But it didn't last long – Tashi fell over again in peals of laughter and the clatter of his kettle, which was still tied to the top of his pack. More than once the spout got bent. We helped each other up. Sticks broke but were not discarded, kept for the evening fire, and others were cut on the way.

We made good progress. One or two miles were very fast, then there was a major hold-up and a bottleneck to get round an obstacle, or else the ice ran out. Sometimes this happened where other smaller rivers joined, creating turbulence not just at the junction but downstream as well. The odd invisible whirlpool could make the ice very thin and unstable. Sometimes you stabbed the ice with your stick and it went down into a new layer of soft crystals. This was not good news. There were air pockets, and if the ice was not solid and stable it could react very quickly to changes in river level.

This stretch might have only been about twelve to fifteen miles but it felt much longer. Cut hands were common – ice was rough. In the afternoon there was slush on the edges of the ice where it chafed the rock. Beware the slush; it froze hard and cut the boots. You trod very gingerly.

Above our heads on the sides we saw the summer water level,

a reminder of how transitory our path really was. The only distance that mattered was how far away the next cave was, the only time that mattered was how long it took to reach the next stopping point, to get cold, to make tea. Time was elastic but interrelated, recycled. The rocks kept their Buddhist, geological time, but the river was of the moment, *au point*. Being time itself. Being ice, frozen yet moving.

Time to get up. Time to be going. Half an inch on the map might take six hours but maps were only rough guides. Landscape could not be reduced to a few lines. How could you map the ice? The ice could not be easily charted because it was always changing. We knew its contours. The real map was within the Zangskari mind and never written down. It lived in their subconscious. It lived in our thoughts. Mountains lived within their minds.

What fascinated me was that the frozen river was beyond language and yet firmly lodged within memory. I would have dearly loved to know the way in which the older men who had made the journey many times registered the ice and read it and then remembered it. On each journey they were laying down one memory on top of another about a certain stretch of the river. Rocks at least were more or less constant, as were the points at which the side valleys entered the system, but each year the flows and thus the levels fluctuated. Temperature patterns varied, as did the timing and depth and frequency of snowfall.

This was the sort of memory that nomads had, where they returned to certain areas annually and registered minute changes in climate or vegetation cover. This was what happened on the higher pastures in the summer, where they shifted two or three times at least and then back down again. But here in the midst of winter it was not about grazing or water for a herd or flock, but about safety, survival and success. Kinship with ice. As if there were words to describe all the differing colours of the ice, reflected rock walls and patches of sky that changed colour as the sun set and rose. Beauty intertwined with danger and the passage of time.

Maybe *klu*, the water spirits, would have something to say. Maybe there were frozen water spirits trapped in the ice, just as there were in the hanging glaciers and cornices and the spirits of avalanches. Ice had many dimensions. If I could have, I'd have mapped the river from end to end, not just in my own mind but in the minds of the older men who knew the frozen river well and passed that knowledge on. A map of images and poetry, fear and wisdom.

They talked about Bakula Bao, a cave where the last Bakula Rinpoche did not just sleep the odd night but stayed a whole winter meditating. He must have had a good store of firewood, food and a devoted cook.

How extraordinary to spend a few weeks in a cave contemplating the ice. It had a certain Tantric edge to it, as if the nuances of the river were mirrored in the mind, the various mental states and visualisations passed through one by one till the mind dissolved just as the river finally melted.

How then to describe the fluted beauty of a frozen waterfall a hundred feet high or a stretch of ice a mile long, pure and simple? Beauty and danger went hand in hand. Sometimes we only had a few minutes to register such things before we moved on.

The men knew every bend, they knew where the caves were, even when they were hidden up narrow side *nallahs*; they knew where the ledges were; they knew which ones led to safety and which ones were dead ends. They knew where we could find firewood and water. They knew which side of the river to take in emergencies, which side gave out and which side didn't.

Knowledge passed on from one generation to another. Your life depended on it.

Boots and kindling

The Zangskaris wore woollen boots with a smooth leather sole and strong felt uppers tied below the knee, rather like elaborate moccasins – and very effective they were, but not so good for climbing. The soles were flexible, and their smoothness led to quite a few falls on the ice and accompanying laughter. In the evenings in the caves around the fire there would be a circle of boots all steaming away, drying out. The leather came from yak or goat, tougher than sheep, and was usually treated with butter or apricot oil. Like the Zangskaris, strong but flexible. Only if the boots got really wet was there a problem, but they would be dried out beside the evening fire. Great care had to be taken. Too close and they would burn or singe, and they needed to be careful not to let the leather crack. A wet boot was a frozen boot, and a frozen boot was a dangerous boot. Frostbite was a real problem. You also had to leave room to wriggle your toes. Socks, three pairs or four? A daily debate. So long as they were warm and dry. The smell of sweat, wet felt and wood smoke. Zangskar had its own fragrance. Yak dung burning – pure nectar – mountain incense.

Everything was a joke, which endeared the Zangskaris to me no end. Mr Tashi in particular – with his multi-coloured darned cloak, who had been an excellent court jester and mimic for the monks at *Losar* – was a wonderful companion. They joked that his brother the monk might even be sleeping with his wife while he was away, but no one seemed to mind very much. The circle of boots was always fascinating, and men wriggled their toes, trying to get some of the warmth back into their feet. They were very hardy. Foolhardy sometimes. But they knew the river backwards.

The first man to arrive at a cave would light the fire, find water and get the tea ready, no easy task if the river was completely frozen, but with the friction between the ice and the side of the gorge there was sometimes a small band of water an inch or two wide, and a cup or old tin could be used to get the water. We had no stoves. To carry kerosene or petrol complicated matters, so we travelled light. No tents. This was a trading trip not a joyride.

Kindling was vital. Dried twigs and small branches were bleached by the sun and the constant passage of the river when in flood. We became connoisseurs of kindling and knew just where to find it, where to stretch your hand under a boulder. There was always a line about ten feet above the ice, which was the flood mark. Very obvious when you looked for it. Hunter-gatherer stuff. A wild harvest.

Zangskaris never complained of the cold, although their fingers and toes must have been very close to getting frostbite. Some never even wore gloves. They just had hard, calloused hands that were more like claws by the end of the trip. Grasping a stick all day did not help the circulation. Over the centuries they had adapted to the cold and the altitude, and had, I was told, more capillaries in their extremities. It made sense – better circulation. No doubt they had also inherited genetic advantages from living at high altitude. More oxygen in the lungs.

Sleep always came easily when you were that tired. Mornings were the worst. Dark before dawn. Rocks hard in impossible places. I would crawl out of the sleeping bag like a caterpillar leaving its chrysalis. Boots stiff. Hands frozen. Must take care of the leather. Socks had holes from the fire. They looked singed. Others woke up.

Where's my spoon and mug? Tea and *tsampa*. One lived on basics and every day gave thanks for that alone. Plastic or wooden cups much better than metal cup. Lips didn't stick to the rim. Shoes stiff, very stiff. Sleeping with them in your sleeping bag uncomfortable but necessary. Trying to put on my gaiters. No foam-rubber mat. A simple thing, your comfort. Heat loss astronomic if sleeping on ice.

Breakfast: solid frozen bread or rock buns, slightly sweetened with sugar. One was left on a rock for me by Dorje Tsering. Gladly I took it. One bite, then I put it down. I savoured the texture of the bread. Precious, as were wheat and barley. The only food I would have for the next three hours. No time to cook.

The Zangskaris again pulled down their balaclavas. It was such a signal of defeat that they hardly ever did it. Only if the blizzard came at them or if it was very cold in the morning. Then they got great white beards that grew from hoar frost beneath their chins. Every man became his own continent. The river became ours for a few days and nights, we were that close to it.

Culinary matters

That day was very good going. Then there was an obstacle. Slowly we edged round a big rock. There was slush up to our ankles, not a good sign. We manoeuvred ourselves gingerly, one at a time, agony if laces came undone. Gaiters froze up, and then I spotted someone starting to collect wood. That meant the midday stop was within an hour. Hopes rose. One twig or root at a time. Soon there would be a bundle.

Then by late afternoon we saw a bridge made of birch twigs stretched over the ice high above us, slung between two boulders. Elegant in its own way, a catenary curve; even spider's webs formed these curves, natural, pleasing on the eye. Tibetan necklaces also formed catenary curves. But we were still a long way from the wonders of Leh bazaar. We were close to Nerag, the only crossing point for thirty miles in either direction, on a path that was used in summer to get from Zangla to Lamayuru. Nerag – this was where Tashi Namgyal's father Iche Namgyal came from, summoned by telepathy from Nerag by the previous Khushok Bakula.

Here we stayed not in a cave but in a small sheep house. The smoke was truly awful, we choked and retched as it filled our lungs. It was so cramped and smoky that I decided to sleep outside. Fresh air was vital, however cold. We had already slept in two caves. I preferred caves. Better ventilation. Three stars, but no running water.

Invariably they made *tukpa*, a kind of soup with water, turmeric, salt, small slices of leg of yak, small dumplings or large dough balls and *churpey*. Rice took too long to cook. Cooking on trek was not that different to cooking in their homes, only here you had to be more careful of the wind. No one went hungry.

The more you ate, the less you carried, but the men were mindful that they were carrying supplies for the return journey. I reckoned each man got nearly one kilo of *tsampa* a day, around 3,500 calories, enough for the trek but only just – it depended on the temperature. *Tsampa* is two-thirds roasted barley and one third dried peas ground down. Very nutritious, and I loved it. Easy to digest. Without warm food we would not have made it.

Days merged. It seemed as if we had been on the frozen river forever. There was a kind of luminosity about our thoughts, an inner radiance that came with confidence. Time had passed us by.

We tried to keep track of it by the number of caves we had slept in.

Tashi dances on ice

At night the stars seemed very near as we looked up through the corridor of rock. But we only saw a fraction of the night sky. Instead of the whole sky moving and shifting, the stars were held in a narrow band that was bordered by the peaks and ridges, so relative to these they did move quite fast. They were bright. Even in our sleep we were still moving on the ice, confronting walls, treading slowly, balancing on boulders. Men turned a little and jostled in their sleep, an arm flung out here, an elbow there. They were also still travelling on the ice. I knew it.

Our minds were focused on our journey. And after the meal, before they settled down, the Zangskaris danced and sang to keep warm, telling stories before turning in, an ancient rite straight from the heart of Central Asia. This journey had a shamanic feel to it, as if we were descending into the bowels of the earth, into the heart of the mountains for seven days and seven nights. Eventually we would be regurgitated out into the mouth of the Indus. Mountains breathed life into our tired limbs. Mountains kept us on the move. Noting each change of rock, each shift of colour, each strata with its own mantra, layers twisted and turned, almost vertical, the ripples of rock pushed skywards. Himalaya in motion, embedded, exultant, exhilarating.

Day five. Fingers were like dull pegs. In the half-light we groped with bare fingers, as if our life depended on it, which it did, more or less. If you lost the feeling in your fingers and toes you'd had it. This was primitive stuff, but a vital reminder of the fragility of life. 'Hurry, hurry, hurry,' blow the flame, light the wood. Straw helped. Flames caught. Here was a bit of dried yak meat to chew on like biltong. At least the twigs were dry. It was the dry climate that made living and travelling practical, almost piratical, as if stealing a march on an enemy or rival. We were wedded to our strange migration. We lived in the moment, our lives depended on it. But it was damned cold. Cold that penetrated to our very bones. Keep moving, keep moving. Not too fast, not too slow. No time for words. No time to think.

There were always stories of people trapped in caves, neither able to go backwards or forwards because the ice had broken up and the river flexed its fluid muscle. Then there was the cave where the king threatened to eat his cook. They were stranded for ten days and the food ran out. The king kept eyeing his cook up and down as he got hungrier and hungrier. And just as he decided that he would have to kill his cook, the river froze over again that night and thus saved the cook's life and the king's honour. Yet another miraculous, apocryphal tale worthy of Milarepa.

Occasionally if spirits were high and the sun was out we would dance on the frozen river. The Zangskaris danced traditional dances and then they asked me to dance. I had been in the army long enough to have picked up a few bawdy songs, and one particular song and dance routine appealed to the Zangskaris no end. I was asked to do it more than once. It was certainly not suitable for the monasteries, having more in common with their ibex routine at *Losar*. 'Old MacDonald's Farm' (the army version) bears little relation to the children's rhyme of the same name, although the tune, most of the words and certain intonations are the same, as well as the progressive farmyard experience, which is earthy to say the least. 'Old MacDonald's Farm' is very suitable for Zangskaris who have the required bawdy sense of humour.

With a partner you imitate all the farm animals one at a time in certain erotic poses and gestures that left little to a fertile imagination. MacDonald also acquired a few yaks and *dzos* along the way.

It takes two to tango, so I chose Mr Tashi as my partner and we gave the whole group, including the lamas from Zhunchul, a very vivid rendering of the nursery rhyme, which runs through a large number of farm animals and shows their various antics when procreating on the ice. The Zangskaris thought this was hilarious, just as good as anything they had seen at New Year and in the monasteries. They understood every nuance. The choreography was finely tuned and we performed the routine several times. It even helped that we fell over once or twice. Mr Tashi was the ideal companion. Nothing shocked him at all. He soon knew every word off pat.

The more raunchy the song and choreography, the more they laughed. They were earthy spirits, for whom life was just one long Buddhist joke.

Snow leopard tracks

Only when you were moving could you begin to feel normal. We were very small dots compared with the mountains. It was as if we were living in the ice age, treading gently on the pathways of history. Survival and speed. We faced much the same problems as hunters two thousand years ago.

You could only think of the next stop, and it was not worth stopping until there was some sun to warm your hands. It was far too cold to sit in the shade, and the gorge was so narrow, twisting and turning, that the sun only got into it for an hour or two every day, if you were lucky. Sometimes you could feel the heat draining right out of you. But today was a good day, plenty of sun.

A bit further on we saw fresh prints of snow leopard. Coming in from a side *nallah*, using the frozen river for three or four hundred yards, then crossing over to the other side. Snow leopard tracks, without mistake. Large pads. Fresh that morning. Maybe only an hour old. Four toes. Clear, sedate, as if the animal had just walked ahead of us. Maybe it had heard us coming and decided to watch us from above. Still watching. Hunter and hunted. Padding along with purpose.

Snow leopards feed off ibex, markhor, burrel, marmots, even sheep and goats if they have strayed. Very secretive. Masters of camouflage and ambush. We marvelled at the beast. Its numbers in this range were quite good. In Ladakhi they are called *shan* – the grey ghost. The elusive one. Ancient rock carvings of snow leopard can be found alongside carvings of ibex. The prints in the snow were large and occasionally you could see where it had swished its tail. They usually attack from high above or lie in wait on a ledge. They can even tackle a young yak if there are two of them and they manage to get on its back. Often they take old, ill or injured beasts. Even to see the prints was quite something. Snow leopards were out there watching you. We were potential prey.

For days we lived on the ice between walls of rock. Only occasionally did we see sun or blue sky. Sometimes it snowed, sometimes it didn't. When we passed a juniper tree one morning, the Zangskaris broke a few small branches off and burnt some for incense. The smell was wonderful and intoxicating as the smoke went skyward to the gods, hoping to propitiate them for a safe journey and a safe return. It seemed appropriate as an offering. Incense in Zangskar is often pine needles brought from the south.

A feeling of reverence. We had entered the realm of the *klu*, the water spirits.

Several more waterfalls were frozen solid. Great nuggets of ice, hanging silent, noble, not a squeak, an architectural solidity that took our breath away. We rested our packs on a rock to admire the waterfall's fluid beauty. Fleeting in the sense that we were passing by. Entranced by its pale elegance. Fluted ice, its own history, its own provenance.

Five minutes rest, and then we moved on. Hands cold, the heart of the river. A symphony of ice. If I had crampons and a rope I could have been tempted. The ice axe was useful for breaking ice to melt to drink.

Suddenly the river took on a new dimension. Unstable, fragmented. Cracks appeared, ice floes locked in intimate embrace, rocks obliterated, paths appeared and disappeared, footsteps mingled, some frozen, some fresh, ice, snow and slush made their own textures. The sun melted only a token gesture. Breath hovered, cold and icy in the shadows. Hoar frost and rime, winter merchants hovered.

Always there was the tapping of the sticks, a slight show of uncertainty, a faint whiff of hesitation. We fell silent and listened. Ice was weak, water swirled underneath. We could hear it, even see it – ice was honeycombed with air and had no real strength. Danger lurked.

A man went on ahead gingerly. We waited and watched. No ropes here. No safety lines, only nerve and intuition. A brave venture – back and forward till a path was found. Edging back onto the ice we rejoined the silver path. One at a time. And then the pace picked up again as the river improved. Always we read the ice, looking for imperfections, the swirl of the river underneath, wafer thin, air entrapped, slender fragment, always risky, places like these, under rocks, beside overhangs. Then there were slush pools.

Occasionally we had to climb like monkeys up and up and then along narrow ledges, not easy with a pack and soft, smooth shoes. Climbing is a matter of balance, skill and confidence. We managed by edging forward, fifty or even a hundred feet up. One slip and we would end up in the drink. Not funny at all. Not easy with a pack on. Hanging on with cold fingers, not easy either. Felt on ice, leather on ice, ice on ice, the straw in the boots seeping up between the toes. Even blood began to freeze. Skin turned pale. Only when it was black did you really worry. Mountaineers always tended to lose toes. Frostbite crept up on you unawares. Numb. The next cave was called Tip Yongma Bao.

Ice haiku

Ice – pale sheets
Twist this way and that –
Clear air fractures silence

        Brittle – Broken words
        Stifled by cold –
        Tongue tied – River frozen

Pale solidity flows
Between rock walls,
Slender canyon – home of ibex

        Cutting through the heart
        Of a mountain range – flowing

Every minute of the day –
Even in moonlight

        The frozen river lives within us.
        Winter's path – Sleeping in caves
        We dream about ice
        As if we have known the river
        Since birth – Kinship

In our sleep we imagine gliding
Along its sinuous back –
Hypnotic.

        Silence from within –
        A vast unopened book

We read the river – So cold
Fingers can hardly turn the pages

                Curved contours – invisible lines
                Underwater charts –
                Worn smooth like a ship's hull.
Survival depends on reading the ice
Sullen echo, tapping its very heart –
Beware whirlpools

                We admire its beauty –
                Wrestle with its pale strength –
                Glistening waterfall
Always we test the river
As the river tests us,
Deeply aware –
Its shortcomings and ours –
Merged

                Weakness and fracture.
                Small signs written
                Into the frozen world
Tread carefully
Many miles of ice –
Tango in slow motion,

                Trapped between walls of bare rock
                River's curves – Hollow caves
Slithering into the future.
Past – present and correct

                Slowly the river flexes its muscles –
                Draws us into its icy world

Sometimes we move fast –
Like the river beneath our feet –

On a good stretch we race ahead
Pause in the sun – Fire takes
Midday – a few minutes to spare
Again – We dance on the ice
Happy to be alive
Buddhist mantras –
Incense – Chanting
Spiralling upwards
Echo of echoes
Om mani padme hum
Into the land of ibex and snow
leopard –
The scent of Old Tibetan gods
Chen Regzig lives here.
Impermanence and emptiness
Contemplating snow and ice
Winter gives birth to avalanches.
Each year feeding the river
Passed on from hand to hand – the route
Invisible, intuitive,
Each generation making
Its acquaintance
The ice road –
Survival against the odds.
Frozen Wisdom

Solitude, danger	Hidden meanings –
Inner freedom	Rite of passage
Resonance and pitch	Listen again for the echo
Fragile navigation	Solid waterfalls
Shifts of light	Glimpses of caves
We move fast	At night we hunker down.[42]

Tashi's wife

Zangskari carrying frames were ingenious and lightweight, made from bentwood willow, locked together with goat- and yak-hair rope. Most things were carried in a sack or two in between the frame, with yak hide forming the base. The ropes were used over the shoulders for holding the whole frame together and were on a quick-release system like a timber hitch if anyone ever fell in. They had round willow rings for tensioning the ropes.

'Sonam, old man, how far is it to Leh? Only two more days? Phew! I thought it was another two weeks.'

'See the rocks?' he replies. 'Less snow. Means we are nearer Ladakh, nearer the Indus.'

Always they talk about reaching Ladakh as if the central Indus valley were a different country, as if Zangskar were still its own kingdom, which it always was. They had a quiet pride in their valley, with its own dialect and old Tibetan pronunciation. A tribe apart. Scholastic too.

'What about Tashi's wife? Very nice, how many children have you got, Tashi? Your brother's a lama, Tashi? How many children have you got? One, two, three? Better keep an eye on your brother, Tashi. Monks aren't all saints. Buddhism isn't all that holy in the red hats. Now you are on the ice, I bet he isn't studying in the monastery any more ...'

When the going was good, it was very, very good. Like ice hockey, you held your stick out in front at a 45° angle ready to balance yourself in case you fell, weaving it from side to side. The stick was useful in case you fell in – you held it out and others could grab it.

Tashi tried to pass me going fast, and fell over yet again. He laughed, his kettle clanking away like a bell. I helped him up and on we went. He was quite a character. Sometimes he danced on one leg, which was not easy at all with a pack, gliding, almost as if skating. Then he would change feet.

He was a mime artist, sometimes with an aluminium cooking pot on his head. He loved being asked to do certain skits. 'Imitate your wife, Tashi …' 'Ha ha, Tashi is brilliant.' No doubt about it. He imitated his wife, wiggling his hips as if dancing erotically. Then I saw it on his lips. He pursed them, pretending to kiss the air around him. Life was a joke. The harder life was, the bigger the joke. It was as if they were on holiday, yet there was an inner strength that was hard to match, a rich seam that kept them alive throughout the winter. Full of fun, these Zangskaris. Someone even bought a puppy for five kilos of peas, so we called the puppy *Panj kilo*. Travels in a satchel.

Ice floes

You followed the older men, even when they climbed steep slopes. If you caught up with them and they managed a smile, that meant the river was all right. Everything hinged on that smile. The great fear was that we would be trapped if the river broke up and there was no way out back or forward.

In some places the ice was dark green like bottle glass. It depended on the reflected light and colour of the water. Green like the window in my room back in Padum. Green was somehow reassuring. Again Dorje Tsering was ahead of me – we were in rhythm, that was often the secret. Many people instinctively walked in pairs. You walked looking down at the next person's heels, seeing where they put their feet; you were almost in a trance, so good was the rhythm, and yet the river was only two or three feet away. You got a sense of its energy, its majesty.

Then the ice opened up just a few paces in front of me, between Dorje Tsering's feet. I don't think he even noticed. No noise. No warning. The crack swiftly came between my own feet, and I only just had time to transfer my weight to my left foot and stop myself falling in. You quickly slew yourself off balance. An instinctive reaction. A second or two more and I would have gone in. The water was moving very fast and deep.

I watched Dorje Tsering's ice floe for a minute or two as it broke off and continued downstream alongside me. When it came up against an ice sheet, I saw it hover and then disappear as the current took it under the ice lip. Just a scraping noise as it made invisible progress. That is where I would have ended up.

The river like a snake rippled through the mountains, making its path. Alluvial deposits. Stones hung as if in mid-air, teetering. Up and down, we rose and fell. At one point a pot disappeared into the river, rumbling down the slope. I said that it was on its way to Pakistan. They all laughed.

Up and down, there were small figures ahead on the ice, a mile away, the spirit of endeavour. It was always good to spot others ahead and see which side of the river they were on. We exchanged information about the ice, where to be careful, which caves they had slept in. We shook hands and chatted for a few minutes, then passed like ships in the night.

Habitation?

Day six. We saw some dried dung and made a fire with it. That was progress. It meant that we were on a summer grazing route. Or maybe the yak had strayed. Whatever the reason, it meant we were not alone. The side valley led up towards Markha. There had been one other valley on the same side that led to the

Junglam, the middle way, the northern border post of Zangskar. Markha was a big valley with many villages, and quite a few snow leopards and wolves.

Even the cliffs seemed to be opening up a little. We felt that we had left Zangskar far behind and were entering a new domain of winter. No man's land. Snow had all but gone from the peaks, and we contemplated bare rock walls and a thin ribbon of ice on either side. Problems indeed. Our options narrowed down. We trod even more carefully, well aware that the narrow width might not be as strong as it looked, with air pockets underneath or bands of ice needles that could fracture under load. The ice floes were also increasing in number and size. Not a good sign.

My fingers were often very cold, so writing notes was almost impossible — photographs would have to do. Anyway, there was no paper, ink would have frozen, no light, too much to do. And my pencil was broken.

In a smaller cave we slept as best we could, jostled together higgledy-piggledy. For Zangskaris a trip to Leh was the highlight of their year, like going to the cinema. The big town, the capital. In summer it took ten days over several high passes. If you went via Kargil it was eight days plus a day or two in trucks. Ten days again. So the *chadar* was quicker by far, and cheaper. Cost zero.

Often there was no time for meditation and it was far too cold to sit, except around the fire at night, looking into the embers, watching shadows dance on the walls of the caves, a primitive form of reassurance that went back thousands of years. We were reliving the conditions of the ice age. Every man within his own world, yet acutely aware of who was in front of us and behind us and how they were doing, how they were coping. We always had each other in mind and knew whose stick was whose.

Even looking at the frozen river, hour after hour, was a form of walking meditation, but of an unusual kind. In the language of Chan or Zen it would be called *kin hin* – a hundred miles there, a hundred miles back. When we stopped we were 'doing nothing but sitting', and when walking we were 'doing nothing but walking'. Gathering momentum was a wonderful experience, and within that rhythm freedom generated its own energy. Without thinking, we were moving very efficiently. If the ice was good we tapped into the energy of the frozen river and used it to our advantage. Ice meditation. Minds became very sharp indeed.

Days and nights seemed to merge. This was still day six. Maybe we should have cut small notches in our sticks to keep track of time. One got to know the rock, particularly when it changed colour. Grey, reddish, almost orange in places, then purple and back to pale khaki, the strata always rippling, tipping, doubling back on themselves. Himalaya in action, buckling and twisting. Shear planes, rifts, erosion. The whole spectrum. With ice, the texture changed day by day. How fast could one go? Was it getting dangerous?

Then the rest stops. First one man sat down, followed by another. If it was a long stop a cigarette came out for Thubsten. If not, we moved on again after two minutes, just time to catch your breath before getting cold. Sweat froze. Their homespun was brilliant – it was wool, flexible, soft, strong, warm. Sheep were essential to their survival, as well as all the carding, spinning, plying and weaving. A good wife was a good spinner. Usually men did the weaving on small mobile hand looms. A joint enterprise. Homespun trousers kept their legs warm. It was a miracle that the Zangskaris did not break anything when they fell over. Sometimes a stick broke and they had to cut another one if there was a sapling close to hand. Even getting up off your knees with a heavy load was not easy, so we helped each other. The main problem was if a man slipped and then slid towards the open water. But he was up again within seconds and on his way ... tap, tap, tap. Keeping the momentum – both inner and outer – was important. The psychology of travel.

We were nearing the end, yet we were so self-contained and confident that we had become wary of habitation. Maybe we had learnt to think like a snow leopard. Biding our time. Independent and on the hoof. Sniffing the air.

Coppersmiths

Each cave was different. Each had its own atmosphere and dark-ened walls. Some were up side valleys and used in emergencies, but you had to know where they were. They all had names. Your mind on the ice was working out which cave was best for that stage. Timing was everything.

At the end of day six we were at Chiling, the coppersmiths' village.[43] The houses were larger, it was a prosperous place. Once more we crammed into a small stone building and as the fires were lit I was again fighting for fresh air. Villagers were well used to passers-by. Firewood was very scarce.

The village of Chiling had quite a reputation and was famous for its fine copper work, silver and brass. Here they made ornate tea urns and kettles, tea pots, braziers, sieves, *chang* jugs, charcoal burners, cups, bowls, spoons, *mani* wheels and the long trumpets used in monasteries. High-grade copper and brass work. There were silversmiths and jewellers who made bracelets and neck-laces, earrings and ornaments. They also worked with gold.

The craftsmen were apparently brought here from Nepal several hundred years ago. Newaris. And very fine work it was too. They even made Buddhas. They say that Zangskar once provided the raw copper, which would account for the village's location. The smelting skills were passed from father to son.

There were many poplars. Trees seemed to grow better than in Zangskar as there was more shelter. The village of Chiling did not give us firewood. I don't blame them. With three hundred to six hundred people passing every winter, that was a heavy toll on your supplies. You couldn't just give firewood away.

It was not so cold here, and the bare rocks retained more of the heat from the day's sun. Although still about -15°C, it was positively balmy compared with Zangskar. We slept in an outhouse. It seemed a different land, more prosperous, almost with a Tuscan feel.

Day seven

The last day was a very fast run down to the Indus. Twenty miles or more at high speed. The mountains opened out and we were straining at some invisible leash. There was a side *nallah* to Sumdo and a narrow path that led to an ancient temple with paintings. About half a day's walk up the same *nallah* there was a very old wooden statue made out of juniper wood, about a thousand years old. I did not see it then but visited it later. A Maitreya known as the Gopko.

Here, within spitting distance of the Indus, there was hardly any snow, only ice and bare rock. The opening skies were bright blue but the ice thinned out on either side. We speeded up when we realised the end was in sight, and this now became something of a race. The ice was very good and we were in fine fettle. We started to take risks we might not otherwise have taken. Back on the river we were laughing and joking.

'Hurry, rush. Hurry, rush. Off before dawn. Last day only about twenty miles to go, a doddle under the odd bridge, slip, slip, tap, tap. What's that over there? That was a box pulley bridge.' You hauled yourself across. Very clever. We slipped underneath. For several hours we made good progress, and then after the midday break the landscape really changed.

Another ridge? Is that the other side of the Indus in the distance? Five, ten miles to go. God, this is crazy, like the Grand National. They all sped up. Tap, tap, tap. 'Ah, there's Tashi, tap, tap, tap. Can't be far now.'

The stops became fewer and the speed increased. We might even spend a night under cover. We moved very fast indeed, about twice the speed of normal walking. Exhilarating, as if we were skating along, which we were.

How far is it now? Six to ten miles? How many times have you done this, Tashi? Five or ten times? Sometimes twice a year. Now we were really motoring, the mountains started to open up. We had a strong sense of purpose. Everyone had a new energy. And then a shout went up. Someone had spotted a truck far away in the distance, a dark speck moving slowly.

Is that a road I see before me? A real road on the hillside opposite? I almost enjoyed following its curves uphill. But there were no more trucks, very few and far between at this time of year. Fuel was precious. Would we get a truck tonight? What sort of food would they have in Leh? Tibetan *mok mok*, by the sound of it. Steamed dumplings filled with finely chopped vegetables and mutton.

Then we saw the Indus. In fact we sensed the river long before we saw it. A thin, narrow gorge with thin, narrow ice. The lion river, one of the great rivers of the world. It gave its name to India and rose far away in western Tibet near Mount Kailas. It was narrow compared with the mighty Zangskar river but over two thousand miles long, one of the four arms of the mystical swastika. The others were the horse, elephant and garuda bird. Mount Kailas, holy of holies, centre of the Indian and Tibetan world.

But where could we cross it? A mile down? The ice was thin, only a foot wide. One of the lamas from Dzongkhul nearly slipped in, a close shave. You had to keep your wits about you right to the very end. One or two hundred feet wide, the Zangskar river, it looked magnificent, much stronger than the Indus. Maybe at one time they thought Zangskar was the centre of the universe. Pure, unadulterated river. I looked at a whirlpool, the water gyrating. Four miles to go. We saw the tall poplars of Nimu on the other side, swopping solid rock for conglomerate, old river beds filled with pebbles.

We went a mile downstream before crossing. It was like reaching the far shore, very strange at first to be walking across fields again, as if we had sea legs. Dry, dusty fields, then seeing houses and people, the road running through Nimu. Another world. Our ice journey was suddenly over. *Finito*. This was Ladakh.

Nimu

The village of Nimu was on the old caravan route from Kashmir to Leh, about midway between the old fortress of Basgo and Leh itself. Long *mani* walls, larger fields, larger houses set back from the road, a more prosperous air. Civilisation, as far as we were concerned. We had suddenly re-entered the real world, leaving the world of frozen rivers far behind. Where was reality? Ice had ended and tarmac had taken over. A black ribbon danced through the valley and over the mountains towards Leh. This was what we had come for, to visit the central Indus valley, a trade corridor

Gonpo, the well-known meditator from Stagrimo monastery above Padum.

Setting off from Padum down the Chadar with Sonam Stopgyas (far right) and his uncle, Dorje Tsering.

Good going on Chadar.

The ice nearly running out. We soon
started climbing along ledges.

Dorje Tsering.

Problems – Dorje Tsering in the lead.

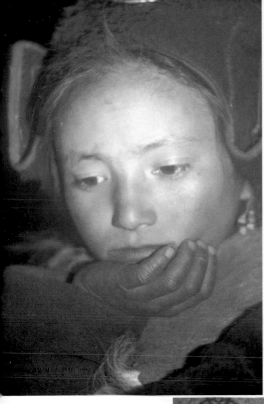

Phuntsok Dawa's
eldest daughter.

Hamid sings while he
plays the jerrycan.

Karsha Gustor.

Nyungney Karsha,
March 1977.

River crossing below Karsha.

Crystal goose – Kushan/
Gandharan Buddhist Reliquary
found in a Stupa at Taxila,
Rawalpindi 1st century AD.

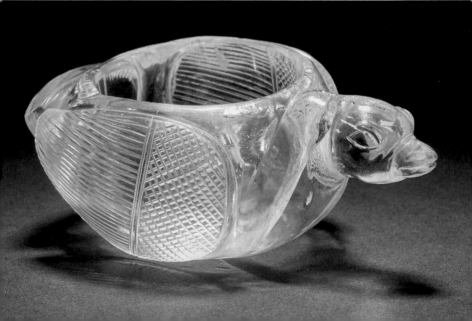

that stretched from one end of Ladakh to the other. We felt very pleased with ourselves for having made it this far, an air of jollity replacing the caution on the river.

Not to be outdone, Tashi found a wheelbarrow and insisted on wheeling each of us up and down the road many times. There was no transport, so we waited another whole day for a truck to arrive.

Everything seemed new, as if we were seeing things for the first time. Could we wait by the bridge? Maybe there was a shop over there. Tarmac – now there's a strange thing. Something coming up the valley. What about an army jeep? They stopped. No room. Tashi did imitations of his wife again. Exhausted but elated, we lay down and rested beside the road. How far was it to Leh? More than twenty miles. What about a truck? There were supposed to be some early paintings in the caves down at Saspol but none of us had the energy to look for them.

We resigned ourselves to not getting a truck that day so we found a remote building. Thirty men in a small space, 10ft by 20ft, about the same size as my room back in Padum. Once again I nearly suffocated from the smoke from the fire. Cramped, I tried to stretch my legs. There was no fuel, so we burnt our sticks to keep warm and for cooking. Farewell, faithful sticks!

Sonam was already chatting up the girl in the shop. I heard someone say, 'Sonam, you're terrible.' But he was just a young lad looking for fun. What about the high pastures? Not just yaks, is it? The girl looked like she could handle him. Although very patient, she did not succumb to his charms. He tried to make her blush, but did not succeed. They knew what Zangskaris were like.

We waited all the next day for a lift to Leh. It was only twenty-five miles. But there was no traffic, no cars, no buses. No nothing. And then in the late afternoon we heard a distant noise, the sound of a diesel engine. Our luck had suddenly changed. We managed to wave the truck down and climb on board in the back. Five rupees each. Not bad.

We all piled in, throwing our bags into the back of the truck, and then we lurched towards the capital. We had made it. The frozen river was now behind us. We were in high spirits. It was like a holiday. We were off to the bright lights, clinging on for dear life. We all ducked passing under electrical cables, then the checkpoint. Round several bends, more prayer flags. Buddhas everywhere, painted on rocks. Drive safely, one false step and you end up back in the river. That would be ironic. That mound up there, that was Leh. Couldn't wait. Burning our sticks was a bit of an error but I was sure we would find more. Essential for the return journey.

'The women in Leh are very beautiful,' Sonam kept telling me, then dug me in the ribs with a wonderful laugh. I believed him. I knew he was right. Mr Tashi smiled. Dorje looked the other way and Thubsten pulled on his cigarette.

Fresh vegetables

About two miles before the town of Leh, Sonam banged on the roof of the truck cab and climbed down. He asked me to follow him. It was nearly dark by now and he had a friend to see, a lady friend, as it turned out. Dorje Tsering came as well. The others carried on into town, and I would see them in a day or two. It was already dark and there were lamps in the windows. The lady of the house greeted us, obviously pleased to see Sonam. I saw a curious look in her eyes. She had long, dark hair. No wonder Sonam liked to come to Leh. She must have been about thirty-five, and I think Sonam used to stay here when he was at school. He told me that he had failed his exams first time round. Now he was studying for other exams.

For an old Zangskari, the delights of Leh must have seemed like paradise. Progress took the form of concrete houses, petrol pumps, buses, lorries, telephone lines, electricity cables, diesel generators and the ever-present army, which brought much wealth to Leh. Boom time in summer for the vegetable sellers who sat out on the pavements and street corners selling radishes, small turnips, carrots, cabbages and all manner of other greens, even small cucumbers.

But here in the middle of winter they also had fresh vegetables in the house. Cabbages and greens. Where on earth did they get these from at this time of year? Flown in from Delhi. My God, they had everything here. We hadn't seen a fresh vegetable for months.

After a race like ours down the ice you took time to catch up with yourself. We savoured small delights. In the house the metal stove was large and solid, 4ft by 2ft wide, cast iron and black, about 2ft high and on its own platform. A wonder to behold after the rough and ready stoves of Zangskar. There were designs on the side, eight Buddhist auspicious symbols in brass: the endless knot, lotus flower, conch shell, parasol, golden fish, *dharma* wheel, auspicious banner and treasure pot. You got used to seeing them around. All Buddhist homes needed these symbols, granting long life and prosperity, with homespun Buddhist wisdom thrown in for good measure.

Here in the house there were floorboards and Tibetan carpets, wooden shelves, large glass windows, even sliding doors. What heaven was this: copper pots and pans, Thermoses, even papers – the *Hindustan Times*, only a day or two old. The good lady's husband had been to Delhi by aeroplane and had just returned.

I wasn't sure how, I would have to check. There was an airfield here in Leh that was open in winter if there was good weather and not too much ice on the wings. The airfield was crucial for the military and was fought over with the Pakistani army, the fighting taking place near Spituk monastery, which overlooked the airfield. There was even a story that when the first plane landed an old man took hay out to the aircraft to feed it, thinking it was a 'wind horse' that had been on a long journey.

The low table was all set for the evening meal of rice and vegetables cooked with a little turmeric and cumin seeds. Heaven on earth. Salt tea, yes, but no butter. The good butter had run out, so Sonam gave a kilo to our hostess. Dorje Tsering watched out of the corner of his eye. He knew what it was all about but kept quiet. The lady friend was fifteen years older than Sonam, but they obviously knew each other very well and joked. Maybe they were related.

The big news was that there was going to be an election next month in March. Mrs Gandhi was still in the driving seat but she wasn't popular. Her Emergency had been in full swing for eighteen months or more. Agitators and journalists disappeared without trace. There were rumours of forced sterilisation. Family planning with a difference. And last year the famous Baroda dynamite case. The good news was that all the 'problem' people who had not been charged and imprisoned would be set free. Everybody hoped democracy would triumph.

But such problems barely touched Ladakh. Delhi was very far away. Here they'd had their own fair share of emergencies. Four major wars in twenty-five years, quite enough for one lifetime. The only real emergency in Ladakh was if there wasn't enough snow and the crops failed or the supply of army rum ran out.

Here in Leh the other big news was that the Queen of Ladakh, Rani Deskit Wangmo, was hoping to stand as MP. She planned to take over from Khushok Bakula, who had been MP for nearly ten years already. This was a wonderful form of democracy, where rinpoches and queens could be members of parliament. In Ladakh, Buddhism and politics were always closely intertwined. Buddha often casted his vote silently.

We slept very well indeed. The fresh vegetables were memorable. I felt as if we had indeed arrived in paradise, a walled garden.

Leh bazaar

The following day I got a lift in a jeep and went up into town with Sonam. The main bazaar was once lined with poplar trees and made up of many shops, mostly with simple shutters or wooden boards that were put back again and padlocked at the end of the day. There were often balconies above. Until recently they used to play polo up and down the main street. Most shops were open and the owners on the lookout for trade. New faces were rare in winter. They sold all manner of goods – hardware, cloaks and cloth, jewellery and foodstuffs, the sorts of thing you might find in Srinagar or even in the Punjab. Pots, pans, rice, dahl, dried fruit, rope, dried beans, ghee, matches, dye, dried yeast, string, shoes, prayer flags, brocades and Kashmir shawls. The list was endless and had probably changed little since the trade routes shut in 1950. One or two sold transistor radios, and Ladakhi music could be heard playing in the bazaar. There was a local radio station that was very popular, with local news, Ladakhi folk songs and even a young stylish woman presenter.

The bazaar was dominated by the old nine-storey fort-cum-palace that had been built by Sengge Namgyal – an old King of

Ladakh – in the 17th century. Although smaller, it pre-dated the Potala in Lhasa. The palace had stood empty since the 1830s and was only inhabited by one caretaker monk. There were many balconies, but it looked somewhat down at heel, impressive but crumbling, a symbol of the past glories of Ladakh with a fine view of the Indus valley. Technically it was still owned by the Queen of Ladakh, but she lived in another palace in Stok.

The first thing I did was get my hair cut in the bazaar and have a shave in an old barber's chair with a cut-throat razor. That was an experience, looking in a mirror. The reddish beard that had got tangled with icicles and hoar frost a few days back was gone. The fresh feel was exhilarating. No razor blades in Zangskar, no hot water, no soap. Sonam said it made me look ten years younger, but I hoped I didn't get frostbite on the way back. To feel the fresh air on my cheeks again was bracing.

We then sauntered around the bazaar and watched as the other Zangskaris traded their butter. Sonam explained that it was becoming more difficult to get a good price as the market was flooded with cheaper Amul cooperative butter that came up from Punjab and Gujarat. The price of Amul butter was around 30 rupees per kilo, but it was white and bland compared with the fine yellow Zangskari butter. There was even Amul cheese, a bit like a mild cheddar, which came in round tins and was not bad at all. Once opened, I used to attack it with a Swiss army penknife, cutting segments one at a time.

The bazaar was very friendly. We were Zangskaris in every sense of the word, wild men from the south with quite a reputation in Leh, like cowboys riding in from the Wild West. The party had now split up, all staying in separate houses wherever they had a connection. We met each other by chance in the streets, like long-lost brothers.

All the Zangskaris smartened themselves up in Leh. Even Tashi, whose cloak was full of holes and patches, put on his best clothes and boots. Looking neat, he sidled up and down the bazaar for a few precious hours, his thumbs shoved into his cummerbund, as if he were lord of all he surveyed. This was his annual holiday for a few days each year. His time out of the valley to see the sights and admire the fine-looking women and vegetables. No doubt they paid a visit to Chang Alley, which lay parallel to the main bazaar but was much narrower. They exchanged their butter with traders in the bazaar and then exchanged goods to take back. You could see Zangskari butter in the stores, still in the goatskins or sheep's stomachs. The genuine article – deep yellow, cut with a knife and weighed out on scales – and they got about 45 rupees per kilo for it. People in Leh always preferred Zangskari butter for their tea. It was pure and had more taste, it was Buddhist butter, local food for local people. A risky business, the ice road, the *chadar*. The butter walk.

Zangskari butter also had a whiff of enlightenment about it, butter churned by young girls on high pastures. It was the high pastures and all the mountain flowers that made the butter so special. Yaks, or to be more precise, the cross-bred *demos* and *dzomos*, were the key to success. All that effort to make the butter by hand, then to carry it down the frozen river for a hundred miles. Extraordinary.

After the traders in the main bazaar in Leh had paid for the butter, an exchange took place. The Zangskaris needed tea, onions, soap, rum, ghee, mustard oil, *chang*, even a night in Chang Alley. They loved Leh, but after a few days their money would run out and they couldn't wait to get back home. They said Leh had become like Kashmir. Soft. Cosmopolitan. If the men returned with any hard-earned cash tucked into their belts from butter trading it was a miracle. Some who had carried five kilos of butter would take home about 220 rupees. Others who had twenty kilos would end up with about 800 or even 900 rupees – a large sum of money for a small farmer. And apart from selling live animals at the end of the autumn, this was often the only cash input they could expect each year. Even Zangskar was slowly becoming a cash economy, but the paper rupee note was still regarded with some suspicion. Some even used the notes to light their fire.

The dentist

Western visitors were still a very new phenomenon in Leh and hotels a rarity. In the backstreets close to a bakery I found one that was still open. The Moonland Hotel was owned by an eccentric dentist called Dr Hussein. The rooms were small and the walls painted green, the beds narrow and the mattresses hard. But a bed was a bed. Pure luxury, in other words. Dr Hussein had six wives but assured me he'd had no more than four at any one time. One died and one left him, and at the moment he was living alone. Wife Number One was down in Kashmir and came up in the summer to keep an eye on him. Where the other three were remained a mystery. Maybe he had one in Yarkand, one in Khotan and one in Kashgar, just like the old traders. He also repaired typewriters.

Dr Hussein loved his chickens and in his surgery he had an ancient dentist's chair. Many old souls came to him to have their teeth extracted. Fillings were a little fiddly these days, the dentist's chair had seen better days and the surgery was alongside the outhouse where the chickens were kept. He had one prize chicken that laid vast eggs. His pride and joy. Chickens sometimes visited the surgery, pecking around on the floor for scraps of grain. The old drills were hand-driven and had all sorts of pulleys. Old Ladakhi ladies came to get gold fillings before a large Buddhist festival. He was the only dentist in town. Teeth mattered.

The next morning I had a good chat with Dr Hussein. What he was a doctor of I was never sure and I never liked to ask. Maybe it was philosophy, maybe chicken breeding, or maybe actually dentistry. Doctor of fillings. Doctor of extractions. Every morning he proudly showed me yet another vast egg. He was very keen on his chickens. 'A man with six wives must keep chickens,' he said. Maybe he was the rooster. He kindly cooked me a meal. *Skew*, *mok mok* and *namkin char* – it was easy to satisfy Zangskaris. Then, miracle of miracles, there was also half a bucket of warm water for washing – utter luxury. He liked his *arak*, did Dr Hussein. He reminded me of certain South American characters brought to life by Gabriel García Márquez in *No One Writes to the Colonel* and *A Thousand Years of Solitude*. Maybe Ladakh was ripe for magic realism.

The doctor, dentist and chicken fancier kept his ear to the ground about Leh politics. Every morning he stood by his *bukhari* (stove) in his raincoat, his long johns tucked into his socks, sucking a cigarette through his clenched fist, planning the day. *Bukharis*, wood-burning metal stoves, are found all over the North-West Frontier. *Bukhār* – a Hindustani word derived from the Persian meaning *heat* or *fever*. Essential in winter.

'Tourists are good,' he said. 'More money, more building. Start in the spring.' He pulled teeth for 10 rupees. And yes, he also repaired typewriters, an interesting combination. His surgery was littered with the carcasses of old typewriters, typewriter ribbons and Buddhist prayer flags, Buddhas on the window sill. His father had worked with Major Peter Hailey as Joint District Commissioner in 1939. The doctor's philosophy was derived from chickens, observing the pecking order.

I explored Leh's backstreets. What a luxury to go into a tea shop and order tea instead of gathering up firewood. Fresh warm bread that was true heaven. Roti and chapatti. The bakery close to the Moonland made Yarkandi nans, like lavash. These were made by throwing wafer-thin, elongated, oblong sheets of dough onto the side of an underground oven, a pit about three feet deep with charcoal at the bottom, which had been damped down before they were baked. A minute or two later they were just picked off with a long bent wire with a hook before they fell into the fire.

For breakfast I ate three of these slightly burnt breads at once, twelve inches long. Very thin. One after the other – nothing better. A little bit of soda had made them bubble up. The *chang* in Chang Alley sat in pale plastic containers and did not tempt me. Women in their long Ladakhi dresses and aprons squatted down on street corners, offering it for sale to passers-by. Tea was only 30 paisa. How cheap were the real pleasures of living. In the tea shops you could sit down on a rickety chair at a wooden table. Even that was a novelty, the height of luxury. You could buy *mok moks*, small neat steamed Tibetan pasties and stir-fry noodle dishes while Ladakhi and Indian music played.

At the post office I was in luck. Two, three, four, five, six letters, as well as a small parcel, but no yellow foam mats. I discovered later that the replacement rolled-up foam mats did arrive in Leh and had been sent back to the UK a month or two earlier. *Quel dommage*. The letters were battered – they looked like they had been in a donkey's saddlebag – but they had got here. I walked around the bazaar in my dirty orange anorak but soon bought a new lightweight cloak that was fine for walking in. Not too heavy. Should be good on the *chadar*.

Karakoram trade

Trade was what made Ladakh prosperous. Sandwiched between the Himalaya and the Karakoram, Leh was the main trading town. Caravan leaders came from all over Central Asia, even as far as China, the edge of the Takla Makan and the edge of Tarim Basin. Much of the wealth of Ladakh was gained not just from trade and the sale of goods but from providing animals, fuel, food, fodder and horsemen along the way, as well as the customs dues and taxes extracted at certain crossing points, usually at bridges or forts that could not be circumvented as at Khalatse, where they grew fine apricots. From Alexander Cunningham's detailed study of Ladakh that I had found in the Alpine Club library, I managed to piece together the patterns of trade, which only ended in the late 1940s.

These tentacles stretched in all directions, offshoots of the great Silk Road albeit very important ones that led down to India and the Punjab, to Chitral and Afghanistan, even to Gandhara. But the routes were far from easy. To Kashgar via the Khardung Pass, the Nubra valley, the Saser and Karakoram Pass was nearly six hundred miles or thirty-five stages. The route Eric Shipton took. I even met an old trader called Syed Ali Shah who remembered him. He said, 'Ah, yes, Mr Shipton he used to stamp our passports in Kashgar.' So his name lived on in the bazaars of Central Asia.

They say you could follow your way up the Karakoram Pass by simply following the bones. People died there as well. The altitude was unforgiving. But that was not the only problem. In 1888 a

Scottish trader called Andrew Dalgleish was murdered on the pass
by one of his Afghan servants. His body now lies in the Christian
cemetery in Leh. To reach the Karakoram there were two other
passes to cross first. The Khardong La behind Leh, which was over
17,500ft, and the Saser Pass; this was worse because it was steeper.
But all three passes were now closed to foreigners.

By chance I met an Indian Air Force helicopter pilot who regu-
larly went up to the Karakoram Pass to drop men and supplies.
He said the glare from the snow in winter was terrible. When he
came back down he stayed in his darkened room in the officers'
mess with a dimmed purple light and an old parachute hanging
from the ceiling. Flying helicopters at such heights in these
mountains was very dangerous as the mountain winds were lethal
and unpredictable.

Other old trade routes from Leh once led to Skardu, Gilgit,
Hunza, Srinagar, Manali, Kishtwar and Kyelong. The sort of prod-
ucts traded a century earlier would have been tea, *pashm* or shawl
wool, *charas*, i.e. hand-rolled hashish, and tobacco from Yarkand.
There was even a *charas* officer to check the quality of the hashish. Some *charas* was consumed in Ladakh, and the rest went on
down to Kashmir and Punjab. The *pashm* came from the fine
underwool of the pashmina goat, which is found in eastern
Ladakh and western Tibet and used to make Kashmir shawls, a
trade that once gave the King of Ladakh and his delegated
merchants great profits, although it was now controlled directly
by Kashmir. There was an even finer product called *shahtoosh*, or
toosh, which is made from the underwool of the Tibetan antelope. These shawls were very fine and very expensive. I have seen
one, brown and very lightweight. Indeed the Tibetan antelope or
chiru was so rare and endangered from illegal hunting that the
shawls were now banned. Nomads picked up stray wool on

bushes when the antelope moulted, and merchants went to the higher villages and collected it once a year.

In the other direction flowed opium, cloth, brocades, leather, spices and saffron. In 1840s about seven tonnes of *charas* went one way and the same amount of opium went the other, no doubt from the East India Company's factories in Rajasthan, although the trade had dropped off a bit since the imperial edict of 1839, when a tonne of opium was burnt in Yarkand. Other goods exported to China included turmeric, chintzes, turbans, otter skins, cardamom, ginger, tamarinds, black pepper, cloves, honey and sugar. In the other direction: gold thread, raisins, dried fruit, turquoise, rhubarb, coral, sugar candy, felts, musk, velvets. Ideas also travelled freely as well as carpets. Central Asia was well connected.

All these and far more could be found in the Leh bazaar below the old palace. There was still a lingering whiff of the old trade route, in the old caravanserais, though most of the yaks were now kept out of town and had been replaced by hauliers with gaily painted lorries decorated with scenes of Dal lake, exotic dancing girls and flowers.

Opium and *charas* had gone underground. The mountain passes to the north were now closed and well guarded, but such items as Mongolian carpets and old jewellery did occasionally slip over the border secretly from western Tibet.

In the past there was a well-known trading trip to Lhasa every three years, called *Lopchak* and many Ladakhis found themselves seconded to help with the trip. It was in effect a tribute. Back came tea, which was often drunk in Ladakh. Downtown Lhasa also had its own attractions.

Soldiers and philosophers

To fully comprehend present-day Ladakh I found that I had to understand not just Buddhist philosophy but the Indian army, including the recent military campaigns on its borders since 1947. For a while Ladakh's position had been very precarious. The old trading town of Leh was surrounded not just by monasteries and crumbling caravanserais but by army barracks, store depots and training camps. In summer large convoys of soldiers from all over India came up the Zoji La. In winter they shivered, many never having been to altitude before. Ladakh was not a popular posting, but the role of the Indian army was crucial in holding a front line not only with Pakistan but with China as well.

Gradual acclimatisation was vital. During the disastrous 1962 war with China many soldiers died of altitude sickness. A whole battalion had been flown into Chushul airfield at 17,000ft and many died just after getting off the plane. That airfield was close to the Tibetan border, the highest in the world and often under fire, with many soldiers being killed just to keep it open. The Chinese had built a road across the Aksai Chin connecting Kashgar with Gartok without being detected. Don't mention the war.

Rumour had it that a patrol of Jammu and Kashmir police saw the Chinese army lorries belting along the highway, went to investigate and were fired upon. Another patrol was ambushed near the hot springs. In the end the Chinese got what they wanted and the border had been relatively stable since then. But it was a close-run thing. It was at the same time as the Cuban Missile Crisis, so the world watched with bated breath. Ladakh could easily have ended up communist, with men and women in blue

suits wielding little red books. What the Chinese would have
done to the monasteries does not bear thinking about. Mao in
Ladakh, a very different type of philosophy.

Many of the Tibetans around Leh had escaped from Tibet,
like the Khampa who had come up on the bus from Srinagar
with me. Most served in the 22 Mountain Regiment. Border
security is a major task and there are many other quasi-military
units, with a bewildering number of names: the Special Frontier
Force; the Border Security Force; the Special Services Bureau;
the Indo-Tibetan Border Police and Indo-Tibetan Border Force.
They all gathered information, and kept a wary eye on Chinese
and Pakistani infiltrators and spies. The last war was with
Pakistan back in 1971, when patrols on the peaks and glaciers
were commonplace. But the most popular unit by far was the
Ladakh Scouts – a fine testing ground for young Ladakhis who
did not want to become monks. Even in old Tibet, monasteries
had regiments of soldier-monks who were more like police but
could also go into action if need be. Even soldiering has its
philosophy.

I was also interested in how Ladakh was administered by the
Indian government. Since I was smartened up and cleanly shaven
I went to see the DC, who had an office down by the new polo
ground. Sayeed Rizvi was a bright-eyed, sparky Delhi man. He
was very genial and delighted in conversation, immediately
welcoming me into his office. The job, he explained, was pretty
much the same as that of the DC of old, only the DC's house had
now been taken over by the army. Leh even had electricity and
an airfield. Sayeed, an economist, dealt with law and order,
together with all manner of local matters, as well as planning the
impending election. Development was top of the list. He was
keen to promote apricots and pashmina, and helped with

constructing new kidding sheds in Changtang. He gave me the first coffee I had drunk for months – and very grateful I was too. With his blessing I was permitted to stay in Zangskar; as he joked to me, 'I was doing no harm.' Laissez-faire is very much the Ladakhi philosophy.

The next day I bumped into another fascinating government official, the Ladakhi philosopher Tashi Rabgyas, the information officer. He knew Zangskar very well indeed. As a young man he had been sent there after the catastrophic snowfall in 1956 and had supervised compensation to all the villagers who had lost livestock. And as he was scrupulously honest he was a hero in Zangskar, feted wherever he went. He also collected Ladakhi folk songs and his ruling philosophy was Madhyamika, the Middle Path. And so in the middle of a dry, dusty road, with Tashi wearing his Ladakhi grey cloak and pink cummerbund, we had a long discussion about emptiness and the Middle Way, dependent origination and the meditative path. His jovial smile won many people over.

This was what I really loved about Ladakh. Buddhist philosophy was a very real, living entity. It was in the streets and in the homes, not just stuffed away in the monasteries. Tashi Rabgyas's parting shot was simply this: 'Madhyamika? Buddha's teaching? Down in India they had it for a thousand years and what did they do with it? They threw it away ...'

He smiled and gave a little chuckle.

Not far away from Leh in Choglamsar was the Buddhist School of Philosophy, where the Dalai Lama had been giving Kalachakra teachings in September.[44] It was the first time he had ever visited Ladakh and most of the country was there. Forty thousand people attended, the majority having walked over the mountains for days on end. Half of Zangskar went.

They listened intently to words of wisdom about the birth and death of universes, the solar system and the workings of the elements, the four states of mind, the path of fruit and fruition, meditation, initiation and enlightenment, as well as the six yogas of Naropa, training the mind and the body. There was a complex series of initiations. Remarkable. Imagine if Wembley Stadium were home to a three-day philosophical colloquium for small farmers and businessmen.

So young Ladakhi men had a clear choice. They could either join the monasteries and become monks, philosophers and skilled debaters, or join the Ladakh Scouts and become soldiers and marksmen. Both paths needed strict discipline. It was all in the mind.

Return journey

The four days in Leh were wonderful, but Tashi's money had run out and Dorje Tsering was heavily laden. He had bought a circular stove, a large shovel, some onions, some tea – red Tibetan and Lipton – soap, cardamoms, chillies, cloves, garam masala, dried vegetables, dried apricots, sugar and shrivelled tomatoes on a string. Fruit had, of course, run out long ago. After a few days we planned our escape, the return journey. This good weather was not good news for the river.

It was now the third week of February, high time we left Leh and went back onto the *chadar*. Adrenalin started to flow, the feet were itchy. In the darkness I hailed a few friends. Thubsten and Tashi were by now dancing in the main street of Leh, their XXX rum having had its desired effect. We all went up the hill arm in arm. For the return journey I bought a bottle of emergencies-only XXX black rum for 30 rupees – about £2. 'For Defence

Services only' was stamped on the label. Smuggled out of the army.

The truth was we longed to be back on the frozen river, back on the ice, deep in the mountains. Solitude. We craved solitude. The return trip up the river should be better than the outward trip, but it wasn't. In fact we very nearly didn't make it.

The last night in Leh we all slept in a small house below the old palace amid a maze of small, steep lanes. The heart of the old city. At dawn, like small gods we strode down the backstreets of Leh. Everyone else was asleep. We meandered towards the new polo ground and took a last-minute photograph with the royal palace in the background. Sonam was not coming back. He had other matters to attend to, so I was under the wing of Thubsten, Tashi and Dorje Tsering. The government flag had not yet been raised in front of the DC's office. Never mind. Six months till the next cup of coffee.

The truck revved up. We got up into the back, our packs taking up quite a bit of room. Tashi hung on for dear life, the gears engaged. Farewell civilisation, back to the world of ice. All we thought about were the upcoming evening and which cave it would be. We were bored of luxuries. Life would soon be pared down to the absolute minimum. That was how we liked it. Language too. We needed solitude and silence. We needed to get moving.

The truck rattled on down the valley past all the army camps, eventually stopping before Nimu at the top of the bend. Far below we saw the river and thin strips of ice, where the Zangskar river met the Indus. We saw the colourful letters of the mantra *Om mani padme hum* painted onto the rock and prayer flags fluttering. Something told me we would need all the luck we could get. We got down. This was it. The other passengers looked at us strangely, as if we were from another planet, which in a sense we were. Somehow the link between faces that you had only known for thirty minutes can be as dramatic as those you had known all your life. The other passengers said nothing, but clearly we were an oddity. Zangskaris belonged to another universe, hard men who risked their lives on the river just to bring butter. Maybe we were a little mad as well. But the Tibetans had a liking for wild men of the mountains. They were survivors and made the best meditators, so I was told.

We sat with our luggage beside the road, contemplating our future as the truck drove off. Thubsten had another cigarette, as did Tashi, the fruits of the bazaar short-lived. They sat beside the tarmac taking a last drag, the last ounce of baccy before getting back down to Zangskar. Just a minute's delay checking everything, making sure it was all secure. Then top gear, slipping, sliding down the shale, cutting sticks, old routine, hoots and shouts of laughter. Tashi was back on good form. Thubsten had his rubber boots and was very proud of them.

Back over the Indus, higher up, the lion river fresh from Kailas. Geographers like length and height in the same way that historians like dates. The Indus was the longer of the two rivers, but the Zangskar always looked as if it had more volume, more power, greater flow. Then we saw trouble, big trouble ahead. To us it was obvious and very alarming.

All the time we had been in Leh, drinking tea and chatting, it had been good weather. The sun had been out for days on end, and the sun does things to snow. Even before we got down to the river we could see that something was very wrong. The ice looked uneven in texture, even from a distance, the light reflecting in different patterns. What was wrong was that the river had risen by about six inches, and that made all the difference. It was crucial. If the water level fell, the ice cracked; if the level rose, it created other problems that we were about to encounter. We crossed the Indus by an old Bailey bridge, and then we realised that the river was far worse than we had feared.

There had been a sudden melt, probably in the Markha valley. The river levels were much higher. The ice was almost covered and no one knew if we would ever get back. Just for starters, we had to go on all fours on our hands and knees, pushing our packs in front of us under overhangs, and this was just on the first half mile or so. Not a good start, in fact very dangerous. The water was less than a foot away and the ice appeared to be only four or five inches thick – if the narrow ice shelf gave we would all go into the river. We crouched down under the river bank and held our breath.

One by one we pushed our packs forward. Twenty or thirty yards at a time, then fifty yards on our hands and knees, edging forward, and eventually we stood up and helped the man behind us. Here the weight of the new purchases began to tell. Some had bundles sewn up in canvas cloth or old hessian sacks. The over-hangs were pronounced – only alluvial rocks compressed together, not very stable anyway, and a small foretaste of things to come. The ice curved elegantly, but the surface was already pitted and crystallised with the new wet ice from when the river had risen and spilled out over it. It meant that our boots could easily get wet, which was not good news. It also meant we could not read the ice, so we had to tread much more carefully. The ice did not respond to tapping. Dull thuds. It had changed character.

If the frozen river had collapsed further up we could be in real trouble, caught between two walls. If the ice had broken up, melted, then re-formed, we would be lucky. We had no idea whether we would get back. We might get stuck halfway. The Zangskaris were unusually silent.

Then there was another problem. The water was in fact flowing over the ice and had been doing so for days on end, setting up its own fragile crystal structure maybe twelve inches deep, so we walked through two or three rivers at once. At one point we had to walk through slush and ice needles, but not before taking our boots and socks off and rolling up our trousers. This was going to be hard. Just getting across the river was bad enough. Dorje Tsering took the lead. The main ice underneath had also collapsed but seemed fairly secure. It had relocked itself. This short bit with Dorje out in front taking the lead and tapping with his stick was not so bad. The ice needles hurt, but it was only for five minutes or so, albeit long enough to lose all the feeling in your feet. Yet there were longer stretches ahead of two hundred to three hundred yards at a time. Yes, the needles were sharp, but you just had to keep going. Every so often we sought the shore, a bank of pebbles or sand, to sit down and have a short rest.

Pebbles stuck to our bare feet and had to be prised off before we could warm our feet up and get some circulation going. Skin came off like parchment. Removing the stones was painful, but at least you knew that your nerves were still working. Drying one's feet, pummelling them back into life became critical. This was an 'emergency', so I decided to open the XXX army rum, much to everyone's delight. You needed it to get the circulation back again, and a quick nip here and there kept you warm. Keeping a towel at the top of our rucksacks was again essential, for rubbing our feet and toes. Getting the feeling back into your feet was a slow process, hard, painful work.

The level of the flow went up and down, just as in streams during the summer. Levels dropped at night, and as the water receded very slowly, long, sharp ice needles formed. These were the ones that cut you. But so long as the main ice stayed firm we were all right. Once or twice the main ice did move, and we saw deep fractures and cracks in it just like crevasses on a glacier. We relied on instinct and intuition, our senses finely tuned, honed down.

My feet started to bleed, so I sacrificed a pair of socks and walked in those for the next stretch or two. We held our boots in our hands or strung them round our necks. The socks went stiff as a board but still gave some protection. Wool is marvellous stuff. Thank you, sheep. The bright lights of Leh bazaar seemed a million miles away.

Dorje Tsering

That first night back up the river we slept in a cave hidden up a narrow canyon. The gap between the rock walls was only three feet wide. We squeezed up there and three hundred yards further on we found the cave. Not often used, apparently, but brilliant for us. Everyone tried to get their boots and trousers dry again. To the Ladakhis, walking barefoot over the ice was no hardship at all. They used the rum medicinally and started singing.

We all had small jobs, lighting fires, gathering firewood, collecting water, melting ice, preparing food, etc. As with mountaineering, the main story was the ascent, getting to the top, onwards and upwards. Only a very few lines are ever devoted to the descent, the anti-climax. But this was often where accidents occurred. The next two days were particularly difficult. We had to be very vigilant, with no time for heroics. Psychologically the return trip was not as exciting as the descent, just basic practical problems that needed solving one way or another. And much more dangerous.

The following day, day three and in the shade, we found a great pool of slush and no way to get onto the opposite bank. The pool was about six feet deep and ten feet across. There was only one thing to do, make a series of stepping stones, so we passed small boulders from one to the other in a great line, creating an underwater pile till one stone came to the surface. It took three hours to make three stepping stones, and even then they were not very stable. To get everyone across was not easy. One slip and that would have been it. That slush pool took up a fair bit of our travelling day and we were still in the shade, which was very, very cold.

Then at one point my right leg got wet up to the knee from the slush on the edge of the ice. Not good. Coming down the *chadar* had been a doddle by comparison. This was painstakingly slow, and everyone had to keep their balance and their sense of humour. More of an ordeal than a pleasure.

Near the big waterfall that looked like a series of frozen organ pipes there was an accident. This was where Dorje Tsering with his heavy stove and all his purchases fell in. I was behind him and heard an ominous crack, then the ice gave way. About twenty yards ahead of me I saw him suddenly disappear, until only his head and shoulders were visible. This was what we had all feared. Falling in and then being swept under the ice. You would have little chance of saving yourself. It all just depended on how deep the river was, how swift the current, how bad the crack in the ice and whether the crack was spreading. Maybe the ice had been worn thin by a small whirlpool underneath.

Without thinking we rushed over. I even tried to take a picture, but his rescue was far more important. Two others got to him first. He was in deep shock and did not say a word. We put our packs down for fear of breaking more ice and edged forward. If one went under, then two or three could easily follow if the ice suddenly broke again. Our outstretched sticks now became very useful. We crept nearer and nearer. Luckily the depth was only about six feet. Another foot or more and it would have been curtains.

As it was, Dorje was in the water up to his neck, half wedged in between the ice, but still in a very dangerous position. His pack had fallen backwards, getting totally soaked and almost lost. His stick saved him as he instinctively lunged with it across the hole. We managed to pull him out, fully aware that the ice could give way at any moment. Once back on the ice we helped him to stand up. He then went to the side of the river, took his cloak off and wrung it out. The water froze almost before it hit the ground. This was also a critical moment because he could easily get frostbite if he did not warm up. His body temperature must also have plummeted and death from exposure was a real possibility. He looked shaken, and I was not surprised. He had nearly gone all the way to Pakistan.

At the next stop on a sandy beach, Dorje laid all his possessions out in the sun in an attempt to dry them out. His matches were a gonner, but the tea stood a chance. And there was soap, dahl and rice, mirrors, cloth and onions. Quite a few onions. The men again talked about the King of Zangla who threatened to eat his cook. Moral of the story: take lots of food with you. But we knew that we were not out of the woods yet. Trees were very scarce.

It wasn't until we passed several turnings for side valleys that things got better. We assumed that the thaw had been in the east, because upstream the ice had not changed at all. The closer we got to Zangskar, the colder it got, the better the ice and the faster we went. Slowly we started to feel better.

Every day we passed other parties coming down, and we warned them of the ice being in bad condition. I recognised one figure, the rotund Nawang Lawchok – the *naib tehsildar* from Karsha, who was carrying his small, beloved dog. He was pleased to see me. We slept in two more caves, ones we had used on the way down, the first Tip Yongma Bao, then Kilima Bao. Rock caves. Rough basic hotels. Fresh air but no running water, with twenty-five people sleeping there. Nothing more to report. Then Pishu, a very smoky old den. It now felt like we were getting near home as the valley opened out once more and we could see signs of habitation, even yak dung in certain places. We speeded up as we got closer, although it was just as cold as when we left.

On day six we reached Karsha and crossed the river again. By now we had become used to freezing water. Tashi and I raced home to Padum. He won by a whisker and laughed. The next day I saw him on his rooftop looking very pleased with himself. 'How's your wife, Tashi?' He puckered his lips and kissed the cold air. It was good to be home again. His brother, the lama, I was glad to see, was back up in his monastery banging his drum, contemplating the universe rather than Tashi's wife.

5

KARSHA
MONASTERY

March 1977

Singing from the rooftops

That afternoon I gave Tashi Namgyal his packet of Lipton tea and had a good chat with Phuntsok Dawa, who asked me to go and stay with him in Karsha. He was a teacher in the local school. It was like old times. Small pleasures made life not just bearable but exotic. Winter had its charms. *Chadar* was indeed a fine education, the philosophy of ice a barometer with which to gauge winter. For many Zangskaris *chadar* was the winter. On my return I offered prayers to the local *lha* and said a few hundred *Om mani padme hums* for good measure. At last I was beginning to think and feel like a Zangskari. I settled back into village life and contemplated my next move.

On the other side of the valley I could see the village of Karsha. It was about six miles as the chough flies but always looked closer. The valley was like a vast open-air chessboard with villages and *mani* walls dotted around, the giant pawn-like *chortens* suggesting that the Buddhist game of chess went on for hundreds of years. A sophisticated glass bead game played out with Buddhist stratagems and philosophies openly debated where thoughts were as powerful as the mountains and glaciers.

In Karsha they got the sun about an hour or so before we did in Padum, a distinct advantage in winter. Padum faced north and lay in the shadow of the main Himalayan range. Snow and ice stayed longer on the peaks and glaciers, so meltwater was at first slower to appear, but then in late summer there was often a torrent. The Himalayan glaciers behind Padum were vast. But in Karsha the snowfields were small in comparison and they often struggled for water when they needed it most. Ploughing and harvesting were a fortnight ahead of Padum, so the two villages exchanged labour and even seed corn. In spring you sometimes saw a man walking to another village with a wooden plough strapped to his back. Agriculture was highly organised.

But as it was still winter it was the elaborate colourful monastic festivals and the old frescos in Karsha that now interested me most of all. From a distance Karsha monastery stood out white, with its many layers climbing up the mountainside. It had grown organically, architecture without architects. Even against the snow it looked like a Greek city state in miniature, complete with philosophers, cooks and trainee monks nestled beneath the mountain of Choralah. A bit like Mount Athos, but women were allowed into Karsha monastery, particularly at festival time. Villagers often had houses within the monastery for their own monks that they maintained. They were honoured guests, for it was their work in the fields that sustained the monks and kept the Buddhist wheel turning round. The Karsha festival, known as Gustor, was the largest in Zangskar.

Each village had its loyalty to a certain monastery and its own monks. Religion was not just a prop or opium, it was the solid

central core to their lives and their progress towards enlightenment, a stage set with its own rhythms, striving for internal
perfection and the art of giving, of wisdom and compassion. To
have a whole valley set on this course at high altitude was
remarkable. I felt privileged and humbled. The soft, delicate
sound of women singing from the rooftops as they worked, spinning and carding out of sight, was particularly moving and
delightful. Their songs were about yaks, sky, flowers and the
mountains, lost sheep and their lovers in the high pastures. It was
time I went to live in Karsha.

Magpa household

In Karsha I stayed in a small room with Phuntsok Dawa in a
house just below the monastery. The room was even smaller than
my own room back in Padum, 12ft by 6ft and with one small
window. There were the two of us and a small stove, but we got
along very well and took it in turns to cook. The main house was
a *magpa* household, where the woman of the house had inherited
the property and fields. She had no brothers and so she took in a
husband, in these situations usually a second- or third-born
brother who did not want to become a monk. Rumour had it
that some women in *magpa* marriages were quite powerful, and
occasionally they could hire and fire their husbands if they did
not pull their weight. It usually depended on how much land
they had. If labour was short, you acquired an extra husband.[45]

The woman of the house was a great character, always laughing and joking. Other women often came onto her rooftop to
work. I once found her daughter feeding a young lamb with milk
from her own mouth, like mouth-to-mouth resuscitation, an
extraordinary and beautiful sight. When she realised I was

watching she blushed. It was an intimate act of compassion. Every life counts in Zangskar, even sheep and goats. Basic agriculture. Survival.

Also associated with this house were two artist monks. On the walls of their cells they had painted roundels about twelve inches in diameter that were filled with landscapes. On one there was a painting of Karsha monastery, and leading up to it a winding road that had yet to be built. I later met them again as they decorated the new temple in Padum. In one painting they put in a Westerner in shorts among the Buddhist landscape, a man trekking. They had to keep up with the times.

This house was just below Karsha monastery, and in the wall above there was a small opening about 3ft by 2ft. Phuntsok told me that if a 'naughty' monk was caught having an affair with a woman or found guilty of any other misdemeanour, he was stripped of his robes, bundled out of the monastery and lay person's clothes thrown down after him. It was a drop of about ten feet onto the rocks. Not pleasant, but occasionally it did happen. The problem was that young monks wanted adventure and ran off to join the Ladakh Scouts, as happened at Stagrimo. But nobody talked about this.

Phuntsok Dawa taught English and Urdu in the small school. He had been posted to many other villages in Zangskar, so he had a very good knowledge of the valley. Most of the lessons were held outdoors, and the children also learnt Tibetan, mathematics and general knowledge. If any of the children were bright they were sent away to school in Leh. Stenzin Namgyal, Phuntsok's son, ended up at Tyndale Biscoe down in Srinagar.

Every day from the monastery we would hear the conch shell being blown to summon the monks to the temple for their prayers. There was a monastic school as well, and in between lessons the young monks did vigorous exercises. Every evening we would hear chanting as they lined up and repeated their daily prayers and texts from memory. It was a pleasant way to end the day, but also very cold. From the rooftop we could hear them chanting Buddhist mantras and sutras in a delightful sing-song canto that rose and fell in a rhythm, like waves breaking gently on a seashore.

Karsha had a very different feel to Padum. It was set about a mile up from the river and was more spread out, enjoying magnificent views of the main Himalayan range to the south. All the peaks were saw-toothed and glaciated, and all unclimbed apart from the one behind Padum with its curved prow that I had climbed with a good friend back in the summer – Fiona Lumsden, Kenneth Lumsden's intrepid daughter. We called it 'Blue Poppy Mountain' as we found wonderful examples of this beautiful flower on its lower slopes. Such a deep unfathomable blue. Next to this was a much higher double peak with fine hanging glaciers that was nicknamed 'Padme Hum'.

The village of Karsha was divided by the stream that came down a narrow ravine. Two halves. Left and right. On one side the monastery and on the other the nunnery. In winter the stream – a raging torrent in early summer – became a series of frozen pools with murky ice, under which water flowed very slowly. It provided drinking water for the whole community, and women and children gathered to fill their jerrycans every morning. In winter water was a scarce resource needed by animals and people alike.

Karsha was the main Gelugpa yellow monastery of Zangskar, for the followers of Tsongkhapa. Religion was an expensive business, and the investment of the villagers' time and labour to keep the Buddha's doctrine alive and well was considerable, like an insurance policy against misfortune. The monasteries were highly organised, and they allowed monks to undertake business ventures of their own. They invested in trading schemes, and would lend money and grain to farmers at 25 per cent interest. The monastery had a vast reservoir of grain that could be drawn upon in times of drought or crop failure. It was their seed bank.

Crop yields were high in a good year, despite the altitude. Maybe it was the increased ultraviolet light, the good soil and the local varieties that ripened quickly, as well as the minerals and nutrients that came down with irrigation. The local spirits and gods also kept the ecology intact, thus ensuring survival and continuity, and the limits of polyandry and monasticism kept the population in check. Women could also become nuns or marry outside the valley, and quite a few lived in Leh or Manali.

Karsha was a large village and I enjoyed living there. There were none of the religious and government tensions that always lay beneath the surface in Padum. The road had yet to arrive. Everyone looked forward to the festival.

Yak tails

Gustor, the great Karsha festival, was the big event of the year, and the monastery was putting on a show, a grand spectacle like a mystery play with many colourful characters in masks acting out the drama. History and teaching. A celebration of good triumphing over evil. Old gods and new gods, and the wheel of life turning. Over a thousand people gathered, with all the women in their finest jewellery and best clothes, hats, boots and embroidered shawls.

The path to the monastery wound up the mountainside, went under a large *chorten* and then zig-zagged its way up to the main temples. In the main courtyard there were six black yak tails tied to the top of the flagpole, as was the custom in Tibet, tails that had once danced around the mountains. In the old days yak tails were used as standards when armies went into battle. Genghis Khan had nine yak tails. He would. Yaks had power within the community, physical and spiritual, totemic and symbolic. The higher the village, the more dependent they were on yaks for their economy. The nomads' best friend. Occasionally choughs balanced on top of the flagpole. Yaks, choughs and ravens, black guardians.

Yaks were almost the opposite in behaviour to the choughs. They stood their ground stolidly and moved slowly, but could be surprisingly nimble if they had to be. Their tails were not just used on top of the flagpoles fluttering with prayer flags in the central courtyard, but as fly whisks and symbols of-authority, even for the Indian kings. Some tails were black, others white. Long after the yak had bitten the dust, the tail lived on. What is last lasts longest.

Conch shells

The sound of the conch shell summoned the whole village. The sound was deep, as if from the bottom of the Indian Ocean, resonating in the thin air, a long, full, rounded sound that reached far back into one's consciousness, as if the ocean that laid down the mountains were itself vibrating, a natural continuum that evolved as you looked up and saw the outline of the monk in his robes playing the conch against the skyline as he stood on a rooftop, an ancient reverberation that had summoned monks since the time of Buddha.

The sound was slightly hypnotic and could put your mind into a quiet space. Each conch had a slightly different pitch. The sound was pure and resonated with the teaching, awakening the ignorant and dispelling fear. In the *Mahabharata* a conch was used by Arjuna to summon troops into battle. In India Hindu priests would stand on a beach or river bank blowing a conch, as if they were a whale calling. They only used right-turning conch shells. Vishnu knew all about that. The conch often featured in paintings as one of the eight auspicious Buddhist symbols. In Karsha you had it all: prayer flags fluttering, yak tails, conch shells and choughs.

Monastic loyalty was very important to villagers, defining their outlook on life. In the mountains there were many paths. Yellow and red, Tsongkhapa contrasted with Kargyu Drugpa, the dragon teachings of Bhutan and the Nyingma yogins, the wild ones with long, tousled hair.

Within half an hour the surrounding rooftops, balustrades, balconies, windows and steps were choc-a-bloc with young and old alike, all jumbled, straining and peering for a view of the courtyard, all dressed in their newest cloaks.

Slowly the monastic orchestra assembled. Long horns were carried down the steps one by one, with a young monk holding the business end, not easy when the steps were so steep. Timing was important. They set up in a corner under an awning and other musicians followed, drums, cymbals and double-reeded *surnas* which were more like shawms than oboes. They belonged to the ancient Indian Shehnai family. Their sound is supposed to create and maintain a sense of auspiciousness and sanctity. (They are also used by snake charmers.) The monastic orchestra was like a large rock band getting ready, only they would have had to play all day in sub-zero temperatures.

Dogs sat in the snow and from an upstairs window a large portrait of the Dalai Lama smiled down. A donkey edged its way into the courtyard. People chatted, strained necks, looking around as young men eyed up the girls. It was a fashion parade, a chance to be noticed. Buddhist teaching came a poor second to flirtation and jokey exchanges.

The *umzad*, the master of ceremonies, came down the steps to oversee final preparations. On his head was draped a large, curved, saffron-coloured hat, and down his back a spine of clumped woollen threads that looked a bit like a horse's mane. Over his shoulders hung a great length of saffron-coloured wool and in his hand he held a large bundle of incense sticks, his badge of office.

The brass horns were now extended as all three sections were pulled out, each section about three feet long with large, open-ended mouths, a bit like the alpenhorns you might see in the Swiss mountains. These needed room and were not easy to play. Sometimes the musicians played them standing up on the roof of the monastery and they could be heard many miles away, like a yak bellowing.

Then a group slowly emerged from the crowd: Karsha Bakpas, *teshispa* and 'crow-headed work leader', bird mask and beak on top of his head, accompanied by Abe and Meme with their wooden masks. The *teshispa* had his bow and arrow of divination. The crow-headed work leader also had a lambswool hat, a necklace of turquoise and amethyst, Chinese brocade and, in his belt, cloth from Bhutan. In Karsha the wooden crow's head not only had three eyes but a silver beak, precious objects connecting them to the world of the ancient sky spirits. Royal flight.

In the opposite corner sat the monastic drummers in the shade, looking very cold. A man with a sword appeared from the top of the steps dressed like a Chinese man, the monastic policeman whose job it was to keep law and order. He had to keep the crowd back, which was already pushing outwards like a football crowd. And so with several long swipes he cleared a path, at which the people laughed and started calling out to him. Even he found it difficult not to smile, although he had an important job to do. The sword was of course blunt and was a bit of a joke, but he had to make sure that there was enough room for the monks to dance and also that the crowd did not become too dense.

All the monks had been training for many months to re-enact various dramas and rituals associated with Buddhism and ancient Tibet. Long lengths of yak-hair mat and carpets were laid out for the lamas not taking part, and even the old men who had been sitting by the kitchen appeared in long yellow robes. This was going to be a real show.

Preparations were made for the high lama's seat. He sat on a throne in the shade and wore two cloaks, just like everyone else – no point in getting cold. He sat behind what looked like long necklaces of bone draped below the awning, there to remind us about impermanence. Human bone?

The master of ceremonies stood on the central platform giving small, unhurried instructions. He was in charge, it was his big day and he had to remember everything off pat – no notes. Practice makes perfect.

The whole reputation of the monastery hinged on the festival, each act had a story and the monks took their dancing very seriously. Everything was in hand. For two or three months they had been preparing and the previous night there had been a final dress rehearsal, but without all their resplendent robes.

The platform for the head lama was prepared with Tibetan carpets and a yak skin. In front of the long, low roof and off to one side sat the monastic VIPs and the orchestra. As a backdrop there was a section of printed Indian cotton with flowers. Monastic theatre, with the courtyard as the stage.

First the musicians came down, headed up by two boys dressed as monkeys beating sticks together and running around backwards and forwards furiously, making the most of it as cheeky little monkeys, pawing people, trying to get tips, their faces hidden behind the masks. They had a really good time. Then drums, cymbals and pipes, the musicians all kitted out in monastic garb and tall yellow hats. The music was written on a goatskin, which was unfurled and laid on the ground. The master of ceremonies handed each of them an incense stick, after which the head lama came across and took his place on his throne, accompanied by three attendants. More tall yellow hats, black, yellow and red shawls, one person carrying a water pot with peacock feathers. The head lama had bushy eyebrows.

There was small delay, a short lull while people chatted away, and I found myself in a quiet space, rather like waiting on the banks of the Thames for the Boat Race to start.

Ritual and dance

There was an air of quiet expectation, humour, even banter. No one minded waiting, and even the sun was shining. You forgot about the cold. Ritual dances were like animated wall paintings, the visible heart of Tibetan Buddhism and its complex philosophy and psychology. In Zangskar rituals were everywhere – funerary rites, weddings, purifications, monthly recitations, exorcisms and large annual events like this dance festival.

Ritual took many forms, both public and private. It could be short or lengthy, it could be costly in terms of time, grain and butter. It could be held in a monk's cell, at home or deep inside a cave. Ritual kept the monastic world rotating. It also gave purpose to risky endeavours and calmed the mind. Psychologically it was very powerful. Multi-purpose storytelling.

The dance festival was a vivid depiction of a complex belief system and philosophy, a system that covered Tantric visualisations, pathways to enlightenment and negation of soul. A rich tapestry of belief and intent, colourful and noisy, a performance worthy of a team of magicians who could conjure up favourable weather, defeat enemies and encourage good crops. Different rituals for different seasons. But the underlying message was always the same, although it worked on many different levels. A powerful etiquette of donations and respect, of prayers and propitiations. Spirits were tamed and subdued, objects imbued with dark powers and then thrown out of the village

The rituals were as perennial as the winter snows, the monasteries and monks as reliant on the villagers as the villagers were on the mountains for meltwater. The Buddhist ecology was fuelled by juniper, incense, the sound of drumming and cymbals, conch shells and *damaru*-pellet skull drums. Each ritual evoked space and majesty, a place within the mind where there was hope, confidence and clarity. Nothing was more important to the villagers than the festival that was about to begin. Entertainment and education. A *danse macabre*. A sacrifice transformed. Shamanic Buddhist Tibet at its very best. Ritual deeply engrained. A form of worship that was both ancient and colourful. Pure theatre. The audience awaited.

Monkeys and skeletons

We had two full days of dance, music, storytelling and mystical play-acting, all in sub-zero temperatures. So many elements. So many characters. So many monks. So many different dances. So much colour flowing, so much silk, so many costumes, so many masks. It felt an enormous privilege to see this particular festival, the first Westerner to do so in Karsha.

First down the steps was Hushang, a Chinese merchant with a large papier-mâché mask. Then the master of ceremonies, then the *bakpas* and the crow-headed work leader. Hushang represented the gentler Eastern approach of Chinese Buddhism, more akin to Zen and Chan – thinking and not thinking, as opposed to the dialectical and debating approach of rationality. Form and emptiness debated in full colour. Then Hushang was helped down. He sat on the far side watching the whole performance, occasionally getting up to meet and greet dancers as they came down the steep set of steps from the upper temple. It was easy to lose one's balance. Hushang's mask was very large and always smiling – a quiet presence in an otherwise wild performance. Hushang had a large, brown, cheerful face with big ears, and the monk could only see out of the mouth. He was a likeable visitor, a man from China.

Scenes were re-enacted from early Tibetan history. Here was Kamalisa from Nalanda, a student of Sangarakshita, who had come for the great debate held at Samye monastery near Lhasa in 793 CE. Sudden versus gradual enlightenment. The ways of Chan and Dzogchen pitched against years of slow philosophical study. Indian Vajrayana or Tantric Buddhism versus Chinese or Eastern Mountain Buddhism descended from the teaching of Huineng. The historic debate was instigated and encouraged by the Tibetan Buddhist King Trisong Detsen and lasted two years. Was it an even contest? Did either side fully understand the debate? The monastic dance retold a simplified version of this story from the Tibetan perspective in which Hushang was slightly subservient and apparently lost the debate. Thinking versus not thinking. But from his standpoint there was no need for debate. Why use words to impart deep knowledge when a smile or simple gesture would do? The flick of a yak-tail whisk?

The exploits of Langdarma, a Tibetan king who less than fifty years after the great debate of 793 CE persecuted Buddhists and reverted to the old Bon religion, were very popular in Ladakhi dramas. He was eventually killed by an arrow fired by a monk called Lhalung Palgyi Dorje, one of Guru Rinpoche's students, who then fled to Amdo, reversing his cloak from black to white and becoming a recluse. Civil war ensued as the kingdom fragmented. Amid the chaos one of Langdarma's grandsons moved west with his small army and took over the kingdom of Guge in Ngari, western Tibet, which included Ladakh. It was from him that all the royalty in Ladakh were descended. He had three sons, and one of them held Zangskar. That is early Ladakhi history in a nutshell.

Other dances depicted certain incidents in the life of the Buddha and Guru Rinpoche. Deer and yaks, monks with horns, bulls, monks with hats, dark hats, blue hats, green hats, black hats, so called devil dancers, the purification of evil, the destruction of self. All featured. In time with the Dharmapalas – Yama, Mahakala, Palden Lhamo and Begtse Chen – quivering at the climax.

With the sound of drums and *surnas*, the head lama, the *Khenpo*, came down the steps into the courtyard and was greeted by the master of ceremonies. Cymbals and *surnas*. Crescendo after crescendo. The pace was accelerating fast. Dragons on silk, flames on hats, skulls and eyes, the faces on aprons, almost in a trance, a kind of ecstasy invoked. Staffs and staves, ribbons, *dorjes* and *vajras*, the dancers whirling almost like dervishes.

A kaleidoscope of colour. The flowing quickstep, dancers in time, almost like the tango, blue, green, orange, yellow, red, a gyrating blur. Bone necklaces, like court jesters, teased and tamed the spirits, sometimes in pairs, sometimes half a dozen at a time. Drums and bells. As if the paintings on the walls of the monastery had suddenly come alive, which in a sense they had. Then there were clowns, young scallywag monks who rushed around with small sticks, begging for money and throwing flour, pawing and tugging at sleeves. Like puppies, they knew they had a captive audience to milk. Then there were skeletons with red ribs and blue headdresses, clowns laughing at life and death, red and blue tutus, fans for ears and tassels, teasing and cavorting. And all the time the man with the sword jovially keeping the crowd at bay.

The boys laughed and played a game. The women all dressed up with goatskin shawls tucked tightly around their shoulders crowded together like a flock, jammed pack tight. They all caught the eyes of the men. Hundreds of *perags* at a slight angle. A turquoise sea. Determined to look their very best. Almost coquettish. A fashion parade. An excuse to put on jewellery and forget the hard work of farming, child-rearing and keeping the home fires burning.

They watched the battles of good and evil, the hand gestures, *mudras*, the act of cleansing. Strong Tantric traditions, a bit like a morality play, time in Bardo, mock battles, death, rebirth, the land of limbo, a ritual offering to deities of the monastery, guardians of faith, spirits of mountains. Existential symbolism. Emptiness without words.

The festival was long and colourful. The villagers understood its importance as a dramatic vehicle, a pageant for telling their story and their role in keeping the story alive. It was a key social event, a communal statement of belief and intent. It is who they are. At certain moments it was like a circus, a pageant, a Buddhist miracle play. Stories that weaved their way around their lives. The miracle was that it survived at all.

Day two

On the second day there was more incense. Horse, yak, dog and ram were brought in wearing special blue, red and gold cloths embroidered with *vajras*, thunderbolts. These were blessed and then let go. Recently married brides and grooms were also brought in and danced slowly, self-consciously, the whole weight of the occasion draped around their shoulders in the form of *kataks*, the white scarves, a symbolic gesture of offering and purity. They gave money. And then the skeletons danced again, the crow-headed work leader and *bakpas* in attendance.

Following this parade of brides and grooms, I was asked to dance in front of the whole crowd. I gave money to the monastery, 100 rupees, a strange and wonderful moment. You pay for privilege, as with horse races and archery in Zangskar, where if you won you paid money, not the other way round. It brought you down to earth. Here they had slow and fast horse races, everything balanced out. Ingenious.

Sometimes there was a flurry at the top of the steps and a dozen or more dancers came down the steep steps at once. Magnificent headdresses with flames and skulls sat on top of their black hats, and many were wearing white handkerchief masks across their faces – a symbol of purity? They had a fine array of silk robes fit for an emperor in reds, blues and greens, all with aprons and with beads criss-crossed over their chests, some red, some white. Even coming down the steps was difficult and dangerous. They danced in pairs, their timing immaculate. Some had masks set on their heads at an angle just so that they could see out ahead but not down. Their sleeves were very long indeed, like magicians, and in each hand they held a metal thunderbolt and a bell, sometimes a staff or even the top of a skull. Some of the beads were made from human bones, not to mention, of course, the thigh-bone trumpets. Known as *kang ling* they are 'leg flutes' and are obtained either from learned lamas or criminals. They encourage fearlessness and summon hungry ghosts during the chod ritual. Normally they are only played by monks at special ceremonies outdoors, or for individual *puja* and tantric rituals and are often used with bells or a *damaru*, a skull pellet drum.

There were more black-hat dances, heruka dances, the drum dance, the four-head dance, the Mahakala dance – the great black god of death – and the dance of the four protectors. Then stags and yaks, followed by the ritual slaying of a *torma* – a small human sacrificial offering made from dough – with a three-sided dagger called a *phurba*. The red-coloured figures are made from *tsampa* and butter and laid on a cloth. This act symbolises the sacrifice of the ego, the cutting loose from *samsara*, the cycle of birth and re-birth. In the old pre-Buddhist days this probably would have been a very real human sacrifice. Every aspect was danced. A Buddhist ballet, exhausting to watch.

The monastic orchestra sat to one side in temperatures again well below freezing. The *khenpo*, the head lama, perched on a temporary throne, a dais with all his accoutrements, holy water and peacock feathers, behind an ornate screen of jewels that dangled from the ceiling. His job was to take part at key moments and escort the *torma* with all the bad luck from the previous year.

At the very end of the festival young monks led a procession, dispensing incense from holders, swaying from side to side. They cleared the way, followed closely by dogs. Then three monks with *surnas*, then the *torma*, then the chief monks followed by two monks with cymbals and three monks with drums on staves that they banged in time as they descended through the village. It had all the feeling of a quasi-military procession. Dogs watched and waited for the final denouement, when the *torma* was thrown away out of the village bounds and they could eat the offerings. The dogs knew their time would come and hovered patiently. The sacrificial offering would be ritually cut into pieces and scattered in the four cardinal directions, its destruction representing the killing of the enemies of Buddhism and the purification of the human soul from the three evils of ignorance, jealousy and hatred, which are somewhat similar to the animals at the centre of the wheel of life ... a pig, a snake and a bird, representing the three poisons: ignorance, aversion and attachment.

Then there was a climax of yet more *surnas*, horns, drums, conch shells and cymbals. An ecstasy of sound that would have frightened off a pack of wolves. The *torma* was thrown out with all the evils of the valley trapped inside it, having been offered to Mahakala, the god of death. Dogs descended on it, scrapping as they went.

Suddenly you felt cold and realised that it was getting dark. *Gustor* had ended and slowly all the monks walked back up to the monastery by way of another path up a rocky ridge, their slender forms silhouetted one at a time against the evening sky as they returned exhausted to the monastery. The village and the monks could now rest, assured that all was well till the next festival. Winter could now run its course.

Tsongkhapa and choughs

Karsha was the Gelugpa powerhouse of Zangskar and had lineages derived from Atisha, the 10th-century Bengali teacher who revived or reformed Kadampa monasteries in Tibet. These were linked to the teachings of Tsongkhapa, the man from the Onion Valley, whose lineage was the same as the Dalai Lama's. These things were explained to me in Karsha as I grappled with the many differing paths in Buddhist philosophy. A complex web of thought.

One of Tsongkhapa's first works was called *The Golden Garland of Eloquence*. For Tsongkhapa, calming meditation alone was not sufficient; it should be paired with rigorous, exact thinking 'to push the mind and precipitate a breakthrough in cognitive fluency and insight'. This led to the regime of vigorous dialectical debating that characterised the Gelugpa school. These debates were very physical and required great skill and intuition, as well as sharp, penetrating wisdom and a deep philosophical grasp of the issues being debated. As they were often conducted standing up, they quite literally involved thinking on one's feet. To watch a debate was like seeing a boxing match or a display of martial arts.

One senior monk would be seated while the other stood up and delivered his points like blows, holding his cap in hand, sometimes almost running at the other monk and slapping his hands together to emphasise a philosophical or dialectical point. Socrates would have been impressed. This technique was inherited from the important monastic universities of Taxila in ancient Gandhara and Nalanda in Bihar, where Buddhist philosophy was honed down over many centuries – the Oxford and Cambridge of the East, only much earlier. At their height, Nalanda and Taxila each had about 10,000 students and were effectively monastic cities. Students came from Tibet, Central Asia, China and Korea, and then took the teachings back to their own countries. The Chinese monk Xuanzang, who studied in Nalanda in the 7th century AD described a nine-storey library 'soaring into the clouds'.

To follow a debate was not easy as it took place so quickly. 'I agree,' 'I disagree,' 'I agree but your reasoning is wrong,' or the question was returned in a different way. Maybe closest to high-level ping-pong, this wrestling with key intellectual ideas was very fast and energetic, like verbal duelling or sword fighting. Usually held outside or in the shade of poplar trees, the debating could be lively, intense and humorous, and was how Ladakhis passed their exams, their *mala* or *mani* beads almost used as a weapon, their retorts like sling shots, their minds very sharp. Honed down. Clear like the air.

This deep philosophy resonated within the walls of the monastery as they practised. I was very impressed at their skill and dedication. Tsongkhapa wrote many other works, including *The Ocean of Reasoning, In Praise of Relativity, The Secret Mantra, Stages on the Path* and *Ruthless Logic*. It struck me as remarkable that over five hundred years later these ideas were still at the forefront of modern Buddhist teaching and scholarship, and that they should be debated in such a remote yet peaceful environment. Examination days were keenly anticipated. Translating texts written down by Tsongkhapa kept the Hungarian linguist Csoma de Kőrös very busy indeed.

Philosophy was one thing, but I could not help noticing the alpine choughs out of the corner of my eye. They said that the yellow-billed choughs nested at Gelugpa monasteries and the red-billed species at the Kargyu or red-hat monasteries. The choughs in Karsha were certainly yellow-billed and nested right behind the monastery on cliff ledges close to the roofs of the temples. Their flight was extraordinarily dextrous – they dived down, pirouetted in the air, then came to a sudden halt on a window ledge or balcony of a monk's small cell and fed from their hands.[46] Spent grain from *chang* making was often laid out to dry on yak-hair blankets in the sun. Choughs loved it.

The flight patterns of choughs were extraordinary. An elegant flip, dive and perch. Black stoop, like the downward dive of a hawk as it hones in on its prey. They were fast and spectacular as they fell tumbling out of the sky in their mock fights or dogfights, then pulled their wings in and plummeted down another hundred or so feet like a black bullet, only to zip out of it at the last minute and perch on the balcony of a monk's cell. They knew they were safe, and Buddhism ensured their survival during the winter. Indeed the story was that a chough flew with a small silver cup from Stonde to Karsha. The monks followed the bird, and when it stopped at Karsha it indicated where they should build the new monastery, which they duly did.

I watched for hours as the choughs fell from the skies like small, dark dive bombers. Brilliant fliers, they just loved showing off to the monks, often in pairs, gyrating and twisting, aerobatics of a very high order. Hover, wheel, dive and jostle, riding the air currents when it suited them. They were perky and cheeky, and must have had a great sense of humour. Jib, jive and dive, backing and advancing, freewheeling, rather like monks debating. They tumbled out of the sky, free-falling, then came to a stop, word perfect.

They were real characters and gave the monks something to think about apart from enlightenment, mantras and sutras. Not at all afraid of humans, no doubt each chough chose its monk carefully, but then again each bird could easily have been a monk who had not passed his exams and had to go round the wheel of life again and again.

Many monks I am sure would secretly want to be reborn as a chough. That degree of control and freedom, which they could only achieve in their minds, would surely set them free. Enlightenment on the wing.

Nawang Tharpa and Tibet

On days off I would go out with Phuntsok Dawa. One such visit was to see the famous teacher Geshes Nawang Tharpa in the village of Hongshet a few miles away. At seventy-two, Nawang Tharpa was one of Karsha's most respected lamas. He had spent many years in Tibet at Tashilunpo monastery in Shigatse and at Ganden monastery, where he studied for his Geshe degree, which was more than just a doctorate in philosophy. Half his lifetime was spent studying Buddhist philosophy.

The size of these Tibetan monasteries was almost unimaginable to Zangskari farmers. Tashilunpo housed over four thousand monks, had four Tantric colleges and was the seat of the Panchen Lama. The current Panchen Lama, the 10th incarnation, would have only been a young boy when Nawang Tharpa started his studies. Apparently there was always some friction between the Panchen Lama and the Dalai Lama, politics getting in the way of religion. Or was it the other way round?

Over a million Tibetans are estimated to have died during the 1959 uprising and in the Cultural Revolution (1966–76), most through starvation, disease and torture. There were major crop failures when the Chinese forced the Tibetans to grow wheat six years in a row to feed the Chinese army of occupation, the local peasants knowing full well that only barley would ripen at altitude. Others died fighting in the uprising. Suicide was not uncommon. Many died of cold or hunger on the passes coming out of Tibet. Tibet got a raw deal internationally and still does. After the Korean War (1950–53) where China was fighting UN forces, Tibet could not use the UN as a diplomatic channel to assert its rights to independence. China knew full well that they could get away with invading Tibet. Jigme Taring told me all this over supper in Bristol in 1975. He had been the English Interpreter to the Tibetan Mission to China in February 1950. As he said: 'If only Britain or India had sealed a treaty with Tibet in the years following partition in August 1947 this would have recognised Tibet's sovereignty and rights to independence.' The Korean War started in June 1950. For many years Jigme Taring's wife Rinchen Dolma Taring ran a well-known children's home in Mussoorie for Tibetan refugee children and orphans, many of whom had fled over the mountains to India. There are now many photographs of Jigme Taring on the Pitt Rivers Museum Tibet website. He was also an officer in the Tibetan army. A very dashing young man and good diplomat. I valued his warmth and candour.

Old Tibet was on its last legs. The monastery of Ganden, which means 'joyful' and was similar in size to Tashilunpo, had been founded by Tsongkhapa. Both monasteries suffered badly during the uprising. Temples were reduced to rubble by artillery, their paintings and libraries destroyed, gold Buddhas taken away. Even Tsongkhapa's mummified body was burnt. No wonder Tibetan monks and nuns fled.

Nawang Tharpa was lucky to have visited Lhasa while these monasteries were still functioning. He brought much-needed teaching, enthusiasm and scholarship back to Zangskar. Old Tibet lived on within his memories and devotions, the spirit of debate buried deep within his bones.

Phuntsok Dawa and I walked to Hongshet just as another snowstorm was brewing. Here we saw an important stone with old carvings of men hunting ibex with bows and arrows. Nawang Tharpa was after different game. He hunted the elusive truth with a razor-sharp mind. He lived in a small, cramped room, with only just enough space for three people. Cut into the rock wall were some shelves and on the top lay bundles of scriptures.

Below, tacked to a wooden shelf, a wrinkled white curtain six inches long like a frill, and beneath that, on another shelf, his precious items of worship: a gold casket, holding an image of Buddha, and inside that a photograph of the Dalai Lama, whose image was now banned in Tibet, five small copper bowls and butter lamps, a small torch with a broken glass, a wooden box with Tibetan prints on the outside, a pair of sunglasses, a *dorje* or thunderbolt, and a conical lamp about three inches high with a woollen wick lit with kerosene. To the right, a small fireplace, darkened by many years of cooking. Pots rested on the stove, jutting out. In the far corner, a pile of firewood.

The cell was like a cave, with bare rock visible, and in the dim light sat Nawang Tharpa, very much at home, quietly contemplative, a wisp of a smile gliding across his lips. He held his head to one side and offered us tea. Little would you guess that he had debated with some of the best philosophical minds in Tashilunpo and Ganden and won. Phuntsok sometimes came to this village to buy butter and wool from Sonam Raftan's elder daughter. Philosophy and butter. Spreading knowledge.

Nawang's title *Geshes* means 'virtuous friend'. He had studied for twenty-five years, then taught the lamas in Karsha monastery

Buddhist philosophy and dialectics. The finer points of debating were an acquired art that needed great skill, theatrical ability and an almost encyclopaedic knowledge of the scriptures. His degree would have involved memorising many texts, then debating them rigorously with other monks and masters. These schools of thought originated in India, and were taught in Nalanda and Taxila. Schools of thought such as Madhyamika philosophy and 'The Seven Attributes of the Mind' were the essence of Gandhara.

Nawang wore the red woollen waistcoat common to many lamas, around his shoulders a shawl, his arms bare. He had a smooth face, almost unlined by his thinking and travelling. On his head, a yellow Gelugpa hat. The flaps were often worn upwards, like small wings, which gave the monks the illusion of flying. He was an ambassador from old Tibet.

He sat on a small carpet, his back leaning against a wooden board, and he sipped his tea sparingly. His movements were neat and precise, measured and understated. The habit of a lifetime. Behind him on the bare rock ledge sat his bag of *tsampa* and beside his shoulder, almost unnoticed, was a wooden cupboard, inside which he kept dried apricots.

His eyes were bright. His language had fluency and rhythm, a lilting cadence and intonation, and slight pauses that lent his speech the semblance of poetry. Years of debating had given him deep insights into the Tibetan language and the art of delivery. A master craftsman. Csoma de Kőrös would have loved him.

He also had the habit of holding his left wrist in his right hand and cocked his head slightly to one side like a sparrow as he listened. As he laughed his eyes narrowed and he held his lips in. A man for whom the world held few mysteries. For Nawang Tharpa philosophy had been his daily bread and butter. Lhasa was a golden memory, the last days of the *ancien régime*. It had taken three months to walk there. The cultural and religious destruction of Tibet was a serious loss to the world, and made Nawang's teaching all the more valuable.

Through Phuntsok I asked him what he had studied. There were many topics: Abhidharma, the Compendium and Treasury of Higher Knowledge; Prajnaparamita, the Perfection of Wisdom; Madhyamika, the Middle Way, with works by Nagarjuna, Chandrakirti, Shantideva and Śāntaraksita. Then there was Buddhist logic, Valid Cognition and the Vinaya, the Morality of Vows. Not bad on a diet of *tsampa*. To be a bit more technical he had also studied Prasangika – rejection of essentialism; Conventional valid cognition; Identifying the correct Object of Negation; Lack of Intrinsic Nature; Emptiness; Non-affirming negation and Rejection of the storehouse-consciousness. All wonderful ammunition for winter thought processes. I felt humbled. My degree in civil engineering was by comparison mere chicken feed.

Nawang was a one-man university. I was very impressed with his knowledge, humility and sense of humour. I also remember asking him about modern Western psychology, whether it had any relevance to Buddhist teaching and whether the different models of mind were compatible. He smiled and said that if there was a house with a monkey living in it and the monkey appeared in the western window, everyone would say, 'There's a monkey at the western window.' And if the monkey appeared at the southern window, they would all say, 'Look, there's a monkey at the southern window.' It is always the same monkey, whichever window he is seen at. This put me right back in my place. All is mind, or in this case 'monkey mind'. To find such a man as Nawang Tharpa living in a small village like Hongchet was remarkable. He was indeed a 'virtuous friend'.

Slowly I began to get a feeling for the depth and breadth of Tibetan Buddhist thought, its vast potential, its ritual structures, the innate wisdom preserved in the teaching of the monks. A mind that can debate with itself on a rational level is to be admired at these altitudes; the intellectual achievement of Buddhism is staggering and the commitment of its followers obvious.

> No flies on Nawang –
> No wonder Zangskar has
> A reputation for scholars.
>> In the depths of a snowstorm
>> We went in search of butter –
>> And found wisdom.

Old frescos

After meeting Nawang I really wanted to see the old frescos, the wall paintings in the lower temple at Karsha monastery. They were not generally on display, so Phuntsok Dawa had to find the monk with the key. We watched as he carefully unlocked the old Ladakhi padlock on a hasp set close to the floor. The door creaked open. We then entered a large room but had to go one stage lower down. In the corner a small wooden hatch was opened up, a bit like entering the underworld or going down into a mineshaft.

I turned around and climbed backwards down a steep, sloping ladder carved out of a solid tree trunk, large notches hewn out of poplar. One step at a time, a slightly strange feeling as I entered the darkness of the void not knowing quite what to expect. There were no windows. I was swallowed up by the dark. Only a small, dusty chink of light could be seen from the central section of a doorway that was permanently closed. Dry and dusty. There was the slight musty smell of grain, for it was a granary as well. A world apart, more like a cave than an art gallery. Yet nothing could have prepared me for the grandeur, beauty and scale of these frescos.[47] One of the side walls had an ominous crack in it and there was evidence that water had been coming in from above for years.

We were now accompanied by the monk, who was called Lobsang Gelik. He had a candle, I had a small torch. When you first entered the temple it took a while for your eyes to adjust to the darkness. Slowly your peripheral night vision came into focus and you began to appreciate the sheer scale of the frescos. The candle guttered and then the yellow flame stood still in the half-light. Momentarily you caught sight of painted faces.

Lobsang and Phuntsok went on ahead, muttering prayers and mantras, nodding and touching their foreheads before each deity. I walked along behind with my torch and saw the images one by one – a subterranean vault filled with rich treasures, a magical realm of colour that lay beneath the surface of daily life, a kind of Buddhist Lascaux. Religion and art joined at the hip. Invaluable lessons from the past.

Extraordinary faces that had been smouldering for six hundred years peered out of the darkness and greeted you. Ancient faces that floated in mid-air, wise beyond words, contemplating the universe, their penetrating gaze seeing right through you, staring into the void, the emptiness of a darkened hall. Walls of silence, old paintings. The regime of colour, coveted, articulated. Countless monks would have meditated in front of these images. I was very taken with them. They spoke to me.

After a while the faces became familiar. If they were in Italy the work would be called *fresco secco*, painted onto dry walls carefully prepared and smoothed down beforehand. Dry not wet. Vast murals depicting the lives of the Buddha – various incarnations, past lives, future lives – old teachers, revered philosophers, Tantric deities, famous yogins and meditators. The Buddha lived on in many guises, his life re-created in visual form, exquisitely drawn and painted. Images revered and worshipped, the deities now old and a little cracked in places. It was like a frozen film, a silent movie, a composite array of characters, a cast list, *Who Was Who*. A Buddhist *Tatler*. Faces blended into the ritual landscape of mantras, incense and chanting, early Buddhism laid out in one vast wall painting as if they were still teaching and meditating. Finely drawn figures, inner diligence and spiritual authority, their state of mind on display. Years of contemplation worn lightly, the long wall from side to side, top to bottom, covered in figures, some faded, some scuffed, some cracked, some almost rubbed away, shimmering in the candlelight, floating, hovering cross-legged as if levitating. Teaching.

The depth of each meditation was transposed in rock colours, paint that had been ground down by hand, fine base colours, rich in reds, browns, greens and blues, figures that came from the mountains themselves. You were in touch with earthy gods. Buddhist geology. They had a refinement and life of their own, painted by skilled masters who worked in mobile gangs. Journeymen on the move. Remarkable works of art.

I followed Phuntsok and Lobsang, trying to listen to what they were saying as they moved along the wall. This was what I had come to see. This was what I had come to photograph. A vast illuminated manuscript filled with teachers and saints, gurus, leading lights from the time of Nalanda and Taxila. In the centre Shakyamuni himself. Two and a half thousand years of history.

I saw the Buddhas one by one by torchlight and candlelight, also conscious of an old man taking grain from the granary down below, climbing up another ladder carved out of a solid tree trunk. He talked to himself as he did so. On his back a sack of grain. Each step accompanied by an epithet. *Konchok sum*, the three jewels, the three truths, Buddha, *dharma*, *sangha*. A kind of trinity: body, mind and soul. As well as *shab, shab, shabas*. It was hard work but he did it willingly, carrying up sacks of grain. Farming and philosophy interlinked. This was his monastery. It was his grain that kept the wheel of life turning here.

Nagarjuna and emptiness

The figures were drawn then painted on a reddish-brown ground, interspersed with hills and clouds, forests, tigers, snow lions and elephants. Slight cracks and surface imperfections appeared. Then there were deeper cracks to do with the structure of the building itself. Some of the figures were severe, some calm, some contemplating life happily, some with jewels, some with tousled hair, some with specific hats shaped by the various sects and beliefs. There were lotuses and panoplies, *apsaras*, musicians and their raunchy wives, animals and birds, textiles. This was a world far removed from Zangskar. A film that stopped in mid-stream. Eyes that looked right through you. It was the eyes that told how far you had come along the journey.

The *arhats*, the saints, the followers, the worthy ones, the ones who had crossed over and achieved enlightenment lived in paradise. Bakula was one of them ... Here was the Buddhist story, the pageant writ large for both monks and lay people, and now for Western visitors. Some parts were the worse for wear, scuffed and rubbed away; others were covered in what looked like mud from the damp seeping down from the roof above during monsoon time. Permanence and impermanence. Form and emptiness. Music to my ears. Even the sound of the hand bell represented the void and the clapper represented form. Wisdom and compassion. The epitome of emptiness. Yab-yum – male and female conjoined, and not just at the hip. Compassion and wisdom. Spiritual union. Bliss.

I could feel the reverence of the painters, the devout skill honed down over many years. I tried to take all this in but the darkness made it very difficult. Yet this added to the sense of mystery, where you caught haunting glimpses of certain faces, never able to see the whole wall at once. How they painted it I knew not, unless they put the roof on afterwards. It was a rare privilege to see such paintings in such circumstances, like having an entire art gallery to yourself.

It was perhaps remarkable that the walls of this lower temple had stood this long. That was quite an achievement. Mud and stone. There were gods with blue arms and faces, dancers, swords of wisdom, pierced and extended ear lobes, thrones and diadems. The patina of six hundred years. There were wrathful kings of the four quarters riding horses and snow lions. Flowers, trees and acolytes, a bevy of scholars and monks in paradise. Something to aim for ...

Here was the philosopher Nagarjuna in all his glory with a canopy of nine serpents and a chequered robe. The serpents were *nagas*, cobras, a deity that took up residence in the snake. His philosophy has survived in many forms for nearly two thousand years, since the 2nd century CE

Nagarjuna's philosophy is well known to those on the Buddhist path:

All is possible when emptiness is possible.
Nothing is possible when emptiness is impossible.
Truth and causality. The two truths –
    conventional and ultimate.
Prajnaparamita – the perfection of wisdom.
Madhyamika, the Middle Way, giving way to Sunyata.
Causality has its own path,
Dependent origination – the essence of all things.
The emptiness of emptiness.

These pithy Buddhist aphorisms trip off the end of the tongue like peas in a pod. Each has its own inner truth.

Whatever is dependent arising
We declared that to be emptiness.
That is dependent designation,
And is itself the Middle Way.

Thoughts deeply embedded in Karsha monastery. Here each face was clearly defined, the robes patched green, red and white, with the hands in teaching posture, the *nagas* wide-eyed and more like lap dogs. Enormous wisdom, enormous presence, penetrating gaze. Compassion, deep wisdom. The *mudra*, hand gestures a key indicator. Thumb and forefinger together for teaching. Seeds of thought, seeds of enlightenment, seeds of wisdom just beginning to sprout.

So from Nalanda to Karsha, Nagarjuna's image was laced with philosophy, lock, stock and barrel. The great teaching. So much philosophy in that one portrait, and the whole wall covered in paintings. The torch flitted across other faces large and small. With these philosophers looking after you, what was there to fear? How many temples in Europe were laden with images of philosophers? And then there were the Tantric consorts Green Tara and White Tara, alongside other fine drawings of horses and elephants, kings and courtiers. A real circus, a cast of thousands.

The darkness felt very alive, but the paintings were I felt also in great danger as the wall on the far side looked as if it might collapse. There were large cracks appearing and mud stains coming from the ceiling, from where the monsoon was creeping in.

Here was Marpa, here was Milarepa, here was Atisha. Here was Amitabha. You learnt to recognise them by their hair and certain characteristics – their *mudras* and hand gestures. Then, next to Amitabha, was a very fine face that caught my eye time and time again. I was drawn to this magnificent figure, which was called Vairocana with three faces – the one who comes from the sun, the flower-garland sutra, the Universal Buddha from whom all Buddhas emanate. There was even a fourth face, much smaller, above the main head. As if there were four parts to the mind.

Vairocana was hailed as the source of enlightenment who resided free from causation and conditions, thus expressing Sunyata – emptiness, the very thing I had come to seek. The wisdom of wilderness. The silent passage of time. Contemplating the void. Philosophy in three or was it four dimensions? I could look at that face for hours on end, absorbing its depth of contemplation. I really felt that I was exploring the mind. This face breathed emptiness.

The two side faces in half-profile at an angle on either side, looking outwards. They were unusual. They had real characteristics, reminding me of Giotto drawing real faces from life, with all the skill of perspective. Almost a sense of longing, a distance and depth, a real achievement that may well have evolved from a late

Kashmiri style. Very talented artists, these followers in the foot-steps of Gandhara. Uncle Kenny would have been very pleased, revelling in their craftsmanship and artistic achievements. This wide and adventurous mural, these frescos – a fine sight that made the whole journey worthwhile.

Permanence and impermanence. Illusion and reality. Exquisite Buddhist art. Zangskar at its best. A rare moment in time. Timeless.

Karsha Lonpo

But there was also an aristocratic edge to Karsha. Phuntsok Dawa's brother-in-law, Sonam Wangchuk, had a family temple set high above the village close to the nunnery on the opposite side of the ravine to the monastery. The paintings there were even older than those in the lower temple and reputedly painted by Lotsawa Rinchen Zangpo (CE 958–1055) who had painted the fine murals in Alchi. Early Buddhist art which had first attracted Uncle Kenny to Ladakh and encouraged him to try climbing the Zoji La. In Sonam's temple there was an inscription but it was dark and too scuffed to read in that light. The temple may date from Lotsawa's time but some art experts thought it was similar in style to a temple in Wanla. Old temples in Ladakh are rare treasures. Apart from Alchi, there are old temples at Sumdo and Mangyu. The wooden carving at Sumdo was believed to be 8th or 9th century CE. One of the oldest wooden carvings in the whole Himalaya and made from juniper.

Sonam, known as the Lonpo of Karsha, the Earl of Karsha, was a tall, handsome man about forty-five years old, with a fine chis-elled face. He was not just a farmer and landowner, but an astrol-oger, historian, teacher of Tibetan and an *amchi* – a Tibetan doctor. A Zangskari Renaissance man. Each summer he went walking in the mountains to collect special herbs, which he then dried. He had a vast collection of medicines that he kept in various leather pouches, wooden boxes or just wrapped in paper. The smell was wonderfully aromatic. It was a great gift to be able to cure your fellow villagers with herbs from the mountains. With Phuntsok as interpreter we discussed many things and enjoyed each other's company. Sonam asked me just as many questions as I asked him ...

Slowly I pieced together the general outlines of Tibetan medicine. Sonam said that everything was made up of five elements: fire, earth, water, air and aether. Tibetan medicine aimed to rebalance the patient with mantras, together with a change of diet and lifestyle. It was very different to Western medicine, as all depended on the relationship between body and mind, acute observation and an encyclopaedic knowledge.

At times Sonam became animated and kept looking at me, hoping I would understand the translations. Tibetan medicine was a mixture of Chinese and Ayurvedic medicine. *Amchis* studied for about twelve years. For the diagnosis they took eight pulses, four in each wrist, much as acupuncturists do. He grabbed my wrist and showed me how he did it. He carefully took the pulse at slightly different spots on the wrist. Each pulse related to a specific organ, some weak, some strong, some hot, some cool. The diagnosis involved the three humours: wind, bile and phlegm. Disease was caused by their imbalance.

He took a great pride in his work. The key aspect, he said, was to treat the underlying psychological causes of an illness rather than the ailment itself, a fascinating approach. Payment was often in kind. I was impressed.

Treatment came in many forms, he added, and medicinal compounds were made up accordingly, mostly herbal preparations and powders, pills and pastes that could be smeared on the skin. A rich field of cures, psychological as well as medicinal. And there, hanging up at the back of Sonam's room, supervising his work, was the image of Sangye sMenla – the Medicine Buddha, the master of blue lapis lazuli light. Rich is the world of the amchi. I once asked a Tibetan doctor why there was so much mental illness in the West. He thought for a while, then said three words: 'Too much choice.'

Sonam then showed me his temple, which had belonged to his family for nearly a thousand years. The walls were covered in fine old mandalas and at the far end was a tall statue of Avalokitesvara, the Buddha of Compassion with eleven heads, the patron saint of the Dalai Lama. Indeed for many the Dalai Lama was the living reincarnation of Avalokitesvara, whose mantra is *Om mani padme hum*.

The Hungarian linguist

When I mentioned Csoma de Kőrös, Sonam Wangchuk's face lit up.[48] It was as if it were only yesterday that the Hungarian linguist had been studying in Zangskar. He proudly told me that his great-great-uncle, a monk called Sangye Phuntsok, had taught Csoma de Kőrös Tibetan. Sonam smiled when he talked about Csoma. One hundred and fifty years had passed in a twinkling. 'Zangskar,' he said, 'was once again opening its doors to Western scholars and adventurers.'

I developed a great admiration for this lonely, dedicated Hungarian scholar. There are few images of Csoma, but one drawing shows that he had thin features and was neatly dressed with necktie and jacket. He was so fascinated by the East that he walked all the way from Göttingen University to India via

Persia and Afghanistan, searching for the origins of the Hungarian language and the roots of the Hungarian people. Brave man.

In Zangskar Csoma was known as the 'foreign pupil', and he stayed with Sangye Phuntsok in Zangla. His room in the old palace was even smaller than mine: 9ft by 9ft. He slept on sheepskins. Later on, from August 1825 till October 1826, he stayed in Phuktal monastery, experiencing all four seasons. Phuktal is set in a large cave above a river in the south-east of Zangskar, one of the most dramatic locations in the whole Himalaya.

Down in Calcutta Csoma eventually published his Tibetan–English dictionary. Without his pioneering work, Tibetan studies would be much poorer. The 'foreign pupil' had come up trumps, Transylvania's loss being Ladakh and Tibet's gain. Sadly, Csoma died of fever in Darjeeling in 1842 on his way to Lhasa. But of the Zangskari winter, the Zangskaris and their culture, Csoma left no trace at all. No diary, no record, no sketches. Not even any children.

The nunnery

After seeing Sonam Wangchuk's family temple, meeting the lama and discussing Csoma de Kőrös, we visited the small nunnery nearby. Sonam had supported it in its early days and one of his daughters later became a nun. Sonam also later became a monk. Buddhism ran through his family's veins. The nunnery was close to the site of Karsha's first monastery and old castle. Crumbling walls. Old statues. Old ruins. Old beliefs. New hope.

The nunnery was started in the 1950s and had about half a dozen nuns. The head nun, Ani Yeshe, had been ordained by the Abbot of Ganden in Tibet prior to the Chinese invasion, and

Nawang Tharpa helped them to set the place up. I was very impressed by Ani Yeshe and these nuns. Tough as old nuts. They had shaven heads, hardworking hands – many were used to manual labour – and cheerful faces. They wore their smiles gladly, and I admired their tenacity and learning. So instead of being married to two brothers they had 'married' the Buddha. Or were they sisters of Tara? At least these nuns could stay in Zangskar, keep in touch with their family, and see their nephews and nieces grow up. They enjoyed a privileged role in the community, although second class compared with the monks, which seemed unfair as they studied just as hard. They were very brave and determined.

In Karsha both monks and nuns had their own watering holes in the stream below, and they each had a long, steep, zig-zag path to climb back up each day carrying the water. Celibacy was a two-edged sword. Monks one side of the ravine, nuns the other, enlightenment somewhere in the void in between. They met every morning to gather water, their icy water holes fifty yards apart.

In summer, close to where they drew water, there was a small, ingenious water wheel with an eccentric cam and extension rod to which a large piece of sandalwood was attached. This was an incense mill, and the sandalwood went backwards and forwards, rubbing on a large, flat stone. The fine fragments were gathered in a muslin cloth downstream, then dried and compounded with many different herbs to make Zangskari incense, which was burnt at festivals. Ingenious. Everything was homemade, even the printing of books with wooden blocks, and the making of glue, paper and ink. Zangskari philosophy – self-sufficiency.

The naib tehsildar

Occasionally there were parties in Karsha, and I attended one given by Nawang Lawchok, the deputy or *naib tehsildar*. Nawang had grown slightly rotund on government pay – not for him, the hardships of the fields. Office work and bureaucracy had their attractions. I found him very hospitable and jovial. For ten years he had been *naib tehsildar*, and in that time he had seen five *tehsildars* come and go. They would stay for two years and when time was up you did not see them for dust. Zangskar was an easy posting as there was nothing much to do and crime rates were very low. But the winter was hard for men used to the milder climate of Jammu and Kashmir.

Nawang's father had been a government official but during the troubles, which followed Partition in 1947, there was war in Kashmir and Ladakh. Pakistani troops held Kargil and entered Zangskar. This was 1948. Nawang's father was effectively taken hostage by Pakistani troops while on his way to Kargil to negotiate new taxes. He was leaving the valley with two other important Buddhists and an escort of Gilgit Scouts, but they very soon realised that they had all been tricked and were under arrest. They had a fair idea what was going to happen to them, so they tried to escape. Nawang's father was shot, along with his assistant. Their bodies were thrown into the river and were swept downstream. The third man, the headman of a village called Langmi a few miles from Karsha, saw it all happen from behind a large boulder. Luckily he survived to tell the tale. A UN-negotiated cease fire came into effect in January 1949 but the remaining Gilgit scouts who were holed up in Stagrimo monastery did not believe it and hung on for many more months. Five Buddhist women were killed by snipers near Pipiting when going down to the river to get water in winter. Was that a war crime I wonder? Zangskar has had its fair share of raids and invasions: Mongols, Moghuls, Kulu wallahs, Kishtwar wallahs, Baltis, Khampas, Dogras, Pakistanis, Kashmiris and now Westerners ...

Nawang welcomed me in and sat down on the carpet. He called for his eldest daughter, who brought in some more firewood. There was a round stove with a pipe that reached up into the roof. Around the walls were the eight auspicious symbols painted in many colours. Beside the window lay his law books and a dusty pot of ink. Sadly he had failed his *teshsildar*'s exam and did not have the heart to retake it, for if he passed he would have been posted out of the valley, something he did not want. It was far more important that he stayed. He knew Zangskar very well indeed.

Master of the jerrycan

News of the party got around. The *naib tehsildar*'s house was well known. In came three policemen, who were warmly greeted – Jamyang Dorje together with Hamid and Namgyal, his two constables, plus the radio wallah, the headman of Sani, a Ladakhi vet and a doctor. Towards evening the party started.

Abdul Hamid was a Pathan. He had an enormous handlebar moustache and shining white teeth, and had brought along an empty jerrycan to play that had a resonance all of its own. He sat down with it upturned between his knees, patted it affectionately, then as he played his head slowly moved from side to side. He got all manner of interesting notes and rhythms out of the metal, and with his eyes closed he entered the rhythms even more deeply, at times going into a trance. Wonderful and completely unexpected. We could have been back in the 18th century. Sufi drumming

from an Afghan policeman in the dead of winter in the depths of
the Buddhist mountains. What could be better?

At Partition, Hamid's family had been trapped on the Indian
side of the Kashmir inner line and he never went back to
Afghanistan. He was the tallest policeman in Ladakh, at over six
feet two inches tall, and if there was any trouble the police just
sent him around and then all became quiet. One smile from
Hamid and you felt better.

Silver cups full of *chang* appeared. Hamid beat his jerrycan
once, looked around and then burst out laughing. He sang the
love songs of Ladakh and Zangskar, as well as those of his home-
land. Occasionally he would strike a pose with his head tilted to
one side, eyes afire, hand poised, then laugh and continue to sing
or play. He was a true performer. People spontaneously started
dancing to the Ladakhi chant of *Shab, shab, shabas, shab, shab,
shabas*. Sometimes he raised his eyebrows and finished with a
flurry of his fingers. Everyone loved Hamid. Impromptu singing
and dancing were among the most endearing of all Ladakhi traits.
He was from a long line of singer-composers that kept people
entertained up and down the North-West Frontier. But who
would sing of Hamid?

When the party was over, ten of us slept in the small room.
Hamid snored. Namgyal grunted in his sleep. No one got up
early.

Fasting and fire puja

The next major festival, held in March, was *Monlam* – the Great
Prayer Festival – which went on for ten days. Butter and dough
sculptures were made, many prayers said, and hundreds if not
thousands of butter lamps lit.

Monlam was followed by a two-day fast, when all the women in Karsha in their finest clothes and *perags* sat in the monastery courtyard all day and meditated. Here vast embroidered *tangkas* – about 12–15ft across and 40ft high – were raised and then suspended from the roof of the main temple. Sometimes two *tangkas* were hung alongside one another. A team of six monks was responsible for raising them, a difficult job superintended from the courtyard floor by a senior monk. Each *tangka* was held in position for about three or four hours, then lowered. A source of inspiration and visualisation for both monks and villagers.

Sitting in front of the *tangkas* were monks, a few nuns and hundreds of women in their finest *perags* meditating on the courtyard floor. Row after row, a sea of blue, turquoise and lapis lazuli, goatskins and *gonches*. A remarkable sight accompanied by a low murmur, like a swarm of bees, as they said their prayers. This festival of *nyungney* – a two-day fasting retreat – was a powerful purification practice that brought much benefit to those undertaking the visualisations, helping develop an understanding of compassion towards those who were less well off than us. By fasting, the body and mind began to understand what it was like not to have food and water. In Zangskar that was a daily problem, so most of the women had no need to be reminded. The period towards the end of every winter was itself a fast, and many remembered the long winter when all the horses and animals died. Food to them was sacred, each jerrycan of water brought up from the river a constant reminder of how much work went into survival. Sharing food was a sacred action, a part of their daily bread or *tsampa*. This couple of days was a rest, a relief from the daily chores.

The women sat in long rows behind a phalanx of monks, their devotion remarkable. Two days of fasting, dawn to dusk, repeating mantras and visualising the emanation of the Buddha in patchwork. Avalokitesvara. It was a spectacle worthy of admiration. To tame and train one's mind was the most important teaching. Several dogs lay flat out in the sun, basking, completely oblivious to the women's devotion. Maybe they were practising the art of dream yoga.

After the second day there was an initiation for the villagers and a few days later a Heruka empowerment. Heruka was a wrathful deity who represented the embodiment of indivisible bliss and emptiness. The fifth day was Heruka burnt-offering day, on the 15th of the first month. Full moon again. Two or three great piles of grain were burnt, and melted butter and ghee were ceremonially poured onto the pile, which was started with dried yak dung, as if all the fruits of the fields and summer pasture were being offered up. In a land where it was hard to produce food it seemed on one level a complete waste of resources.

Long lines of senior monks wore special headgear, with five Buddhas strapped around their heads. They used the bell and *dorje*, the thunderbolt, genuflecting as they chanted. It was a sobering thought that so much grain was being burnt, a bit like a funerary pyre for the ego. A kind of sacrifice. A chod ritual. There was the smell of charred grain and the smoke wreathed around the monks, as if they were themselves being cremated. Annihilation. Loss of self. Burnt offering. This was the fire *puja*.

The 'mother' field – mid-April

Winter continued. Another month passed, supplies dwindled, rooftops became bare. Then, as if to counterbalance the burnt offerings, the next celebration was held not in the monastery but in the fields, even though they were still covered in snow. This was a symbolic ploughing of the 'mother' field, the home field, waking the earth up long before winter ended. Monks stood to one side and a pair of yaks were harnessed to the plough. The plough was seen as an arrow and offerings were made. Everybody watched. It awakened the spirits of the soil. The furrow of intent. A man held the plough and another led the animals. The earth was hard, the ground frozen. The furrow was symbolically ploughed and the power of the earth revealed, woken up. A statement of intent. A rite of spring. Then the yaks were let go.

When the real ploughing started a month or so later, they ploughed in arcs not straight lines. It was a fine sight. Women often went in front, broadcasting seed, and men would sing beautiful songs to their yaks as they ploughed their fields and scattered. It was as if the song were waking up the earth from its slumbers, as if the yaks and the passage of the plough scratched the back of the earth and let the lords of the soil know that it was time they awoke, that the snow would soon be gone, the seeds would come and barley would grow, soon to be rippling in the breeze. The ploughing brought everyone back down to earth.

O you beautiful yak!
Please walk fast so that our fields will be sown quickly.
O you beautiful yak, your horns are so long that they
    reach the sky
And your tail is very long.
Please plough our fields quickly, then you can go onto
    the high pastures
And eat flowers and sit by the water on the green grass.
O you beautiful yak. Please plough our fields quickly.

6

WOLVES AND AVALANCHES

April–May 1977

Sleeping rough

After six weeks in Karsha I went back to Padum and started planning my final winter venture. It was already April and time was running out. I wanted to make a long solo ski trip while snow conditions were still good. Something memorable. Something remarkable. A venture over the main Himalayan passes to the south would be too high and too risky. But the route back over the Pense La to Suru, via Rangdom and the Nun Kun massif, would be a fine way to end the winter. I had no idea how deep the snow would be on the pass – maybe thirty feet deep – or what the avalanche risk would be. Like the *chadar*, this last venture was to test me to the very limits.

Over the winter I had made several experimental journeys around Zangskar with both skis and snowshoes. These trips were very enjoyable. Cross-country skiing was a fine art, and it was very satisfying cutting through virgin snow, leaving two trails, two parallel lines, a long signature that usually ended in a flourish. But if it was snowing your trail disappeared very quickly. You learnt to conserve energy, not expend it – altitude and extreme cold saw to that. A long ski journey with real purpose, that was what I wanted. Economy of effort was paramount and carrying the pack not easy. It hampered your movements, the straps pulling on your shoulders. It came always down to lightness, strength and flexibility. Stamina was a vital ingredient. No one had brought skis into Zangskar before, so this was new territory. The wooden Norwegian skis were good for downhill and contouring, but *langlauf* – cross-country – skis were lighter and easier to use at altitude.

Crucially, I had to learn how to survive in the open if something went wrong or if the weather suddenly changed. Understanding snow conditions was vital. Old Zangskaris pointed to the tops of *chortens* and told you that the snow was sometimes as high as that – i.e. ten or even twelve feet deep. Narrow gorges were a death trap in spring. Two Muslims had been killed the year before in an avalanche triggered by their own shots while out hunting ibex. They were swept to their deaths onto the frozen river far below. Instant karma. I would avoid narrow gorges from now on.

Sleeping rough in low temperatures without a tent was an art form. Snow could work to your advantage. As winter progressed, strong winds packed it into ridges, hard crusts, scudding waves rather like sand dunes, running in the same direction as the wind. *Sastrugi*. Beautiful, curved and sinuous. Windslab. The snow creaked and had a life of its own. The real advantage was that if you had a saw you could cut snow blocks to build a shelter. I also had an ice axe and a snow shovel to dig a tunnel. *Voilà* ...

The snow blocks were about 18in by 12in by 6in thick, so I made a 6ft tunnel with an entrance arch and wall. Not quite an igloo but good enough for an emergency bivvy. It took half an hour to build, just as the light was failing. I was pleased with the results. Shelter from the strong winds that swept down from the glaciers.

So to really test myself I slept out in the snow for two nights in a row. No tent. No stove. Nothing apart from the sleeping bag. Temperatures about -25°C with a strong wind. Bracing … which, with the wind chill, brought it down to about -40°C, the same as -40°F, the magical cross-over point, Celsius and Fahrenheit agreeing with one another for a change.

Sleeping in a cave on the *chadar* with twenty others and a fire was fine, but sleeping out in the open on your own was something else. I was asking for trouble. The second night was spent in a shallow irrigation ditch. I stayed awake most of the night, moving my toes and massaging my feet to prevent frostbite.

These short experimental journeys were essential. I used to go out skiing for hours on end. Sometimes at night, under a full moon and the bright canopy of stars, silence and solitude were indistinguishable, as if they had an energy all of their own. They flowed through your veins. Brilliant, the band of the Milky Way. A glittering river of light.

Sometimes, as I returned to Padum after midnight, I could hear monks in Stagrimo monastery high above the village with their trumpets and drums, conch shells and horns, a strange winter orchestra summoning up the spirits. Knowing that I could sleep rough and survive in the snow was vital for my long ski journey. It gave me great inner confidence. I would certainly need it.

The path to Dzongkhul

But I also had to test the snowshoes. Lesson one: snowshoeing with a heavy pack was not easy. Lesson two: getting the rhythm right was very important. Lesson three: don't trip up. If the snow on the pass was still deep powder I could be in deep trouble.

So I tried to get to a remote monastery called Dzongkhul, up a side valley leading to the Umasi La. But to reach Dzongkhul in winter was ambitious, so I took a sleeping bag and spare food for emergencies. Very different to going down the *chadar*, which had at times taken on an almost holiday atmosphere. This was much more testing, but at least I could turn round if conditions got too bad. This route was used in summer by men coming over the Umasi La from Paddar. When crossing glaciers they wore home-made grass sandals, woven and twisted to help them grip on the ice. Works of art, which when worn smooth or broken, were simply thrown away.

Dzongkhul was the spiritual home of the 11th-century yogin Naropa, who lived in a cave. The cave where he meditated was itself set into the cliff. It was very difficult to get to but they have now constructed hundreds of steps and built a small retreat house where you look out onto a tumbling thousand-foot waterfall. Down in Sani there was a shrine dedicated to him with his statue, which was shown once a year in June for the flower festival where the monks read the scriptures. Mind over matter.

Naropa was almost as famous as Guru Rinpoche. The six yogas of Naropa were highly respected and involve *tummo* – the yoga of inner heat – followed by the yogas of the illusory body, clear light and dream state, as well as Bardo yoga and the transference of consciousness. Heady stuff. I was definitely on the bottom rung of the Buddhist ladder, but there was nothing illusory about deep snow. Inner heat would have been very useful when sleeping rough.

I did try the heat yoga once or twice, which made sense in the winter – 'filling the vase', as they say. Sitting in a meditation posture, breathing in and then trapping the air in your lungs for as long as possible. But you have to be properly taught, make the correct Tibetan visualisations, then not breathe a word.

My knowledge of Naropa came mostly from Dr John Crook, a dedicated Tibetan Buddhist in Bristol, and a paperback by Herbert V. Guenther in Saskatchewan that contained a translation of Naropa's biography and an essay on Tantra. Three things I noticed. First, Naropa was said to be buried in the Kanishka monastery in Zangskar, which was Sani. Second, a few of Naropa's words struck a chord: 'Objective knowledge may be entirely accurate without, however, being entirely important and only too often misses the heart of the matter.' I quite liked that. Third, a quote from Tilopa to Naropa: 'Look into the mirror of your mind, the place of dreams. The mysterious home of the *dakini*,' a phrase often repeated in various psychological situations when Tilopa was testing Naropa. 'The mysterious home of the *dakini*' had a certain ring about it. A *dakini* is a female practitioner who has cut through the deceptions of human life and is depicted as a raunchy topless sky dancer. No mention of snowshoes.

But the real problem for me was not Naropa's meditations or the *dakinis* but deep powder snow that got deeper as I went up the valley. A bit like quicksand, it can impede your journey. Snowshoes were very good to start with but I could not manage to get up much speed. The Labrador snowshoes needed more skill as they were larger and hinged on your toes. I sank in less, but I was a bit clumsy with them. The smaller Yorkshire ones were more handy among the rocks. Walking speed was fine, but my movements were restricted. The secret was good rhythm, an acquired skill uphill with a heavy pack at altitude.

The clouds came lower and lower until I was caught out in a snowstorm. So I spent a night in the village of Ating with one of Sonam Stopgyas's uncles. The next day snow clouds still swirled around, but I pushed on up the valley as I was only going about five miles. I would give it a go.

I took both sets of snowshoes with me. Progress was slow. After an hour or so the snow came down even more heavily and I could hardly see the route. A real blizzard. I followed my nose up the side valley. No path to speak of between the rocks. The snow-shoes did well, but it was tiring.

After two or three miles it became obvious that to reach Dzongkhul was just not possible. I had got halfway. In the white-out I began to lose my sense of orientation, and realised that I could easily miss the monastery and carry on into the 'cloud of unknowing'. To be exhausted and cold without shelter in powder snow was not clever. The snow was thigh deep and coming down fast. Flakes were getting in through my snow goggles. I reckoned that even if I got to the monastery I would then be trapped for a week or two without my own food. So I turned around. Naropa would have to wait for another day.

In fact the path to Dzongkhul was closed for another month. I had missed my chance but learnt some valuable lessons. Trial but no error. Both pairs of snowshoes were good. The reindeer gut and birch Labrador snow shoes if used well would have been magnificent on the flat; the Yorkshire ones were for trudging. I had a pack. I trudged.

Snow puja

After these basic lessons of trial and error, I was confident that when the time was right I could ski out of the valley and survive, even in bad conditions. I just had to bide my time. In late April the days were longer and the snow hardened up. Metamorphosis had done its job, another transformation worthy of Ovid's attention.

Skiing out of the valley was still a major challenge. It was something I had dreamed of doing. No one had been over the pass with skis before, but what concerned me at the time of the ritual ploughing was the lack of consistent good snow. Even the monks in Karsha were concerned. They needed more snow to fill the snowfields high above the village. So they had a special all-day *puja*. This was nothing short of black magic. Cymbals, pipes, horns and drums, even skull-pellet drums and thigh-bone trumpets, fanatically invoking the mountain spirits to bring more snow. Impressive. A deep connection with the landscape and weather. Invoking gods of good fortune, the old mountain gods of ancient Tibet.

At first I was sceptical, not sure how a group of musicians and monks could influence Himalayan weather patterns. Whether it was Buddhism or Central Asian shamanism mattered not. But it had the desired effect, and sure enough more snow came. Dark clouds. Then on 26 April snow fell. Bucketloads of it. Necromancy, or just good luck and timing? Guru Rinpoche was on their side and mine.

Back in Padum I left the Norwegian skis behind and also the snowshoes. I opted for the lightweight cross-country skis, but they needed repair. Going down the *chadar* I had worn a quarter of an inch off the soles of my ski boots, so the clips at the front end were very loose, which was not good. I went to see Ringzin the blacksmith. He cut some metal plate to put on either side of the three-pinned toe clasps. This plate compensated for the loss of leather and worked fine.

To ski out over the Pense La down to Suru was a hundred miles. Five days' skiing, I reckoned, twenty miles a day. Phuntsok Dawa saw me off and suggested that I stay with a friend of his: Beda Amchi in Abrang. A quick meal of dahl, rice and *sabzi* at his house, a little *chang*, a nip of *arak*, a firm handshake or two, and then off the following morning. Tashi Namgyal asked me to find some more Lipton tea.

The yaks looked on in amazement as I left. I had weighed the pack carefully and then locked my room with the padlock. A kilo or two of dried apricots would have been very useful right now ... very useful indeed. Orange anorak, sleeping bag, rucksack, red duvet jacket, Dachstein mitts. Food in three bags, milk powder, chocolate powder and sugar for emergencies. Biscuits. Bread. *Tsampa*.

The crisp, almost metallic sound of hard snow rasping under skis was magic to my ears. Sharp sliding, cutting edge, like tearing sailcloth or canvas. Gliding forward, satisfying rhythm, my ski sticks made their own journey on either side, leaving a trail of oval eyes that looked back at me.

Ibex soup

First stop, Sani. The villagers looked at me a little oddly, but they were now used to my antics. At first they thought it very rude of me to have slept out in the snow instead of accepting their hospitality. The headman Nawang Chastor was very helpful. I had tea with him. Later I helped him out as he had kidney stones from drinking too much Tibetan salt tea. Diuretics can be useful at altitude.

I never tired of visiting Sani, with its half-rounded Kanishka *chorten* and the remains of the Buddha. Many artefacts, ideas and even monks had migrated north over hundreds of years from ancient Gandhara to Kashmir and then to Ladakh where they found sanctuary. Perfumed again. The very centre of Zangskar. Maybe Naropa was 'looking into the mirror of his mind, the place of dreams, the mysterious home of the *dakini*'.

That first day I pushed on and crossed the frozen river beside the bridge near Tungri, where the ice was firm. Progress, slow but measured. In the village of Tungri at night I ate ibex soup. It tasted like venison. The real hunter-gatherer diet. I thought again of the rock carvings of men hunting ibex with bows and arrows. Old ways die hard. Ibex. Real Zangskari cooking. You are what you eat. Excellent for an evening meal washed down with a little *arak*, unbeatable. Après-ski. They used to say the best *chang* came from Tungri. In a Buddhist village the men swore blind that they did not hunt animals, but some had been in the Ladakh Scouts and were good shots. Their cap badge was an ibex.

The snow was by now very good and during the night had frozen hard, no longer powder snow. When it melts and refreezes it is called *firn*. It was interesting skiing beside *chortens* and in some cases skiing right through the middle of them, then looking up at the ceilings, where there was always a mandala on the underside. Buddhist statues looked on impassively like ancient ancestors. Progress was good.

Day two was hard, but the snow was consistent and it was a real pleasure to ski through these villages. To be honest, I had no idea at all whether my ski journey would be a success. It was all unknown. I might be trapped on the pass. I might break a leg or break a ski or be reduced to walking out through waist-deep snow as I had on the way to Dzongkhul. Or worse still be engulfed in an avalanche and be found months later when the snow melted. I was well aware of a 19th-century account of crossing the Pense La with ponies floundering in six-foot-deep snow drifts (Andrew Wilson, *Abode of Snow*, 1875). I did not want to join the two graves in Panikar, much as I would have loved to chat with Captain Herbert Christian and Chimed Gergan. Then again, there were wolves to consider. Wolves get very hungry at this time of year. If I was disabled or hobbling along I am sure a pack would have taken advantage of me, given half the chance.

But I still had no idea whether snow conditions would be good on the Pense La. By the end of the second day I got as far as Abrang. Then the snow really came down. Softly, then more heavily, till it had the makings of yet another blizzard. I stayed in Abrang with Beda Amchi and his family for two nights, waiting for the blizzard to abate. My rations were getting low. I had allowed for five days' bread. Minimal. No leeway.

Meat, *tsampa* and buttermilk. The family were good to me. Everyone slept in the same upstairs room under their cloaks. The father made love with his wife every night, twice a night, no mistake about that. They were only one foot or two to my left. Life is raw in the mountains. Pleasures are to be taken as and when they present themselves. Amchi's son made love to his young wife as well, but they were next door in the woodstore. Privacy was practically non-existent in winter. It was a happy family with several young children. Everyone crowded in together, all sleeping under shared cloaks, animal like, cheek by jowl. There was only one room, and heat was a precious commodity. Like all good Zangskaris they slept on their knees on the floor with an angled wooden board for a head rest. This was rather like living in a cave around a central fire. Yak, sheep, goats and butter – a vital part of their economy.

The whole of the next day it was impossible to go anywhere. The snow kept falling. Amchi's wife was always busy, up and down like a yo-yo. Carrying dung, taking firewood, scrubbing, spinning, cooking. Home economy and very industrious.

And when there was a brief interlude of sun, the girls of the house and both boys practised with the skis. They took their felt boots off, walked barefoot in the snow and grabbed the ski clips between their toes. Then off they would go in gangs, each having a turn, on one ski, two skis, with and without sticks, climbing and descending the bank of the irrigation channel. The girls really loved it and the cold did not seem to worry them at all. They usually ended up in a bundle of giggles, half submerged in snow.

Later that day in a brief respite, Beda Amchi got out his sand board and started to consult the books. He was an astrologer and an *amchi*. Beda meant that he was 'lower' caste, although that term was not used in the Indian religious sense at all, but more in the economic or social sense. Originally his family were musicians. On the roof he cleared the snow away, then laid out his board and worked fast, calculating figures, adding and subtracting. I never found out the result. In the corner his son, aged only seventeen but married last year, practised on a piece of wood with whitewash. The intricacies of understanding the heavens were complex indeed.

Auspicious and inauspicious. Stars and planets, sun and moon, gyrations that taxed even the best of Buddhist minds. Here the peasants, the small farmers, were trying their very best to grasp the deep significance of their universe and landscape. That was very hard indeed. Survival and good luck were paramount. I needed both of these as well.

Wolves

In the early morning of the second day at Beda Amchi's I heard a terrible sound of distress and wailing coming from outside. It was just light and still snowing gently. A woman's voice, possessed. Shrieking, terrified. Beda Amchi's wife was walking around outside in her maroon cloak with her dark hair tousled, weeping, holding up a half-eaten leg of lamb, or was it a goat? She was shouting, 'Shanku, shanku.' A wolf, or rather several wolves, had come down in the night from the mountains and jumped into the outside pen. They had killed half a dozen goats and sheep. It was a bloody mess, and yet there had been no noise during the night. Around the pen were countless paw marks and blood on the snow.

For the family this was a real disaster, and the crying and wailing filled the mountains. Each animal life is precious. Each human life is precious. Farming on the edge like this was extremely tenuous. Wolves were a very real menace, but to see it like this was heart-wrenching. 'Nature red in tooth and claw'. This was the front line, the frontier between farming and wilderness, an invisible dotted line, a line that moved with the seasons, a grey area only half tamed. I also pondered the terror that the sheep and goats must have felt, being powerless to prevent the attack. A massacre of the innocents, or was it fair game? They were silent. We had heard nothing.

I wondered afterwards if I had not inadvertently caused the catastrophe. Maybe wolves had been following me all along. Shadowing me, tailing me, smelling my scent. Then biding their time. Maybe they had been confused by the act of skiing. *Langlauf* has its own particular rhythm with an unusual movement, and wearing goggles can confuse wolves. Eye to eye contact is vital. Sizing the prey up. The main thing was not to appear weak or wounded, halt or lame. They would have been curious about a lone figure moving through their landscape and followed me at a safe distance, hunger and impatience driving them on. Then, getting impatient, they attacked the goats and sheep outside. The pen was a circular wall of stones with no way in or out except by jumping in over the wall and out again, rather like a wolf trap but not as high. The wolves were bandits or guerrillas. Hit and run.

The sight of Beda Amchi's wife weeping, distraught and holding up a bloody leg, and seeing blood on the snow and dismembered bits of goat and sheep – it was all too traumatic to photograph. This was a catastrophe and taught me all I needed to know about farming. It was the real cutting edge, the transition between pastoral and agrarian, between hunting, gathering and herding, the settling down of the half-nomad still at the mercy of the elements and wildlife. Half-nomad, because in summer they live in black yak-hair tents up on the high pastures and move every month or so. 'Transhumance' is the technical term. They follow the grass up to the snowline. An ancient lesson. Raw survival – economy and production. Wolves on their heels all the time, even in daytime.

Maybe I had not shown enough respect to the family god, the *lha* that resided in the house, and perhaps I should have made an offering, but then again I felt a bit like an offering myself. It could so easily have been me. A sobering thought, being surrounded by a pack of hungry wolves with only skis and ski sticks to fend them off.

Beda Amchi tapped me on my shoulder and pointed up the valley. A weight of seriousness and sorrow now lay on the household. His reading the previous day had been auspicious, at least for my ski venture. So, even though the weather was not good and more snow had fallen overnight, I could not delay any longer. On with the pack. I said goodbye to the family, and wondered how I could ever repay them for their hospitality and the disaster that I might have inadvertently brought upon them.

So despite the snow still falling, I pulled my blue balaclava down, mitts on, ski sticks in hand, and then pushed off. I wished them well. I was going off into uncertain snow conditions, a cold limbo, laden with hope and a little fear. The third and final test of my Zangskar trip. The first was climbing the mountain behind Padum – that was remarkable. Then the *chadar* with its broken ice and caves. Now the ski trip with wolves and the potential for avalanches. It felt a bit like entering the cloud of unknowing – 'once again into the breach dear friends', particularly as it was snowing and clouds were all around. More like a cold, thick mist, a gentle, slow blizzard. The phrase 'cloud of unknowing' came from a 14th-century English mystical Christian text which urges the practitioner to explore the world seeking experience rather than knowledge. And that was very appropriate. Almost Sufi. Uncle Kenny knew all about that – when he was translating the poety of Hafiz and Sheikh Sa'adi. Only Zangskar was no *Gulistan*. Only dog roses in summer. Low cloud, snow and wolves. It all depended on scent. Another rite of passage.

Solo

I struck off up the valley following the wolf trail and leaving the houses far behind. There were many paw prints just visible. Intriguing, tracking them. Two front toes and two back pads, just like a dog, but a bit bigger. Four or five sets, I reckoned, weaving their way, criss-crossing in exactly the same direction as I was going. I was now entering interesting territory: their territory, their zone. I wasn't sure whether they were Tibetan wolves, Himalayan wolves, Ladakhi wolves or even Zangskari wolves. Maybe they were grey, brown, fawn, dun or even black. But a wolf was a wolf.

All I knew was that they had been hungry wolves who had just had a fine meal. In Nuristan in the Hindu Kush there is a measurement of distance – a *farsag* – the distance that a wolf travels in a night. About thirty miles. In other words, a very long way. (Years later I heard of an Italian tourist who had gone off on his own near Hemis. When discovered, not much of his body was left.)

A lone beast was what they wanted on the move. But maybe these wolves had already had their fill and were now returning home to digest their night-time bounty. If a pack of wolves had descended on me there was not much I could have done. Ski sticks are not very sharp but conceivably might have done the trick. Yet even a lone wolf would have been a bit of a problem. How long can you fend off a hungry wolf, I wondered? There were plenty of wolf stories from the Yukon, but there they hunted caribou in large herds. Here they lived off ibex and marmots; the marmots were still hibernating deep underground.

I was well aware that there were wolf traps and that these were sometimes baited with a young male goat. Once caught inside, the wolf would be stoned to death. Not sure what happened to the wolf skins – maybe they were sold down in Kashmir. If the survival of your family depended on your sheep and goats, then protecting them against wolf attack was vital. Wolves also attacked young yaks, even horses. Many of the larger animals had chunks taken out of their flanks. Wolves seemed to be here in large numbers, if the frequency of incidents was anything to go by.

Wolf traps were controversial, but this was the front line of agriculture. Often wolves went for young, weak or old animals. Ibex were a favourite. Snow leopards also came down into villages and I was told that a couple of them working together could bring down a yak. They liked attacking from above, from a cliff, and then jumping on their prey. Maybe the wolves just wanted a change of diet. I kept my eyes and ears open. This ski journey would certainly be interesting.

I was now completely on my own. The snow was good and, although uphill, it was possible to make steady progress herring-bone fashion without having to re-wax the skis. The snow slowly became deeper and deeper, and there were some very large drifts to contend with. Some had high cornices but the surface was often good. It was an odd feeling that I was tempting fate yet again.

Hunger

Rations were low, the biscuits and bread had run out, and I had no Primus stove. I now relied on milk powder, drinking chocolate, *tsampa* and sugar, which could all be mixed up in a jiffy in a blue plastic cup – a quick emergency fix. I would make a kind of paste with water that dripped from under a boulder where the snow was thawing around the edges or even from small ponds. Everything was now in flux. I knew that I had to really push myself, as I had to reach a cave just below the pass – a distance of twenty miles, which at altitude in deep snow in cold conditions was not easy. Uphill all the way. It takes it out of you. I had spotted the cave on the pass back in November and hoped I could find it again.

I was not sure if the wolves were still keeping a watchful eye on me. Phuntsok Dawa had warned me about bears. They had been seen up in this end of a valley and were hungry after a winter's hibernation. Unpredictable and grumpy. I had to be on my guard. Snow leopards were more secretive, but they too were on the lookout for an easy meal and had recently been seen at Rangdom.

In deep snow it was almost impossible to see the line of the road, but occasionally you could pick it out. I followed the wolf tracks for a mile or so before they veered off to the right up a *nallah*. Across the valley through the snowflakes I could just see the village of Hagshu, from where a route led up to the Hagshu La and over the main ridge to Kishtwar. A man had apparently killed a bear here ten years earlier with his bare hands. It can't have been a very big bear. Bears broke into houses to get butter. There were also stories about Alu, the Ladakhi equivalent of the yeti, the most secretive creature of all. Later on I saw bear prints.

Everyone was now hungry. It meant winter was nearly over, but when the sun shone there were likely to be avalanches. The hungry gap. Stories of wild animals were never far from people's lips and wolves were a problem from one end of Zangskar to the other. No wonder the local *lha* or spirits of the mountain were feared and revered. It was around here that the *naib tehsildar*'s father was killed back in 1948 by Pakistani soldiers. A very sad tale ...

As the snow was new, the bear prints must have been very fresh. The degree of danger simply depended on which direction the wind was blowing. Having been in the Yukon I realised you don't mess with a bear ... whatever the size. I had met a man there who had survived being mauled by a bear and he said the worst thing was the bear's bad breath. The bear had been feeding off salmon. Uncle Theodore had a few bear stories. 'Always wear a tin on your belt with nails in it so that they hear you coming first.' Then there were stories of eating mammoth, dislodged from the permafrost. I'd stick to yak.

I skied on, and gradually the incline became steeper. These were upper pastures in summer, which in a month or two's time would be rich with grass and flowers, but at the moment a thick blanket of snow was all the grazing there was. How I envied the marmots still asleep, deep in their underground burrows. Hibernation was a great skill.

At times I had to take my skis off, strap them to my rucksack or simply carry them over my shoulder, and climb through deep snow. It was just more exhausting without food. A day's rest at Beda Amchi's house helped, but I now had to dig into my reserves of energy and the persistent cold did not help either. To be moving again was good and my body responded well. The Dachstein mitts were excellent but a little cumbersome. The homemade chest harness to which they were attached was invaluable. The wooden ski sticks were strong and they had small baskets on the end, which meant I got some leverage from them.

Occasionally I wondered if the pass would be too difficult, because there was a very steep climb of about a thousand feet that could become impossible wading waist deep through powder snow. Timing was crucial. Often I would stop for five minutes' rest and no more. I passed several rough old tumbled avalanche cones where avalanches had come down from high up and spread out across the valley floor. These became larger and more frequent as the valley narrowed. I remembered Uncle Kenny's warning: 'Beware avalanches.' Wet snow, dry snow, powder snow. Not a good time of year. I had no idea how long it would take for the sun to start melting the snow and send it on its way down from the peaks above.

When the snow was falling I could see very little. I just knew that I had to keep on up the valley. Head down. With large cornices you had to ski over them or cut your way through first. I had to keep my own inner momentum going. The secret was to focus my mind and body on the rhythm of the skis. Far less friction than walking. I repeated the mantra *Om mani padme hum* with each step. Not very original, but it was Buddhist. It worked very well indeed. Jewel in the lotus ... and all that.

Also I had no idea how much snow there was lurking up above just out of sight, waiting for a trigger. All I knew was that I was aiming for a small cave. Any form of shelter was welcome, even vital. My mind was wandering a little.

Along the way after several short breaks I managed somehow to leave behind four plastic bags in which I had the last of the milk powder, sugar, *tsampa* and cocoa powder. At midday I had stopped at the edge of a small glacial depression with some meltwater in it. I mixed the *tsampa* with the powders to make the paste, which I ate ravenously. Stirring it into the right consistency was important. I lay down and had a kip, just to restore equilibrium. When I woke up ten or fifteen minutes later I had no idea how long I had been asleep for. I quickly jumped up and pushed on, without first checking I had the food with me. The bags were just out of sight behind a rock. A foolish mistake. Rations are your life blood.

The wandering mind. Altitude and exhaustion can do that to you. It meant that I now had no food for the next two days. I still had a long way to go. My bread had run out, as I had shared it with Beda Amchi and his family. I had counted on having food for five days. This was day five. It was the tail end of winter. Dried apricots would have been very handy right now.

The only thing I had to eat was ski wax. I wasn't sure that was a good idea. The notion that it had some beeswax in it was an error, but it kept me going, just the thought of it. I had four different colours to chew on, a bit like the colours of the prayer flags. There was always something very cheering about meeting a prayer flag fluttering in the middle of nowhere. As if you were not alone, part of the Buddhist continuum where your own prayers floated off on the wind to some remote deity that lived in the mountains and kept a watchful eye on you. I just hoped that the monks of Karsha did not chant a second round of prayers that would now inundate me with more snow. The ski wax was bitter and tasted vile, but at least you could chew it. Yak biltong would have been much better.

Finding the cave

Meditation and cross-country skiing go well together, each movement smooth and synchronised like perpetual motion. Each peak came and went. A fleeting glance. The weather became better as the day progressed. You wrestled with your inner self, the landscape and your reserves of energy. No wonder the Tibetan yogins wanted to be alone during winter. But this end of Zangskar in winter was fairly bleak even for them. The *dakinis* preferred a little warmth and a few creature comforts. Naropa knew all about that.

One gets used to being on one's own. Rather like solo climbing, but here there was no one else for many miles. Sometimes I had to take the skis off and climb up a steep slope. I would watch my shadow next to me. Reassuring. But most of the time I skied slowly but surely uphill. Sweat became a problem as it ran down into my eyes mixed with glacier cream, which I had smeared on my nose and forehead. The air became warm.

Everything has to come from within. I found myself smiling from time to time – same legs, same rhythm. A solo ski journey can be exhilarating, all or nothing. The barriers between yourself and the mountains melt away. You just keep the right pace. Solo meant solo.

Sometimes there were enormous drifts fifty feet high with large cornices, thick windslab, curved and wonderful. I had to cut my way through at just the right spot, terrified that the whole lot would break off and carry me hundreds of feet lower down or even trigger an avalanche. Sometimes I had to climb crabwise until the right moment and then take it more gently. These *langlauf* skis only had pin bindings at the toe, and if I lost one ski it would be catastrophic. My wooden ski sticks were invaluable.

With *langlauf* there was no sense of time passing, just the sense of steady movement. I kept up a rhythm, but the effort was becoming increasingly marked as the valley climbed. At one point there was a narrow collapsing bridge over a canyon. If that had gone I would have been in deep trouble. I skied across it swiftly in a flurry of snow, hoping not to be swept down. It creaked a little, and I could see looking back that half of it was hanging down over the abyss.

My face was blistering badly. I wore glacier cream, a pair of goggles and a blue and white spotted handkerchief as a bandana to stop the sweat flowing into my eyes, but the glare from the sun always gets you on the lips and under the nose. Snow blindness when on your own is a terrifying thought. If I stopped for a few minutes I again drifted off to sleep in the sun. Catnapping was a skill I had acquired in the army. Even five minutes can make all the difference, so long as you are not on sentry duty. But here I had to be just as alert. The password was no word at all. Pass stranger. I talked to my shadow.

Every mile was an achievement. Sometimes the snow was soft, at others a hard crust. I knew I had to reach the small cave that I had spotted like a Cyclops eye in the cliff face. I had no idea how big it actually was, but I knew it would be something to aim for before getting dark.

As I got closer to the pass I could see the steep bluff ahead of me on the skyline and knew that it would take all my energy to climb up to the cave, which I had by now spotted. My mind was going in circles. I was so exhausted I had only one thing in mind: to get to the cave before the wolves got to me. The thought of wolves kept me going. It was as simple as that. I had no stove and no means of creating a fire. I was now very tired. The journey was beginning to take its toll. Shelter was vital.

The last five miles were hard, a real slog over old moraines, and I had to dig deep into my reserves to get there, brushing past clumps of willow as I went. I don't remember much except that it flattened out and then the climb was very steep. My hands got colder as the sun went in and the temperature dropped very quickly. Everything was focused on that small, dark spot of a cave, a sanctuary. It would probably only give me scant shelter, but that was better than being out in the open. The snow was not hard enough to make a snow hole or small tunnel. I had to keep going. I had no food or heat. A matter of endurance. I had to get there before dark.

Physically I was pushing myself to the limits. The skis were slung on my back as I struggled up the steep slope with only my ski sticks to help me. The wind dropped. I was very cold.

Exhaustion. I had to keep my core temperature up. Exposure beckoned. That cave drew me on. Being drowsy was not good. Your sense of balance starts to go. All I had to do was get into that sleeping bag as quickly as possible, keep my head down and maintain my body heat. That thought kept me going.

When I eventually got to the cave I was almost too tired to register it. There was a sheet of solid ice on the floor and there were some rocks that I tried to move out of the way, but they were frozen in. For a moment I looked back down the valley. It seemed remarkable that only ten hours earlier I had left Beda Amchi and his family. No time wasted cooking. I knew that I had get into my sleeping bag as soon as possible. At least I wasn't talking to myself yet. Or was I? I prayed for good weather, but also realised that might mean avalanches.

I put my skis crosswise across the entrance, hoping that I could get a second's alarm and that the clatter might frighten the bears or wolves off if they were thinking about a quick snack. The ice was uncomfortable, so I put my rucksack under me. A lot of my heat went down into the ice, but I managed to crawl into my sleeping bag and pulled my balaclava over my head. I knew it would be a very cold night but fine the following day. The last light was a deep shade of blue. A handful of stars glittered above the peaks. Minus 20°C at least, I reckoned. That should stabilise the slope for tomorrow. Twenty-two miles. A cave was a cave. Home from home. This was still day five.

Crossing the pass

The next morning, after a rather uncomfortable night, I saw first light hit the mountains opposite. There were icicles over the mouth of the cave but fantastic views back over the long valley that I had slogged up the previous afternoon. Shimmering, streaky colours – pink, blue and green – lightened up the jagged horizon as the last stars vanished. I felt rested. Even though I had no food, my body had an amazing ability to repair itself, to recover its energy. The joys of ski wax.

I rose and put my boots back on, no easy matter. They had been inside the sleeping bag but were still stiff and my fingers numb. No time for breakfast. There was no food anyway, which made things very simple indeed. No stove, no petrol, no kerosene … no matches, no hassle. Then I carried on upwards very slowly, pacing myself. The skis were strapped to my rucksack and I used my ski sticks for support. Every now and then I stamped my feet to get some life back into them. My limbs ached from sleeping on the ice but they were glad to be moving again.

Climbing in *langlauf* boots is not so easy. Here I needed proper rigid climbing boots – and crampons where it was icy. But they were back in Padum, as was my ice axe. Snow gets down into the boots, so my snow gaiters helped. You have a certain distance from your limbs early in the morning, they seem to belong to someone else. You have to cajole them into action. Caress them, massage them and induce some feeling back into the extremities. Keep checking them out. You have to talk to them. Frostbite lurked in the shadows.

Not a whisper, not a creak, even from the Durung Drung glacier, which was sleeping round the corner. A strange and wonderful feeling to be this remote, to be this alone, so much in control of one's own destiny. Invigorating. Hard summons. Short commons. No commons at all. Call of the wild. Onwards and upwards, as they say. No food was a bit of an error. My energy was slowly sapping at every turn. So I had to pull on yet more reserves. But I was young and foolish, merely a small dot in the landscape deep within all these incredible mountains.

The self became smaller and smaller as I pushed on upwards. You became less aware of your own boundaries. Isolation slowly vanished as I relished the views and sun touched my shoulders. Warmth – that was a blessing. Winter was a force to be reckoned with, but this was the end of winter. What would it have been like here in the depths of winter in a real blizzard with no one to witness it? An interesting thought.

This was another zone entirely. No sign of habitation, only ice and snow, the lie of the land almost unrecognisable since autumn. The Durung Drung glacier was magnificent, vast and elegant, a mile wide and about twelve miles long, the glacier yawning, but snow covering most of the crevasses. Dormant, as if in suspended animation, curved, almost voluptuous. I felt like embracing it.

I watched my own shadow as I climbed. I was not alone. The shadow again followed me up the slope, tagging on behind like a faithful dog. Surreal with the glacier in the background. You talk to yourself, you talk to your shadow, to your alter ego. 'Greetings, fellow traveller.' Just the shadow of skis and ski sticks. You smile to yourself and move on upwards. Very steep: ten, twenty, thirty steps at a time – a climbing meditation. You count. Fifty steps, then pause. Then another fifty. You slowly gain an inner strength from the mountains. The structure of breathing. The glacier is broad, vast and hungry. Old ice from hundreds of years ago on the move. What was Ladakh like then? Was Gandhara alive and kicking? You take your mind off the hunger, but it comes back to bite you from time to time. You have to pace yourself. Slow but sure.

I tried chewing on the ski wax again as a form of light breakfast, but I got nowhere fast. It was the psychology of chewing that helped. I can't say that any one colour was any better than any other. They were probably all toxic. If only I had some proper beeswax with me. My father used it for preserving threads, an old sailmaker's trick. I can now see why people chew on their leather boots. It just relieves the boredom. Shades of Bishop O. Stringer (who later banished Uncle Theodore from the Yukon), and Charlie Chaplin. This was more like the Yukon than I realised. Even Akong Rinpoche, who ran a Tibetan monastery in Scotland, had chewed his boots when escaping Tibet. Out of three hundred in his party only thirteen survived. Incarnate leather. Buddhist initiation. Akong was interested in my trip. I would save the boots till later.

Waxing lyrical, I realised that I had to get over the Pense La as quickly as possible. The sun was now out, which made it more dangerous. All the peaks, row after row, a sight that would have thrilled Eric Shipton. Something primaeval, something wondrous to behold, to see a whole range of unclimbed, unnamed mountains. Infinite possibilities. Virgin snow, virgin peaks. Danger beckoning. Raw beauty. But you cannot stay still for more than a few minutes.

The scale of the glacier was impressive and I was soon a thousand feet above it. Yet I was climbing blind. The snow was so deep that there were no obvious landmarks and I somehow veered off to the right without realising it, maybe climbing an extra seven or eight hundred feet above the actual pass by mistake. How exactly that happened I am not sure, but it cost me dear in time. I just kept on climbing mechanically. Head down. Counting breaths, stopping every ten minutes or so, then waiting two minutes, then continuing. Breathing by rote. It was impossible to gauge one's exact whereabouts as the snow was so deep. In my desire to push on upwards I had not stopped to fully orientate myself. The landscape had changed completely with the windblown snow.

You lived in your own world. Just your mind, your body, the steep slope and the desire to get to the top. That was all. Hunger and cold came and went. So long as you could feel life in your fingers and toes, nose and ears, that was good. You would survive. The moment one part of you slowed down or stopped, then you were in real trouble. I thought of the Norwegian writer Knut Hamsun, whose book *Hunger* depicted a man walking around Oslo, starving. Hunger does strange things to your mind. You can start to hallucinate. Altitude and cold also have the same effect. Not unpleasant. The mind does indeed do strange things. Yet this was the zone of clear thoughts, the mind unimpeded, dancing with itself.

You also begin to think of food. Just very basic food like saffron buns, currant buns and ship's cocoa. Even pasties. You are brought right back down to earth. You fixate on one thing and begin to imagine it in all sorts of ways, linking memory with anticipation. Hunger has its own inner patterns and pathways. At altitude, some prefer sweet things and others savoury things. Imagining flavour is interesting. Smoked bacon, toast and marmalade. Roast beef – a dash of horseradish. Powerful visualisation. One item at a time as I climbed the shoulder of the mountain. I was very much a savoury person. I needed Bovril or Marmite.

But I had climbed too high. Far below I could just see the top of a *chorten* poking out of the snow and the cairn that marked the top of the pass. It was around there that Chimed Gergan had met his end. The topography had changed markedly with the snow. But the landscape was waking up. The snow had sculpted the pass in many different shapes. White waves sculpted by the wind. *Sastrugi* and great cornices.

When I crossed the Pense La I had no idea what day it was, but I calculated backwards and found that it was May Day, 1 May, an ancient time of celebration. The Queen of Ladakh's birthday. I sat down and mopped my brow. It was getting warm. I felt elated but knew that the worst was yet to come. The sun was doing its best to uncover mountains, to unmask slopes. I was now entering the most dangerous part of the journey. A race against time. The peaks were beginning to wake up.

Avalanche

The feeling of exhilaration at crossing the pass was very welcome but short-lived. I rested for ten minutes, then skied as best I could down to the *chorten*, trying to make up for lost time. Battered prayer flags fluttered forlornly. Green, red, blue, white, yellow. The sun was strong. The peaks and gullies were warming up nicely. Snow melts from the bottom up, and when the point of friction starts to give, the rest follows. Often small trickles from the edges of rocks that ease under the ice and slowly allow the slabs to release their awful energy. I had crossed the pass at about midday. But I had no watch, just the sun.

The gradient lessened. I took in the joy of the new landscape opening out. Pure pleasure, a just reward for all that climbing. To ski downhill was ecstasy, the feeling of gliding effortlessly across a slope. I savoured the sensation and made it last as long as possible, but I was keen not to lose too much height in one go.

Downhill skiing is very different to *langlauf*. New freedoms, new possibilities, new movements. Speed is of the essence. Your mind is very alert and fluid. The landscape unfolds at a faster pace. You manoeuvre with split-second decisions and changes of direction, no easy matter in pin bindings. Elegance comes with form. Beauty is within the daring. Mountains hold you within their grasp. But the snow conditions were critical. Danger lurked. You do not want to trigger your own avalanche or ski into the path of one. Your perceptions are honed down. Tired but alert.

Skiing is not easy when the slope is about to give way. At one point a ski came off. I had twisted my foot in a turn, and the ski shot fifty feet or so down the slope and had to be retrieved. The only bindings I had were the three pins on the toe, so I tied a spare pair of shoelaces to each ski binding and then around my ankle, so that if the two became parted the ski would not shoot off down a precipice. Then I saw another wonderful clean slope to ski across. It looked very inviting, but my instinct held me back and told me to get on down as fast as possible. Some inner guide was at work. A sixth sense. Danger and beauty, a lethal combination. Echo of silence. The sun had already made its mischief.

The air was too still, the snow too beautiful. For a moment I stopped and looked more carefully at the slope I was about to cross. There was only one other option and that was down to my left. Steep, but just possible. And that is exactly what I did. High-angled, alpine-style downhill skiing with *langlauf* skis and a pack is not easy. If you take a turn too sharp or make a jump turn, the ski comes off. But something had made me very uneasy.

Within two minutes there was a barely audible crack somewhere high above and an awesome rumble from a *nallah*. A large avalanche then swept down just where I would have been if I had crossed that slope. It spread out like a vast fan as it gathered pace.

The 45° slope looked so innocent, but intuition and mountain sense had saved my life. Another close shave.

It was about here six months earlier that I had heard the late Beethoven string quartet, with all its dark energy and vitality. Never more poignant than now. What would Beethoven have written if he had felt the power of these mountains? Vast, uncontrollable energy. Opus 133 was about right. Avalanches come in three sorts. Those that you survive, those that you narrowly miss and those that you do not survive. I was incredibly lucky that day. That was the first of many avalanches. I watched till it came to a halt.

I then skied on down to the valley floor maybe a thousand feet below. But even then I was not safe. The first part was fine, a vast white expanse of valley floor along which I skied. But the meandering river was treacherous – you could not always see it. It was beginning to melt and open up. What at first sight looked inviting was often very dangerous under snow cover.

At a small pool I drank some water, a rare commodity up here. I began to feel drowsy and again fell asleep in the sun. The second day without food. I knew that I had to reach the village of Tashi Tanze, which was about fifteen miles way. I knew I could not last another night outside without food and shelter. With exposure you slowly slip away. The warmth of the sun was deceptive, lulling you into a false sense of security. But there was no lasting value in its warmth because the shade and shadows were devilishly cold and crept up on you. The sun went down and the temperature once again plummeted at around 1°C per minute, 20°C to -20°C in forty minutes. Rule of thumb. Just like a mantra. You could not stop for long.

The bottom of the valley was just as dangerous as the peaks. I faced the dilemma of skiing on an invisible frozen river that was breaking up or under cliffs that were constantly being avalanched from above. Invisible because the snow was on top of the ice, and until you went on it and heard it begin to crack you had no idea how firm it was. A strange choice to make. So I chose one path and then the other. Neither was pleasant.

The river was fine in certain patches, but the snow was wet underneath and the moment I lifted a ski up, five kilos of ice stuck to it, frozen slush that froze the moment it hit the air. Sometimes I spent ten to fifteen minutes scraping the ice off from the bottom of my skis with a penknife. Sometimes I retraced my steps and lost ground. If I had fallen through the ice into the river and got completely soaked it would have been disastrous. To lose sensation in either hands or feet was a slippery slope. A slow end. I was still a long way from Rangdom.

It was a hard choice. I was exhausted and my hands were by now very cold. Nothing for it but to push on with the skis as best I could. Under the cliffs was daunting. It was now three or four o'clock in the afternoon, and avalanches were coming down thick and fast, one after the other. Not healthy at all. From a distance they looked small, but to be caught by one would be disastrous. Snow is very heavy indeed. Even powder snow on the move is lethal. New snow, old snow, wet snow. Spectacular but dangerous. The cliffs were unhealthy, yet I was inexorably drawn to them. The curves of the river slowly pushed me in their direction.

The closer the river got to the cliffs, the less room for manoeuvre I had until I was right under them. It was the peaks on the northern side with their slopes facing towards the sun that were the worst offenders. Obviously all the fresh snow that had fallen in the last two or three days was pouring down on top of the hard-packed ice. For half an hour at least I was in the main danger zone and I hugged the apparent safety of the rock, hoping that if an avalanche came down I could shelter under an overhang. But safe areas were few and far between. Speed was vital. I was always looking for protected spots in which to shelter under the cliffs, but with avalanches coming from above I would have little or no warning at all. I had to trust to luck and hope that the slopes had refrozen. If I had been an hour earlier I would have been caught.

I was very glad to be past the cliffs, as there was only the width of the road between the rock and the river, whose ice banks were continually being undermined. And then the wind got up. 'Beware avalanches.'

Exhaustion

I now had to ski into the wind, which was very strong – about Force 6 – hurtling down from the glaciers. The valleys were strangely linked, like a set of wind tunnels, and at first the sun was still shining. Katabatic wind, fierce, late afternoon wind, just as it had been when I walked in. Instead of dust it was throwing up snow. I had my goggles on, my hood up, balaclava pulled down, handkerchief over the mouth, Dachstein mitts, everything I could muster. The wind was not good news and my strength was not what it was, slowly getting weaker and colder. Not a good sign. But you keep going – one ski in front of the other. The gliding motion, hypnotic. Addictive. Swish, swish, swish. The sliding, rasping, grating noise that means slow progress.

Conditions were deteriorating fast and my lack of energy from not eating was taking its toll. I was making about one and a half or two miles an hour at best, which on skis was very slow indeed. Sometimes I could ski properly, at other times the powder snow was too deep. It went in waves. In the distance I could see the valley turning a corner and start to open out. The village was somewhere at the foot of the mountain on the right-hand side, but still about five miles away. I knew the light would soon start to fade, so I had to find the village before dark. One ski in front of the other, as if being back in the army again. Left right, left right, left right. I could hear the sergeant major bellowing in my ear. The dull monotony ate into my bones but the momentum kept me going. The mantra was 'Swish, swish, swish'. Left ski, right ski, left ski, right ski. 'Swish, swish, swish'. The mind takes over and the body responds. But the wind did not let up. You had to crouch down as you skied. Hard work, because you could hardly see where you were going. And more than once I ended up falling over into snowdrifts. I even invoked Guru Rinpoche from time to time.

Two days without food is really nothing at all, but with altitude, snow, cold and the strong wind, a great effort was required to make any progress. Energy and the desire to survive come from strange places. The image of the village came and went, a bit like a mirage. At times I wondered if I was hallucinating. Strange to say, I heard no voices.

It was around here back in the late autumn that I had heard the silver bell of a lama's horse. But all I could hear now was the sound of my own skis, sliding through the snow or rasping on ice, and my own breath inside the blue and white spotted handkerchief, which was now freezing up. The sound of the wind in winter is lonely, an eerie whistling noise that sharpens itself on ice ridges. I knew that I was having to draw upon yet more hidden inner reserves. I knew that I was acclimatised to the altitude and to some extent the cold, so I stood a fighting chance. The saving grace was the length of daylight. In May you get long evenings. *Sastrugi* were forming and the patterns of drifting snow looked so elegant, wisping, curving, racing, darting, sliding.

When you are up against it, you can't describe the peaks, the shape of the clouds, the fall of the snow, what it is like to be cold to your inner core. Survival takes over. You can only look ahead. The moment you collapse you are lost. These things are deeply embedded. You are so much part of the landscape that there is nothing to say. Words do not even form in your mind. There is no one to talk to, just the wind. Snow engulfs you as it gets deeper and deeper and the drifts start to form again. The surface snow skids along at high speed. Snow gyrates, dances and pulls at your clothing, tugs at your sleeve. You keep going mechanically. Something in your mind – or is it your soul? – keeps your legs and arms moving. Army training kicked in again, and for that I was very grateful. They toughen you up no end. The mind just locks into movement – and yet you are distant, at one remove from your body. Dispossessed.

If you are struggling through the snow, where is your mind? Your body responds mechanically, even when the elements slowly creep inside you. Does the wind give you energy or does it take it away? In these vast mountains does your life actually have any meaning? Do you exist at all? The Buddhist answer is of course that it is all in the mind. Let go. Your ego is diminished, but then without the ego there would be no journey. No spirit of adventure. You have an inner core that is the central part of your being and then your mind, which can float above it all. The ego is brought down to size – and no bad thing. You just wrestle with the wind, think like a yak, run like a wolf, pounce like a snow leopard.

Danger was always there, of breaking a leg or more likely just getting exhausted and going to sleep in the snow, or falling into the river, or being crushed by an avalanche. But right now it was just sheer exhaustion. Giving up was not an option. The main thing was not to lose momentum. Every shadow you entered was like entering a deep freeze. I could have made a snow hole, but I did not have the saw with me to cut blocks and build an igloo. The village, so near and yet so far.

When you become drowsy your mind wanders. Words only half-formed rise to the surface and then sink back again unspoken. The mind is full of unfinished sentences and images. No structure, no logic. No punctuation marks and commas. Full stops appear meaningless. Weaving in and out of sense. I try to reconstruct language but without success. The world of snow was the only world I knew and yet I felt at home. Felt again. Wool sacred, for without wool you cannot survive in these mountains. Like sheep we wander. I was now in no man's land, limbo, an afterworld where exhaustion took over and you had to fight the desire to lie down in the snow. Keeling over was not an option.

How I made those last five miles I shall never really know. If you are young and very fit, determination carries you much further than you think is possible. Skis were invaluable. As darkness fell I came upon the village of Tashi Tanze. In the far distance, under the lee of a ridge, I saw the faint yellow glow of what must have been a small oil lamp in the window of a large house that I half recognised. I kept going, as if aiming for a lighthouse, any port in a storm. It made it easier having something to aim for. The lack of clear landmarks in the snow meant that distances were very deceptive. You had no idea how far or how fast you were progressing. The snow was knee deep and skiing was not easy, but still easier than walking, where I would have sunk in much deeper and floundered. Snowshoes would have helped here.

The village of Tashi Tanze was dispersed, like Zhuldok, although the key houses were fairly close together. I aimed for the house with a light at the window. I just hoped it wasn't a mirage. I half expected it to disappear in a flurry of snow, but every time the wind whipped the snow up and then subsided it was still there, which I took to be a good sign. The last two miles were not easy, but hope is a fine companion. Eventually I reached the house, took off my skis and propped them up. I knocked on the door. There was no response, so I let myself in and moved very slowly among the animals in the dark stable. I valued their warmth and could have just stayed there. It was the main house in the village. I felt my way round each of the walls, and eventually knocked on another inner door and called out '*Juley*' several times in welcome, to warn them of my approach.

A young boy was sent to see what was happening. He showed me where to go. I came into their sitting room, sat down and could hardly say a word. They looked at me as if I had come from another world. Another mile or two and I would probably have collapsed in the snow, or at the very least slept in another snow hole and not woken up. I was lucky to have made the village by nightfall. Just to get out of the wind was a relief in itself.

They had no idea where I had come from and did not believe at first that I had crossed the Pense La. But they took me in and gave me tea, the first warm drink I'd had for two days. Then slowly they fed me. It was a wonderful experience and I slept very well indeed. In fact I rested all the next day. How something as simple as a bowl or cup of soup can revive your spirits is remarkable … and the humanity that goes with it.

I was forever grateful to these villagers, as I was to Beda Amchi in Abrang. I brought a message with me for the *amchi* in Rangdom. I just hoped that the wolves had stayed at home and weren't following me again. How they survived a long winter was anyone's guess. One had respect for wolves. And the snow leopards. But it was these villagers that I respected most of all. Compassion in the midst of winter, deep in the mountains, is indeed a fine gift. I fell into a very deep sleep.

Tashi Tanze

The snow reduces the world almost to one dimension, at least on the valley floor. No colour, no rocks, no cliff faces, no trees, scarcely any bushes, no shadows, only snow and shades of snow, and yet within that framework there are many subtleties. Lack of perspective, as if the whole mountain range is simply painted onto canvas like scenery in a theatre or opera house. The lack of perspective also affects one's vision, as there are rarely any points of reference that stand up above the snow. *Chortens* and *mani* walls, *lhato*, ibex horns and prayer flags. These are markers in bad weather. Points of reference. They give the inner world hope. The mind something to absorb.

But the lack of perspective and reference points also occurs within one's own mind. There is a larger canvas, like being in a desert, and here I was in the grip of a vast mountain desert. Focus can become distorted and diffracted, like living on the edge. Life in the mountains is reduced to a few basic variables. The harsh environment teaches you reliance upon other people and reliance upon yourself. Inner strength comes from within. The mountains have many pastures. For in these vast mountains man is very small, like a grain of sand or speck of dust. To survive here in winter is a real achievement. To survive I had to rely upon human nature – Buddhist nature – in these two villages once my food had run out. The kindness of strangers, the traveller's dilemma. It is this sense of giving that makes Ladakh what it is, where its heart truly lies.

Amchi Saab in Tashi Tanze was a gentle man. He gave so simply, so unselfishly, that I almost wept. His wife stoked the fire up as if they had always been expecting me. When I awoke he asked me where I had come from, what my name was. He took out a small book and made me sign it, then he pushed a cup of *chang* towards me. In these parts *amchis* are valuable men, particularly in winter. They look after the villagers, they tend to their physical needs. They hold the village together. There is no one else.

Sitting down on a Tibetan carpet, that was the greatest luxury. Dark blue, it had a thick woollen pile, a change from rocks and a sheet of ice that had been my bed the night before. I sank back in euphoria as soup was prepared. Sometimes, even when you are grown up, this feeling occurs. When you are a child it is one of the happiest things, to know that you are safe and warm and someone is going to look after you. In his hands I was like a child, exhausted, tired and hungry.

The meal he gave me was no different to others I had eaten in Zangskar, but inside I felt that it filled me more completely, giving me a sense that I was more at home, a sort of *tukpa*, a gesture that I had made it at last. I had found the true worth of human nature, and food was all that I needed. The importance of the agriculture and farming that produced that food stayed with me for the rest of my life. What else is there to study? What else is there to learn? That *tukpa*, that soup was all that stood between myself and the wind. Food is life itself. A gift from the gods of the soil.

I was reluctant to leave that house, so warm and comforting. I could have spent the rest of the winter there, staring out into the vastness of the space that is Rangdom. I had been made to feel very welcome. The next day I rested and the *amchi* had a party. I drank *chang* and danced with his mother, who must have been in her seventies. The whole village came, and the lamas. One was old but strong and striking. Known as Dorje Shuglden, a spiritual *onpo* or incarnation of a minor deity, he was important to followers of his sect. He certainly drank more than anyone else. He reminded me of Gonpo the wild monk in Stagrimo with long tousled hair. The look in his eyes was very intense. No doubt he used the winter for his own meditations; it was said that he meditated all night and rarely slept. Shuglden was controversial and the Dalai Lama had forbidden him to practise, but I was not sure of the details. Even Buddhism was not always plain sailing.

The *amchi* had seen me in the autumn on the other side of the river with four horses. I knew that I was being watched. I waited for the next day, but the weather was still bad. There were three prophecies from several hundred years ago about Rangdom that Phuntsok Dawa mentioned. 'One day they said that men would fly in iron birds, that one day there would be too many foreigners and one day they would grow rice there.'

The day after the party the *amchi*'s children started to make more *chang* to replace what had been drunk the night before. A vast cauldron outside had a fire made from dried yak dung under it, and in spite of the snow the children stoked it for many hours. I helped the *amchi* sow his vegetable seeds in small troughs on the roof. He gave the seeds to the little girls. Here they had only a few fields, just yaks, *dzos*, horses, sheep and goats. Each year he sold around a hundred kilos of butter. That is a lot of butter and a lot of money, which is why they could afford good windows and glass.

The road, he said, was already under construction, but they were waiting for a certain bridge to be built. These always took time and in the winter the concrete foundations cracked from the frost. It was always bridges that were important and bridges that got washed away in the spring.

At 13,000ft in winter, the land was harsh but beautiful. This central plain was four or five miles wide, and with its five valleys the winds shifted, pulling and tugging you in every direction at different times of day. A contrast to the avalanche-prone slopes further up. The face of the mountain was white, each ridge telling its own story. The land was deeply embedded. Rangdom monastery seen from afar was a haven of philosophy, an island of fortune, a symbol of scholarship, a castle of learning. A firm rock upon which the teaching rested. This was indeed an interesting place.

Bar-headed goose

In the afternoon I skied across the plain from Tashi Tanze to Rangdom. It was flat and good going. This side of the monastery was whitewashed, the red walls at the back and sides of the monastery standing sombre against the peaks, alone on its pedestal in the middle of the windswept, snow-swept plain. It took an hour or more to reach the monastery, and then I climbed the slope leading up the ramp to the monastery gates. I entered via the great wooden doors that creaked open. I saw no one, just a few dogs sleeping in what was left of the sun outside the temple. Then I heard noises from the kitchen. The lamas were preparing supper, *tsampa* by the look of it. I skied across the courtyard and took my skis off. I peered into the dark recesses of the kitchen. I was welcomed into the smoky den, given a cup of tea and then I showed the lamas how the skis were used. They were most amused. This was a new phenomenon to them.

Here was the frontier, the invisible inner line, a bastion that linked villages and mountains, where yaks and prayer flags mingled, where Buddha's message fluttered. Monks. Yellow hat.

Tsongkhapa. An outpost of Tibetan thought. The front line, a reality check. Gelugpa.

I stayed about half an hour and made an offering to the temple, *Buddha, Dharma, Sangha*, 10 rupees each. An offering to the four kings that guard the temple and the four Tibetan regions – north, south, east and west. One king hears everything and is in charge of wealth. Another causes roots to grow and is ruler of the wind. The third is in charge of music and upholds the realm, and the fourth sees everything and has a snake that represents a dragon. They stand guard over the monks' shoes as they are inside making offerings and reciting mantras and sutras. While I was leaving, the sound of the *puja* rang in my ears as I picked up its slightly syncopated rhythm.

When I eventually reached the next village of Zhuldok, I slept in an outhouse storeroom. The first and last of the Buddhist villages. They made me welcome. It was here that the woman had leant out of the window and offered me yogurt on the way in. Then I had four horses. Now I was reduced to one rucksack. Simplicity itself.

That night it snowed, which was just what I wanted. The dry, cracked lips, the tired body, the first sip of tea, even the taste of ski wax. When you eat, you eat, when you drink, you drink, when you sleep, you sleep. When you go down the frozen river or over the pass, you keep all your senses alive. Skiing made sure of that.

I still had two more days skiing till I reached the Suru valley and the roadhead at Panikar. Two long days, but at least it was mostly downhill. I hoped to do most of it in one day – swish, swish, swish – unless an avalanche from a side valley got me first. But I was out of their range, at least in the middle of the valley. It is amazing what one day's rest and some *tsampa* can do for your constitution.

As I skied down the valley that morning I heard a strange noise, totally unexpected, almost eerie. I was no longer alone. I was being followed by a strange, haunting sound, insistent, an eerie echoing that crept up on me. At first I could not quite work it out. But then I turned my head to the left and saw a lone goose flying alongside me – a bar-headed goose, less than fifty yards away, neck outstretched, legs tucked in and, clearly visible, two black bars at the back of its pale head. Flying low, flying slowly, maybe only twenty or thirty feet above the snow, no doubt well and truly exhausted from crossing the Himalayan range, honking as its wings beat the cold air. *Aang, aang, aang.*

Grey on white, *Anser indicus*, the great migratory goose, highest flyer of them all, frequenter of Tibetan lakes, Central Asian nomad on its own path. Alone, yet flying very well. The goose has a special place in the hearts and thoughts of Buddhists, a symbol of strength and purity, of completeness, of non-attachment, beloved by Gandhara and Tibet, flying high over the highest mountains, even spotted over Everest. Here today – gone tomorrow – a homing instinct. We were both going in the same direction.

Every spring, bar-headed geese take off from marshes in northern India at night, then catch the thermals and fly over the Himalaya, eventually coming home to rest and breed on the shores of quiet, reflective lakes high up on the edge of the Tibetan plateau. They can be seen in great skeins. A real sense of pilgrimage. To see a single goose and to hear the bird honking *aang, aang, aang* was a small wonder. It gave me strength and assurance. I was not alone. A kinship of snow, long journeys, migration, even identity.

Back in the summer when climbing the mountain behind Padum I had noticed a single goose footprint at about 18,000ft on a snow ledge. Only one print, which puzzled me, but maybe the goose was standing on one leg, resting before descending further, just having a shufti at the vast mountain ranges and working out the next leg of the route.

The goose was flying faster than I could ski, but the distinctive noise of its repeated call sign and wings rhythmically undulating echoed up and down the valley. *Nangpa* and *nan pa*. Insider and goose, both of us headed in the same direction, though the goose was much faster and slowly became a dark dot receding down the valley.

For Buddhists the goose arriving at a vast mountain lake is like enlightenment, part and parcel of the early Buddhist beliefs of Kanishka and Gandhara. Geese feature in prominent positions on many old carvings and even gold caskets, an important aspect of early Buddhist art from Ashoka's time onwards, in Sarnath, Taxila and Peshawar, stored away in reliquaries and ornaments. As if the goose represented not only the disciples but the very soul of the disciple. The *atman* and *hamsa*. The soul striving for enlightenment.

The archaeologist and Buddhist scholar Alexander Cunningham once found a fine crystal goose that contained a small bone relic of the Buddha at Taxila. Now even that has come to rest in the British Museum. An expression of beatific contentment. It was the one that Uncle Kenny had pointed out to me all those years ago. Buddhist migration to the land of enlightenment.

I also thought of Uncle Kenny trying to get up into Ladakh via the Zoji La at night with burning torches and being turned back by avalanches. I hoped he would be pleased with my progress. Something to talk about. The Buddhist flight path. The sound of the bar-headed goose flying alongside me and its lonely call sign

was all that was left of Gandhara. The sound echoed in my mind
for an hour or more. Maybe Gandhara was still there after all.
The perfumed land connected by an invisible thread.

You learn from mountains, you learn from snow and ice, from
monasteries and monks, from villagers and the steadfastness of
their animals. You learn about compassion at high altitude,
wisdom in the face of dust storms. You learn from frozen rivers
and frozen waterfalls, the inner mind of the landscape. Absolute
silence. You are humbled by the Zangskaris, their peace and
confidence. You just hope that you can take back just a little of
their own inner strength to keep your own life progressing in the
right direction. Only taking what you need from the land, but no
more. A rich philosophy, debated endlessly by each generation.
Then the idea came to me, that if I could find some alpine flowers lower down I would put them on the graves of Herbert
Christian and Chimed Gergan down in Suru, grateful not to be
joining them just yet.

Impermanence – migration.
Self – no self.
Absolute zero – absolute silence.
Winter, winter
A season much maligned
For it hath in its grasp
Many beauties undefined.

AFTERWORD

Large parts of *The Frozen River* were scribbled down in note books over forty years ago whilst it was still fresh in my mind, and then typed up on an old Olivetti typewriter. Since then I have worked sporadically on the text, often with long gaps while I worked on the land and wrote other books. An interesting apprenticeship – writing on the hoof. Recent editing and rewriting has enabled me to relive the winter in Zangskar. And that has been pure joy. The note books were stored in a garden shed along with each year's crop of apples. And as the apples matured each year maybe the writing matured as well. Nature has its own pace.

The path has also been quite interesting. Back in the 1970s I left the army because there was not enough time to think and the mountains were calling. I left Oxford because I could not write the sort of book I really wanted to write. I became a boatman in Bristol docks and for the next twenty years became a casual farm labourer working as a shepherd, sheep shearer, forester and cider maker – and even lambing on the Pitt Rivers estate. After Ladakh that made total sense. I wanted to understand agriculture and anthropology from within. I also wanted my writing to be as accurate as possible, and yet to read fluently and appeal to many different types of people. For a book to be two or three different things at once is not easy.

Good travel writing evolves, and yet I wanted above all not just to record the hardships of travel in sub-zero temperatures but also the unspoken messages that Zangskari Buddhist culture, both lay and monastic, was trying to transmit. The sort of things that a child might pick up in any community. Learning by osmosis and careful observation. Subtle nuances that cannot be analysed on a computer. I wanted to sketch pictures and portraits, to record small vignettes and photograph village life. So by trying to be original and inventive, it has been a long but fascinating process, a distillation of ideas and images.

That Zangskar and Tibetan Buddhism have much to teach us is obvious. The road from the Suru valley will by now have made a great difference to life in Zangskar, but I hope that the depth of commitment to a Buddhist religious life is not undermined by 'Western' values and Indian commercialism. Economics and agriculture still underpin life in the valley, but the construction of a road from Lahoul in the south and another from the north down the route of the *chadar* promises to make Padum into a small town. Even a large town.

Change is in the air. In August 2018, from the balcony of a small hotel just before supper in the evening light, I saw the first tarmac being laid by a construction team at Mani Ringmo, the crossroads at the very centre of Padum bazaar. Villagers stood around in amazement looking at the wild machinery, sweaty road workers and the sheen of steaming black tarmac. It was over forty years since I had seen the first two jeeps arrive in Zangskar back in November 1976. I wonder what Henry Thoreau would have made of all this.

However, there is something much more serious on the horizon. Global warming. The elegant peak that stands behind Padum now has hardly any snow on it in summer. The snowline has retreated to nearly 18,000 ft. In the village of Kumig where Thubsten's daughter was taken by the horsemen after her wedding in Padum, the small glacier above that village has died a death. About ten years ago the villagers of Kumig abandoned their fields and moved down the mountain closer to the river to till new fields and receive more water from a new but costly irrigation channel.

Other villagers at even higher altitudes near Shun and Shadey have moved 30 miles east to a new valley where there is more grazing. The nomads carrying salt in small saddlebags strapped to the backs of 1,000 sheep and goats no longer come from the salt lakes of Rupshu. And in Karsha they now only plant 60 per cent of their fields because their own glacier is shrinking. Even the magnificent Durung Drung glacier near the Pense La has retreated a mile or more as has the great Parkachik glacier on Nun Kun. These are serious times and Zangskar along with all of Ladakh is in the front line.

Even winter is not what it was. The *chadar* is now very dangerous and in 2018 two local people died because the ice gave way. One was a local woman. The *chadar* is shorter and far more unpredictable. It is also a tourist attraction. In spring the passes into Zangskar open much earlier even in March instead of June. Many Zangskaris now live outside Zangskar but it is not always safer. Once on the way up to Stagrimo monastery I met a man trying to irrigate his small plot of trees. He was clearly very distraught and fighting back tears. He had just heard by mobile phone that his 23-year-old daughter, a young graduate arts student in Jammu, had died because of a scooter accident. I went to the commemoration service with half a dozen monks. Butter lamps flickered and the house was filled with chanting. One of the men had been down the frozen river with me and we talked about how it had changed. The wild monk Gonpo was his uncle. Prayers lasted for several days.

But winter still flexes its muscles. In January 2019 tragedy struck north of Leh close to the summit of the Khardong La (17,500ft), a pass that leads to Nubra, when ten Zangskaris were killed in an avalanche. They were collecting snow for a large state-owned military aeronautical firm to test-land a new experimental helicopter on snow down in Leh. One theory is that they may have inadvertently triggered the avalanche whilst working, but it could just as easily have been a major powder snow avalanche. The men and two mangled tipper lorries were buried under 20 ft of snow. The bodies were found by army teams using long poles and sniffer dogs. Then dug out by hand and airlifted back to Zangskar, ironically by helicopter. Ten bodies of ten young Zangskari men trying to earn a living as manual labourers. Ten villages that lost their sons. Compensation was paid. The mountains are still unpredictable. Life is short. 'Beware avalanches.'

I realise now how very lucky I was to survive a winter in Zangskar taking the sort of risks that I did. The Mountain Gods must have been looking after me.

ཨོཾ་མ་ཎི་པདྨེ་ཧཱུྃ༔

ACKNOWLEDGEMENTS

I am deeply indebted to many wonderful people who encouraged and inspired me with my ventures in Ladakh all those years ago. First and foremost, Fiona Lumsden, who came with me on my initial reconnaissance to Zangskar in summer 1976. She walked with me from Sanku in Suru with packhorses right through Zangskar and then over the Shingo La down to Darcha in Lahoul, a distance of about 250 miles. She also bravely climbed the mountain behind Padum. A noble first ascent. Through Fiona I met her father Dr Kenneth Lumsden, who lent me his Norwegian skis. He had been in Tibet in 1936, as had his friend Major Peter Hailey, Joint British Commissioner in Leh in 1939. Peter had also been in Gyantse as Trade Officer. They both gave invaluable advice and support.

Thanks to my parents Guy and June Crowden, who brought me up on the western edge of Dartmoor, and encouraged me to explore anything and everything from an early age. To the many other experts who guided and helped me back in England, including Professor K. de B. Codrington – alias Uncle Kenny

– whose own journey to Ladakh in 1942 I was completing. To Dr
Schuyler Jones at the Pitt Rivers Museum, Oxford, for valuable
advice on anthropology. To Dr Peter Steele of Whitehorse in the
Yukon, who had been in Bhutan. He helped me with medical
matters and lent me his Labrador snowshoes. It was in his Bristol
house that I met Jigme Taring, a Tibetan prince, politician and
soldier, who told me about the plight of Tibet and her refugees.
To Stephen Macfarlane, an architect from Bristol, who lent me
his Norwegian cross-country ski boots and a set of fine wooden
ski sticks. To Eric Shipton, the doyen of Himalayan exploration,
who supported my solo expedition and gave me good advice on
maps and Primus stoves. To Professor Kenneth Mason of the
Survey of India and Hertford College, Oxford, whose 1929 book
on Himalayan routes was invaluable. He had been in Ladakh in
the 1930s when on his way to Shaksgam. To Harry Wilson of
Worcester who tipped me off about Zangskar back in 1974, and
to Nicholas Pitts-Tucker, the colourful and energetic bank
manager of Grindlays Bank, Amritsar, whom I first met in a
flea-ridden tea house in Kunduz in northern Afghanistan. To Rev.
John Ray, the stalwart and highly respected headmaster of
Tyndale Biscoe School in Srinagar; the anthropologist and expert
on polyandry HRH Prince Peter of Greece and Denmark; Dr
John Crook, an ethologist, ornithologist from Bristol University
for his knowledge about Tibetan Buddhism; Dr Henry Osmaston,
a geographer, forester, farmer and mountaineer, also from Bristol
University. To Anne Davies of the Lake District, who had been
to Zangskar on a remarkable all-women's expedition back in
1958. To Ewald Ruf and Sigmund Rittler, two German mountaineers who visited Zangskar in summer 1976 and filmed the
salt caravan. To Uncle Theodore Fleming, who was a mounted
policeman in the Yukon during the tail end of the gold rush. He

gave good advice on dog sledging and travel in Arctic conditions. He had experienced -86°F (-65°C), had eaten roast porcupine and defrosted mammoth. To Major John Drewienkiewicz, 'DZ', my old adjutant, who managed to get me out of the army in time for the expedition. He later became a major general. To Captain Julian Oswald RN, who helped my father smuggle Survey of India maps out of the basement of the Ministry of Defence. Julian Oswald later became First Sea Lord, so it didn't dent his career one bit. To Venerable Akong Rinpoche, Tulku and Abbot of Samye Ling Tibetan Monastery in Eskdalemuir, who gave me sound advice on Tibet, and Sherab the Tibetan artist, who escaped Tibet with a bullet in his arm.

Thanks also to various august organisations who helped with funding and advice: the Mount Everest Foundation, British Mountaineering Council, Royal Geographical Society, Alpine Club, Churchill Fellowship, Bristol University, Knowlson Trust and Expeditions Fund, Drapers' Company, Gilchrist Educational Trust and Harveys of Bristol.

Thanks also to Sir Peter Scott, Marco Pallis, Michael Aris, Sophie Day, Maria Phylactou, Nicky Grist and Clare Harris. To Sayeed Rizvi, the DC in Leh and his wife Janet Rizvi, the revered Ladakhi historian; Tashi Rabgyas, the revered Ladakhi philosopher; Ved Prakash Gupta, the *tehsildar* in Padum, and to the many Zangskaris who helped me in so many different ways, and in particular my very good friend Phuntsok Dawa, his father Tashi Namgyal, and his son Stenzin who is now a doctor in Padum. To Sonam Stopgyas and his uncle Dorje Tsering, and Lama Sonam Wangchuk, Lonpo of Karsha. To my neighbour Tashi Tantar, for being so amusing. To many people in the International Association of Ladakh Studies, in particular John Bray. To Helena Norberg-Hodge and all those associated with

ISEC and Secmol. To Nawang Tsering Shakspo, Tashi Morup of LAMO, Dr Anchuk Katpa of Sankar and my old friend Tanu Ringzin.

For encouragement to write this experience up over the years I must thank Rayner Unwin, John Fowles, Fay Weldon and Osyth Leeston, as well as Charles Foster, an eccentric badger-loving, cider-drinking don of Green Templeton College, Oxford. He is a vet, and a barrister but somehow finds time to teach medical ethics; Seb Mankelow, for looking over the *chadar* sections; my brilliant and patient literary agent Jessica Woollard of David Higham Associates; my energetic and equally discerning editor at William Collins, Grace Pengelly; and Katy Archer. A very good team. Thanks also to John Gilkes for the drawing of the map, and the Trustees of the British Museum for permission to reproduce the image of the Kushan crystal goose. And to my wonderful wife Carla, who has been a constant source of support over the years. I must also mention my daughter Nell, who returned with me to Zangskar in 1989 when she was only three. She rode a horse, sang songs and slept in a wolf trap on the high yak pastures. As you do. Many years later when she was at university she scanned all my slides for which I was very grateful.

Above all, this book is dedicated to the people of Zangskar, who were an inspiration and still are, particularly as they are now in the front line of global warming and Himalayan glacier retreat.

James Crowden, September 2019

NOTES

1. *The Frontier Mail*, then known as the '56 UP', now terminates in Amritsar.
2. Grindlays Bank, founded in 1828 by Captain Robert Grindlay, were bankers to the Indian army. The bank manager in Amritsar was Nicholas Pitts-Tucker, a classicist from Oxford.
3. Banihal Pass, 9,921ft. The tunnel was built in 1956 and remained open most of the year, although avalanches were still a problem.
4. Tyndale Biscoe School, founded by Canon Tyndale Biscoe in 1880, was a bastion of muscular Christianity: rowing, boxing, football and mountaineering. Rev. John Ray was headmaster for twenty-five years, also Honorary British Consul, 'Our man in Srinagar'. He has just written his memoirs. Chandra Pandit's father was sirdar on the unsuccessful 1939 American K2 expedition.
5. The Queen of Ladakh, Rani Parvati Devi Deskit Wangmo.
6. Zoji La, 11,575ft, low by Himalayan standards but lethal in bad weather. The pass was recaptured from Pakistan in *Operation Bison*, November 1948, a surprise attack by Indian tanks operating on the mule track. Ladakh's fate hinged on this operation.
7. Mrs Gandhi's Emergency (June 1975–March 1977), a very dark period in India's history.
8. Khampas from Kham in south-east Tibet were often parachuted back into Tibet to gather information and shoot up convoys. If caught by the Chinese they did not fare well.
9. Ngari Tsang was involved with border security. Many Tibetans belonged to the '22s' 'Two twos' (22 Mountain Regiment), also known as the Special Frontier Force, which provided cross-border intelligence.

10. Mount Ararat, sacred mountain of the Armenians.

11. The Dasht-e-Lut, one of the hottest places on earth. Next door is the Dasht-e-Kavir, the Salt Desert. No habitation. Extreme silence.

12. The adjutant was Major John Drewienkiewicz, known as 'DZ', who ended up a major general. I rather liked him.

13. Small crystal goose found at Taxila in 1866. Gandhara and Kushan, 1st century CE. Museum No 1867.0427.2.

14. There were at least ten different varieties of apricot in Ladakh, and apricot oil was used for women's hair, the skin and in lamps. Its kernels reputedly prevent cancer.

15. Kargil was known as the town of eight days: eight days north to Skardu, eight days to Srinagar, eight days to Leh and eight days to Padum. The wars were in 1947/48, 1965 and 1971.

16. Government caravans into Zangskar carried *atta* (flour), sugar, rice, salt and kerosene.

17. Naswar – made from powered tobacco and slaked lime – is terrible stuff, causing cancer of the mouth. It's an acquired taste.

18. Matsuo Basho (1644–84), Japanese poet credited with pioneering the 5–7–5 form of haiku poetry. *The Narrow Road to the Deep North*, his masterpiece of travel writing, was written while on a journey of 1,500 miles that took him 150 days, ten miles a day.

19. Mount Everest and geese quote from *Three Years in Tibet*, 1909, by Ekai Kawaguchi (1886–1945), Zen monk, doctor and linguist. He often travelled in disguise and made a circuit of Mount Kailash. He could pass for a Tibetan, but had to flee for his life from Lhasa when his cover was blown.

20. Tsongkhapa (1357–1419), the 'Man from Onion Valley', born in Amdo. A great scholar who streamlined many past traditions.

21. The mantra of Avolikitesvara – *Om mani padme hum* (O jewel in the lotus) – has many interpretations: spiritual, Tantric and sexual. It encourages transformation of the mind, a path that eventually leads to emptiness. Body, mind and speech: three jewels purifying the mind.

22. In a *chorten*, four steps signify earth and underworld. Thirteen rings on the parasol represent thirteen steps to enlightenment. The sun and moon poised on top represent the duality of absolute truth and relative truth. Seen from above *chortens* are mandalas. A complex Buddhist philosophy which becomes a visible strategy for survival and enlightenment in cold mountain air. The double symbol (Surya Chandra) of Sun and Rising Moon on top of the *chorten* is an emblem of the Twin-unity of the Absolute Truth (of the sphere beyond normal comprehension) and the Relative Truth (of the worldly sphere).

23. *Sastrugi* is a Russian word for windblown ridges that often form on large lakes and open seas. Ice crystals behave rather like sand; once blown, they form their own dunes and ripples, which solidify.

24. A katabatic wind is a wind descending the mountainside. It can be very strong in winter.

25. *Tsampa* – marvellous stuff with a fine roasted, nutty flavour and excellent on a long journey. Simply add warm water or chang and stir.

26. A *tehsildar* is a government official in charge of a *tehsil*, in this case Zangskar. Originally tax inspectors, they now have an administrative role.

27. A *lha* is a local god. They are everywhere. *Lhato* means god stone, a designated place where a god can be propitiated.

28. I once read that NASA was looking at the marmot's hibernation patterns to see if they could help their astronauts on long journeys to other planets.

29. Nawang Tsering (1717–94) was a key Kargyu meditator.

30. Junu Tunglak is fearsome and wields a sword. Early pre-Buddhist spirits were linked to Tibet, and spiritual possession was not uncommon.

31. Major General Sir Alexander Cunningham, officer in the Royal Engineers and Buddhist scholar, founded the Archaeological Survey of India.

32. Guru Rinpoche: in Sanskrit his name Padmasambhava meant 'lotus-born' – the sacred lotus root, symbolic of purity of body, speech and mind.

33. *Dzos* and *dzomos* fetch higher prices than yaks. *Dzomos* produce more milk and *dzos* are more biddable for transport and ploughing.

34. A bodhisattva is a being that is able to reach nirvana but delays doing so, so that he or she can stay on earth to help others.

35. The *Gesar* epic is vast and Ladakhis, like the Tibetans, have extraordinary memories. The poem, about King Gesar, dates from the 12th century, and is also known in Bhutan and Mongolia.

36. *Tangkas* are small portable Buddhist paintings that can be carried anywhere, rolled up and then hung in temples or in people's homes.

37. The 1962 war with China was a disaster for India. The Chinese occupied Aksai Chin and built a road across it without the Indians realising.

38. Thinley Dawa died a few years later in a road accident on the Pense La when the brakes on a bus failed and it plunged a thousand feet down the mountainside, killing seventeen people.

39. The *I Ching*, the Book of Changes, is as old as the hills. The sixty-four interlinked hexagrams curiously have an echo of binary code used by computers today.

40. Kangyur is the Buddhist scriptures, all 108 volumes. The Tengyur, the commentaries, run to 224 volumes i.e. a six-yak load. Going to Leh was a relatively short journey.

41. Snow leopards are very elusive and known as *shan*, or 'grey ghost'. The Zangskar range is probably the best place to find them as they live off ibex, bharal, blue sheep, urial, argali (*Ovis ammon*) and livestock.

42. Basho would have liked the frozen Zangskar river.

43. The coppersmiths – Newaris from the Kathmandu valley – were brought by the King of Ladakh from Nepal in the 17th century and have been there ever since.

44. Kalachakra teachings are very important events, often given in the open air over several days. Since giving teachings in Leh, the Dalai Lama has visited Zangskar twice.

45. *Magpa* marriages are not uncommon. The groom moves in with his wife's family, i.e. matrilocal. In *Bagma* marriages the couple live full-time with the groom's family and the parents will move out after two years to a smaller house to give them more room.

46. Resident choughs often rely on monks for food during winter. I have seen choughs feeding from a monk's hand. They nest on the cliff behind the main courtyard buildings. Red-billed choughs are slightly larger. Both species have red legs.

47. These remarkable frescos were painted by Lama Dzadpa Dorje in the 14th century. He would have had a team of itinerant painters working for him doing the initial preparation and infilling the background. Often the lead painter outlines the design and works on the main figures. The master painter gets all the credit and is mentioned on any inscription and dedication. Sadly, the side wall has since collapsed but work has been done to restore the remaining paintings. There are now windows.

48. Csoma de Kőrös (1784–1842), born in Transylvania, the son of a border guard. At Göttingen he became acquainted with Latin, Greek, Hebrew, French, English, German and Romanian. In Calcutta he mastered Bengali, Marathi and Sanskrit. He met William Moorcroft and George Trebeck by chance in 1822 in Dras, near the Zoji La on their way to Bokhara. They arranged a stipend for him and recommended that he went to Zangskar. Csoma then wrestled with Tibetan for the next twenty years.

BIBLIOGRAPHY

Alder, Garry, *Beyond Bokhara*, Century Publishing, 1985

Ali, Salim, *Book of Indian Birds*, Bombay Natural History Society, 1972

Basho, Matsuo, *The Narrow Road to the Deep North*, Penguin, 1966

Bray, John and Nawang Tsering Shakspo, *Bibliography of Ladakh*, Aris & Philipps, 1988

Chang, G. C. C., *The Six Yogas of Naropa*, Snow Lion Publications, 1963

Clarke, John, *Jewellery of Tibet and the Himalaya*, V&A Publications, 2004

Crook, John and James Low, *Yogins of Ladakh: A Pilgrimage Among the Hermits of the Buddhist Himalayas*, Motilal Banarsidass, 1997

Crook, John and Henry Osmaston, *Himalayan Buddhist Villages*, University of Bristol, 1994

Crowden, James and Fiona Lumsden, *Bristol University Ladakh Expedition*, unpublished report, 1976

Cunningham, Alexander, *Ladak, Physical, Statistical, and Historical; With Notices of the Surrounding Countries*, W. H. Allen, 1854

Deacock, Antonia, *No Purdah in Padam*, George Harrap, 1960

Drew, Frederick, *The Jummou and Kashmir Territories: a Geographical Account*, London, 1875

Föllmi, Olivier, *Zanskar: A Himalayan Kingdom*, Thames & Hudson, 1989

Foucher, Alfred, *The Beginnings of Buddhist Art*, Geuthner, 1917

Francke, A. H., *History of Western Tibet*, S. W. Partridge & Co., 1907

Francke, A. H., *Antiquities of Indian Tibet*, 2 vols, SGP, 1914

Guenther, Herbert V., *Life and Teaching of Naropa*, Oxford University Press, 1963

Harvey, Andrew, *Journey in Ladakh*, Jonathan Cape, 1983

Hewson, Eileen, *Himalayan Headstones from Ladakh Kashmir*, BACSA, 2002

Hopkins, Jeffrey, *Meditation on Emptiness*, Wisdom, 1983

International Association for Ladakh Studies, *Ladakh Studies Journal and Conference Proceedings*, IALS, 1988–2014

Jäschke, Heinrich, *A Tibetan–English Dictionary; with Special Reference to the Prevailing Dialects*, Routledge and Kegan Paul, 1881

Keay, John, *Where Men and Mountains Meet*, John Murray, 1977

Lopez, Barry, *Of Wolves and Men*, Charles Scribner, 1978

Marshall, John, *A Guide to Taxila*, Cambridge University Press, 1960

Mason, Kenneth, *Routes in the Western Himalaya, Kashmir, &c., Punch, Kashmir & Ladakh*, Government of India Press, 1929

Mason, Kenneth, *Abode of Snow: A History of Himalayan Exploration and Mountaineering*, Rupert Hart-Davis, 1955

Moorcroft, William and George Trebeck, *Travels in the Himalayan Provinces of Hindustan and the Panjab, in Ladakh and Kashmir, in Peshawar, Kabul, Kunduz and Bokhara, 1819 to 1825*, ed. Horace Hayman Wilson, John Murray, 1841

Neve, Arthur, *Thirty Years in Kashmir*, Edward Arnold, 1913

Neve, Ernest F., *Beyond the Pir Panjal*, Church Missionary Society, 1914

Norberg-Hodge, Helena, *Ancient Futures*, Sierra Club Books, 1991

Pallis, Marco, *Peaks and Lamas*, Cassell, 1939

Peter, Prince of Greece and Denmark, *A Study of Polyandry*, Mouton & Co., 1963

Polunin, Oleg and Adam Stainton, *Flowers of the Himalaya*, Oxford University Press, 1984

Rabgyas, Tashi, *127 Ladakhi Folk Songs*, Cultural Academy J&K State, 1970

Rizvi, Janet, *Ladakh, Crossroads of High Asia*, Oxford University Press, 1983

Rizvi, Janet, *Trans-Himalayan Caravans: Merchant Princes and Peasant Traders in Ladakh*, Oxford University Press, 1999

Rizvi, Janet with Monisha Ahmad, *Pashmina: The Kashmir Shawl and Beyond*, Marg Publications, 2009

Royal Geographical Society, *Hints to Travellers*, Vol. 2, RGS, 1937

Shakspo, Nawang Tsering, *Cultural History of Ladakh*, Centre for Research on Ladakh, 2012

Snellgrove, David and Hugh Richardson, *A Cultural History of Tibet*, Weidenfeld and Nicolson, 1968

Snellgrove, David and Tadeusz Skorupski, *The Cultural Heritage of Ladakh*, Aris & Phillips, Vol. 1, 1977; Vol. 2, 1981

Thomson, Thomas, *Western Himalaya and Tibet*, Reeve & Co., 1858

Thoreau, Henry, *Walden; or, Life in the Woods*, Ticknor and Fields, 1854

Tucci, Giuseppe, *Religions of Tibet*, University of California Press, 1980

Waddell, Austine, *Buddhism and Lamaism of Tibet*, W. H. Allen, 1895

Wilson, Andrew, *The Abode of Snow: Observations on a Journey from Chinese Tibet to the Indian Caucasus through the Upper Valleys of the Himalaya*, William Blackwood, 1875

INDEX